HEMI

A History of Chrysler's
Iconic V-8 In Competition

CarTech®

CarTech®, Inc.
39966 Grand Avenue
North Branch, MN 55056
Phone: 651-277-1200 or 800-551-4754
Fax: 651-277-1203
cartechbooks.com

Edit by Paul Johnson
Layout by Monica Seiberlich
Design concept by Connie DeFlorin

All photos courtesy Geoff Stunkard unless otherwise noted.

ISBN 978-1-61325-188-1
Item No. CT537

Library of Congress Cataloging-in-Publication Data Available

Written, edited, and designed in the U.S.A.
Printed in China
10 9 8 7 6 5 4 3 2 1

Front Cover Photos

Top: *Bobby Isaac became the 1970 Grand National champion driving the #71 Dodge tuned by Harry Hyde at the pinnacle of the Race Hemi's dominance in motorsports. He is seen here racing the similar #22 Dodge Daytona driven by Bobby Allison during the wing car era. (Copyright CR Racing Memories 0502045, Ray Mann Photograph)*

Bottom: *Shirley Shahan and her A990 Hemi-powered Drag-On Lady Plymouth are seen during the 1965 NHRA Nationals in Indianapolis; she became NHRA's first female event winner in this car the following year at the 1966 Winternationals in California. (Photo Courtesy Ray Mann Archive, quartermilestones.com)*

Frontispiece: *The 426 "elephant" engine in race trim resided under the hood of many successful Mopar drag and stock cars during the 1960s. Here is the engine in the restored Landy Dodge. The WO23-coded race cars were referred to by Dick Maxwell as SS/B Street Hemis, and were quite similar to what could be purchased that year. Note the fitted aluminum hood plate on the OEM Hemi air cleaner baseplate.*

Title Page: *At its apex, the Hemi dominated racing. This is John Hagan and Herb McCandless at the 1970 NHRA Springnationals in Dallas, Texas; McCandless went on to win the NHRA U.S. Nationals and the AHRA GT-1 circuit title, while his boss Ronnie Sox took home the 1970 Pro Stock crowns in both sanctions. (Photo Courtesy Jon Steele Archive, quartermilestones.com)*

Contents Page: *Dave Strickler and Ronnie Sox (in a Comet) race at a converted airstrip during the 1964 United States Drag Team tour of England. The transition toward altered-wheelbase stockers had begun. (Photo Courtesy Kramer Automotive Film/Print Library)*

Back Cover Photos

Top: *The engine and cars that made history: The 1970 World Championship Dodge of Bobby Isaac and Harry Hyde (left) one of the lowest-mileage Street Hemi Daytonas in existence (right) are behind an original 1966 426 Street Hemi auto-show cutaway engine at the Wellborn Musclecar Museum in Alexander City, Alabama.*

Bottom: *Race versions took over on the track and street examples became iconic muscle cars. Here is the first pilot Hemi Charger built for 1971 in red along with one of the final examples created before the Hemi nameplate disappeared from the order book. Both cars are from the collection of Tim and Pam Wellborn's museum in Alabama.*

Author note: *Some of the vintage photos in this book are of lower quality. They have been included because of their importance to telling the story.*

OVERSEAS DISTRIBUTION BY:

PGUK
63 Hatton Garden
London EC1N 8LE, England
Phone: 020 7061 1980 • Fax: 020 7242 3725
pguk.co.uk

Renniks Publications Ltd.
3/37-39 Green Street
Banksmeadow, NSW 2109, Australia
Phone: 2 9695 7055 • Fax: 2 9695 7355
renniks.com

CONTENTS

ACKNOWLEDGMENTS

When Paul Johnson, senior acquisitions editor at CarTech Books, first broached this opportunity with me, frankly, I was not interested. There were too many stories, too much information, too many opportunities to make errors in this project. However, after prayerful consideration, I agreed the job was for me. I had been fascinated with the subject matter, Chrysler's outrageous racing efforts of the 1960s, for most of my adult life and had actually interviewed many of those racing participants during my journalism career. My father had taken his new 1966 318-ci Dodge Coronet to Ray Nichels' Firestone franchise in Highland, Indiana, for tune-ups when I was just a youngster, and thanks to him, I had the privilege of calling men such as Dick Landy, Ronnie Sox, Herb McCandless, and Tom Hoover friends.

Nevertheless, I understood the magnitude of the task, and I could not have begun to accurately complete the tome you are holding without the help of those below. Furthermore, based on my own sometimes faulty memory, I know I will have probably left somebody out of this list; please accept my apologies if so.

Tom Hoover, former race coordinator at Chrysler Engineering: Without the friendship, courtesy, and encouragement of Mr. Hoover, whose name is almost synonymous with Chrysler's Hemi engine, this book would have been very difficult, if not impossible, to write. With an engineer's wit and diligence to this day, he was the one who made sure the engine made the history I have recorded here, and he gave direction and insight throughout this project. To him and the men of Chrysler Engineering, I dedicate the story of the Race Hemi. Thank you, Tom!

A big credit goes to the ones who were there during more than 30 years of interviews: Don Garlits, Mike Buckel, Dick Jones, Bob Tarozzi, Arlen Vanke, Ed Miller, Dave Koffel, Jack Werst, Butch Leal, Bob Harrop, Buddy Martin, Herb McCandless, Ted Spehar, Dave Christie, Forrest Pitcock, Ramo Stott, Richard Brickhouse, Norm Krause, Gary Dyer, Chuck Comella, Tom Myl, Roy Hill, Arnie Beswick, Hank Taylor, Ray Jackson, Gordie Blankenship, and many others. Plus immense posthumous gratitude belongs to Al Eckstrand, Ronnie Sox, Dick Landy, Bud Faubel, Ken Montgomery, Bill Flynn, Jim Thornton, Dave Duell, and others.

Fellow editors and journalists who assisted now and over the years include Elana Scheer, Randy Bolig, Greg Rager, Cliff Gromer, Roland Osborne, Rob Wolf, Jeff Burk, Mike Matone, Rick Voeglin, Marty Schorr, Arvid Svendsen, Dave Wallace Jr., (the late) Chris Martin, (the late) Steve Collison, and the herculean publicity efforts of (the late) Frank Wiley.

Archivists for racers and museum curators Don and Donna Garlits, Gean and Richard Landy (for the late Dick Landy), Brian Greer (for the late Shirl Greer), Ryan Owens (for the late Cotton Owens), Bruce Ramey/Talladega, Doug Schellinger/Daytona-Superbird Club, and a very special thanks to Brandt Rosenbusch of Chrysler Historical for going the distance on every request.

Research paperwork, factory data, and memorabilia: Jim Kramer, Greg Lane, Tim Wellborn, David Hakim, Tony D'Agostino, Chuck Comella, Steve Lasday, Richard Landy, Norman Hecktkoff, (the late) Bob Plumer, (the late) Dick Towers, and special thanks to Mike Goyda.

Race car owners and restorers Erik Lindberg, Mike Guffey, Jim Kramer, Clark and Colleen Rand, Greg and Kathy Mosley, Tim and Pam Wellborn, Don and Mary Lee Fezell, Tony D'Agostino, Robert D'Agostino, Doug Schellinger, Todd Werner, Nick Smith, John Mahoney, Ken Garrett, Dave Blankenship, John Gastman, Le Hodge, Ray Dupois, Jet Townsend, Tim Dupont, Bill and Suzanne Turner, Len Grimsley, Fred and Adam Englehart, Allen Coard, George Nesbit, and Brian Kohlmann.

Authors: Willem Weertman, Dr. Dave Rockwell, James Schild, Marty Schorr, Don Garlits, Frank Moriarty, Anthony Young, and William LaDow.

Last but not least, photographers and photo archivists: Charles Milikin Jr., Jim Kramer/Kramer Automotive photo archive, Calvin Lane for CR Racing Memories, Tim Wellborn/Larry Knowlton and Harry Hyde collections—Wellborn Musclecar Museum, Tommy Erwin and Keith Low/University of South Carolina Photo Archive , Lynn Paxton/Eastern Museum of Motor Racing collections, David Hakim/HP2 Communications, Tom Myl, Doug Schellinger, Dale Matthews, and my son John Stunkard. CR Racing Memories provided a majority of the color NASCAR images, also shot by Ray Mann/Racing Pictorial. Images attributed to me and my archives (Ray Mann, Jon Steele, Lynn Wineland, Phil Smith, Bryan Flach, Pit Slides) are available at quartermilestones.com.

To my wife, Linda: Patience is your virtue; thank you for your love and encouragement.

To the CarTech crew led by Mr. Johnson: Thanks for your confidence and direction while we worked through this project over the course of a year and to its completion.

Finally, to the grace of Jesus Christ, which gave me fortitude, inspiration, and purpose to pursue a project about a subject that has touched so many people for so long. To His Kingdom is the glory.

FOREWORD *by Herb McCandless*

Yeah, it was the Hemi. . . .

I'd say that the 426 Hemi was the best thing that ever happened to drag racing, especially if you were driving a Mopar. I know; I was there.

In late 1964, I was living in Memphis, Tennessee, and driving a '57 Chevy equipped with a Z11 in Modified Production. One Saturday night, a gentleman named John Moore, who raced against me in a Plymouth, literally changed my life. He approached me and asked if I thought I could drive a 4-speed Hemi Plymouth Super Stock car. Being a cocky 21-year-old, I answered, "Of course I can."

Well, it turned out that Mr. Moore was assistant regional manager for the Chrysler Zone Office. So he arranged for me to purchase a new 1965 Plymouth and I became a lifelong Mopar fanatic because of it. John was also the one who named my '65 car *Mr. 4-Speed*, and I kept that name on all my cars until I went to drive for Sox & Martin in 1970. That name has followed me through the years.

At the time, I did tell Mr. Moore that I knew nothing about a Hemi. That is when I learned that Chrysler had a week-long school for people who were driving these Hemi cars. So I went to class in Detroit and learned all about the engine; our instructor was Tom Hoover himself. It was at this school that I also learned just how serious and committed Chrysler was to racing and winning with their new Hemi.

Beyond my own career, the world of racing itself changed because of the development of the 426 Hemi. It created performance and speed like we had never seen before. Racing fans crowded the racetracks to see these very fast cars and whatever the competition had to try to stop them. Drag racing here in the South, booked-in match racing, and heads-up 3,000-pound "run whatcha brung" was what we did every week. The competition among the Ford, Chevy, and Mopar cars and fans was amazing; we drew sellout crowds wherever we went.

I worked very hard to learn all that I could about the Hemi. That '65 car was very fast and I won a lot with it. This caught the attention of the Chrysler people and they started furnishing me with parts and tech support. Then, after Buddy Martin hired me on full-time, I was getting paid to do what I loved with the best people and equipment in the business.

Back then, Chrysler had a weekly test program that was run at Milan Dragway. If we were anywhere in the area and they were testing, we would go. Because of it, when something was found to make a car run faster, Chrysler was very good about passing that information to the other racers. Because it might take two weeks to get the word to everyone, I liked to go test with them and get that two-week advantage!

Looking back, I cannot imagine what I would have done with my racing career and my businesses without that relationship with Chrysler. Even 50 years later, I remain grateful every day for my racing successes and my involvement in Chrysler performance. The 426 Hemi played a large role in giving me a lifelong direction; my life has been very good. I suppose I was never meant to drive anything but a Chrysler car. Once we had that '65 Hemi Super Stocker, we never looked back. We never had to. . . .

Herb "Mr. 4-Speed" McCandless
McCandless Performance, Burlington, North Carolina

- Winner – 1970 NHRA U.S. Nationals, Sox & Martin Duster
- Winner – 1970 AHRA GT-1 World Champion, Sox & Martin Barracuda

INTRODUCTION

Yeah, It's Got a Hemi

For years and years, knowledgeable auto enthusiasts worldwide have been aware of the heritage of Chrysler's Hemi engine designs. During the first years of the new millennium, the company itself has been very proactive in promoting this, and the engine's famous moniker. Indeed, the word Hemi is now a trademark of Chrysler Group LLC, successor of the original Chrysler Corporation.

Although the overhead-valve hemispherical combustion chamber design did not originate with Chrysler, the company has repeatedly used its association with this engine design's performance for marketing over the past 50 years, and for good reason.

Chrysler's 426-ci second-generation Race Hemi was born in a perfect crucible to meet its objectives. Moreover, it both entered and left the street production environment without being castrated into a caricature of its former self. Rumors of its extinction have never proven to be true; the basic layout still exists in various forms of racing, while the equipment aftermarket and the company itself, through Mopar Performance, continue to sell both built-up examples and peripherals to those wanting a touchstone to its heritage. Beyond its mechanical identity, today the word Hemi is found on performance-oriented Fiat Chrysler Automobiles LLC vehicle packages, race engineering powerplants, and associated apparel and accessories.

But the Chrysler Hemi engine was much more than just a gimmick. Initially developed by the firm's engineers for a government contract on aircraft engines, the automotive variation followed an investigation into the most effective engine design in the years immediately after World War II. Without prejudice or assumption, the objective was not performance, but rather the creation of Chrysler's first V-8 engine. What came about as the indirect result of selecting the hemispherical configuration changed automotive culture and racing almost from the beginning. After all, from the beginning, engineering had always been a focus of the company Walter P. Chrysler had founded in 1924; this effort took that to a new level.

Before I delve into the story of how the Chrysler Corporation found itself as the proprietor of the Hemi's notoriety in the 1960s, a quick look at combustion chamber designs is in order simply to understand what makes an engine a Hemi. The term itself refers to the shape of the combustion chamber built into the cylinder head, which in this case is a dome, or hemispherical shape. In actuality, the Chrysler variant used about 40 percent of this for the sake of compression and efficiency, making it spherical in shape rather than a full 180-degree hemispherical-shaped half dome.

Three factors critically influence the effectiveness of this shape: surface area for combustion, valve placement for intake and exhaust events, and cross flow to allow the cylinder to fill and expel the fuel charge effectively. After ending production of the first hemispherical engine designs in 1958, Chrysler V-8s went primarily to a wedge-style chamber with paired inline valves, but development of the original Hemi design was integral to the later competition version, first introduced in 1964.

One crucial factor was the angle relationship between intake and exhaust valve locations. In testing, 58.5 degrees offered optimum flow between the valves' timed openings. A four-cycle internal combustion engine has four strokes. Induction is the downward stroke drawing fuel into the cylinder. Compression is the upward stroke that compresses the fuel mixture for ignition, normally by a timed electrical spark. Power is the downward stroke from the release of energy after ignition. And exhaust is the upward stroke pushing spent fuel out of the cylinder.

In a performance-designed hemispherical engine, the piston is domed to partly fill the chamber in the head, helping the combustion and exhaust cycles. However, this requires precise calculations to keep those cyclical events in rhythm and balance without the damaging effects of parts hitting one another.

The hemispherical design began to show its merit, even in the early 1900s when several European makes incorporated it into luxury and racing automobiles, in minimizing heat loss to allow more efficient combustion. Friction and heat are the two biggest detriments in any

Marty Robbins, popular country music star, was also an occasional pilot during the halcyon days of Chrysler's NASCAR program. He is seen here with the #42 Dodge wing and his guitar at the only event he competed in during 1970, in October at Charlotte Motor Speedway's National 500. (Photo Courtesy CR Racing Memories 0301011/Racing Pictorial Collection)

engine; minimizing them increases power. In the 426 Hemi, both the larger domed piston surface and deep combustion chamber help dissipate heat. The valves, located across the curved plane from each other, augment this by a cross-flow configuration. This means that the fuel mixture comes in cooler from the intake side, is spent, and is exhausted on the opposite side, again creating efficiencies.

The Hemi design had two significant drawbacks. One was the complexity and cost of the valvetrain needed to actuate the design. This was one of the unfortunate realities that caused Chrysler to cease using the engine's initial configuration in the late 1950s. The second was the weight and design of the reciprocating pieces (piston, rod, crank) in the bottom of the crankcase. It became a serious problem with the advent of engine designs permitting greater RPM levels.

This is the engine and cars that made history. The 1970 World Championship Dodge of Bobby Isaac and Harry Hyde (left) and one of the lowest-mileage Street Hemi Daytonas in existence (right) are behind an original 1966 426 Street Hemi auto show cutaway engine at the Wellborn Musclecar Museum in Alexander City, Alabama.

In simplest terms, an engine is an air pump. The faster a pump of a given size can spin, the more power it is capable of creating. The desire for lighter bottom-end parts, coupled with a greater understanding of flame travel and airflow characteristics, eventually made the true spherical chamber design less attractive in many forms of racing. The sheer durability and effectiveness of the basic Chrysler design, however, left it as the sole powerplant in professional nitromethane fuel racing on dragstrips and other environments where this fuel is legal. Various lower-class cars also use the Hemi in competition.

Fiat Chrysler Automobiles has continued the use of the term Hemi to describe engine efficiencies and designs even if the actual combustion chamber is now refined from a true half-dome configuration.

At the time of the 426 Hemi's arrival, certain realities were unforeseen: the auto racing sanctioning body's disdain for true dominance, the coming challenges of emissions controls, and the frank advent of political correctness in marketing automobiles. These factors hastened the end of the engine in its most visible environments before other technologies exceeded it.

In the following pages is the story of the second-generation Chrysler Hemi, released in 1964 and measuring 426 ci. The story is not relayed so much in mere technical terms, which has been told before, but in reference to its race-bred successes, challenges, and packaging. The young engineers who brought this engine into America's popular culture did so during a time that was ripe for generating mass appeal. Television broadcasting, car magazine proliferation, the "youth culture" with its postwar money and ideals, horsepower technology, and new car sales markets all came together in this crucial decade. The Hemi became not only a race legend, but also *the* iconic powerplant of the American muscle car when racing needs resulted in a mildly detuned street version. In the ensuing decades, that notoriety was passed down, rarely seen but frequently mentioned when it came to recounting American performance automobile racing and manufacture in the period of 1964 to 1972.

Even on its golden anniversary, 50 years after arriving, the classic second-generation Chrysler Hemi engine remains today as a testament to the efforts of the engineering and executive minds at Chrysler Corporation. The objective to win (hearts, minds, and races) was met and actually exceeded all expectations. Here is its story. . . .

CHAPTER ONE

1953-1962
A Revolution Begins
The First-Generation Hemi

It was the most powerful internal combustion engine that Chrysler Engineering had ever built and remains so. Surely its goal was performance. It had hemispherical combustion chambers, an aluminum block, twin magnetos, forged pistons, and a dry-sump oil system. But the goal of the first Hemi that Chrysler engineers created was not winning an event on a Sunday afternoon, but helping to end a vicious, bloody war that was engulfing most of the world.

The first Chrysler Hemi engine, XIV-2220, was not an automotive engine. Rather it was a contracted project for the U.S. Army to create a 2,500-hp airplane unit for the war effort. Begun in 1939 and worked on for much of the duration of World War II, the piston-driven powerplant was designed for unheard-of durability and power; it first flew in July 1945. The engine was inverted with the crank above its 16 cylinders (each with its own cylinder head similar to a radial airplane engine), displaced 2,200 ci, and became XP-47H once installed in a fighter plane for testing. However, the promise of jet propulsion was on the horizon, and the explosive advent of the atomic age was less than a month away. Before being fully refined, the Hemi program was canceled and the experiment ended.

It was a shame that founder Walter P. Chrysler did not live to see XP-47H tested. By all accounts, he would have loved the ideas incorporated in the exotic design. Chrysler succumbed in 1940 to the effects of a stroke when the Battle of Britain was raging and before the United States was involved in the conflict; the attack on Pearl Harbor was still more than a year away. It was a true honor that the military had come with a project of this caliber specifically to Highland Park, Michigan, where the company and engineering department that bore his name was headquartered.

Choosing a Course

Chrysler the company, founded by its dynamic leader in 1924, was the final member of what had become Detroit's Big Three auto manufacturers. It had

survived the Great Depression and World War II that followed. However, a group of executives who continued to embrace the ideals of the prewar era remained as

the great, new Chrysler
FirePower Engine
the sensation of the century!

This color cover from the 1951 Chrysler FirePower engine brochure announces a new engine for America's postwar consumers. The term FirePower had connotations unforeseen at the time. (Photo Courtesy Chrysler Group LLC)

This 1951 cutaway 331-ci Hemi display (in the Garlits Museum Engine Room in Florida) shows the internal workings of the early engine. This opening salvo was the basis for its legacy in various forms of motorsports into the next decade. Even after being discontinued by the company for 1959, the bigger-displacement examples were highly valued, especially in nitromethane-legal racing classes.

Chrysler Corporation's leadership in a world that rapidly changed as hostilities ceased and more personal desires took over. The story of the Hemi as a racing powerplant is the coupling of the war effort's development, the need for a V-8 passenger car engine (Chrysler had remained with straight cylinder designs throughout the period), and the need to occasionally overcome internal forces that stoically held to tradition.

Within just two years of the war's conclusion, single-cylinder testing that had already determined the hemispherical combustion chamber design in the V-16 was confirmed as optimum for an automotive engine as well. Plans were laid to begin development and construction of a suitable version to power the company's vehicle line. After adapting both a double-overhead cam and pushrod-actuated prototype hemispherical cylinder head to a traditional Chrysler straight-6, a 90-degree V-8 version was completed. This was first designated the A182, which became A239 as it achieved refinements for possible manufacturing concerns. Set at 331 ci, the engine had an oversquare design (determined by a greater 3.81-inch cylinder bore and lesser 3.63-inch reciprocating stroke), and the noted cylinder head configuration. Both helped with its efficiency.

Inside each spherical combustion chamber, carved into the head casting above each cylinder, were valves measuring a 1.81-inch intake and 1.5-inch exhaust opposed on an optimally determined angle difference of 58.5 degrees. Dual rocker shafts were required in each head to actuate the valve gear because of these valve locations. This engine entered the new-car market in late 1950 as part of the 1951 Chrysler model line under the

This detailed image of a 1954 cutaway engine at the Garlits Museum shows the camshaft and pushrod styles, twin rocker shafts, and valve positions.

In this image of the same engine, note the first-generation port shape and size, something that was addressed with good success by the second-generation version thanks to Harry Weslake.

FirePower name, a marketing term that became almost an understatement in the ensuing decades.

The war had resulted in changes to popular culture. An innocence had been lost, and a sense of determination to succeed regardless of setbacks had been instilled. This was no more evident than in what became known as the car culture. Hot rodding had begun before the war, but its popularity was tuned and fueled in the years following, helped by a cadre of men with war-honed skills and imaginations. The need for speed, the semi-recklessness of youth, and an unstated determination that the old had passed and new horizons were ahead added up to a focused desire to make it better, make it faster, and make it to the finish line before the other guy.

Wally Parks, a former California dry lakes racer, became the visionary of this movement when he created an association to help channel these pursuits from the boulevard onto measured, timed courses nationwide. This was the National Hot Rod Association (NHRA). Robert Petersen saw publishing as a way to stimulate further interest in racing and cars, founding *Hot Rod,* then *Motor Trend,* and then a string of other magazines that made him an empire builder in his field.

As the work was going on in Highland Park to create the first Hemi V-8 prototypes in the 1940s, Bill France gathered an assorted cast of characters in a Daytona Beach hotel to discuss a combined effort for stock-bodied racing, a popular pursuit on fairgrounds and temporary courses where open-wheel exotics were not prevalent. He called his new group the National Association for Stock Car Auto Racing, better known as NASCAR.

The A311 Record Setter

The new Chrysler engine quickly made itself the focus of interest in all these places, somewhat to the chagrin of Chrysler's conservative management, who were more enthralled with its fuel efficiencies and market competitiveness with Cadillac and Lincoln. Regardless, the company's inherent desire to pursue engineering possibilities led to the engine being reworked for performance venues with a hands-up directly from Vice President of Engineering James Zeder, who had helped spearhead the engine's approval. Although Briggs Cunningham, a wealthy sports car builder, went racing internationally with Chrysler Hemi power in those formative years, this prospect for power found its most focused calling with the A311 program. That program began in earnest after the long-standing American Automobile Association (AAA) sanction announced the possibility of allowing a 335-ci stock block program for the 1953 Indianapolis 500.

Previous work on an engine test program named K310 used modest aftermarket changes, and it had already found that a gasoline-burning, multicarbureted 331-ci Hemi was capable of 353 hp; now all the stops were pulled out. Leaving it at the stock displacement, engineers John Platner and Don Moore experimented to come up with a 400-horse version burning methanol, with bigger valves, a roller camshaft, and fuel injection.

Upon hearing of its success in testing with drivers Rodger Ward and Joe James, the AAA quickly rescinded the offer in the face of opposition from well-heeled Offenhauser-equipped competitors, dropping the displacement limit to 270. A smaller version was built but did not prove to have the required ability for a number of reasons; it was pulled from the 1953 event before qualifying was over.

Nevertheless, the company still saw the A311 as having promotional possibilities, even if it was not screaming at the Brickyard. The first to take advantage of this was Firestone Tires, which supplied a majority of the competition shoes at that time for the Indy cars and wanted a less-finicky tire-test engine than the full-tilt Offy. The answer was the A311. Fortunately, Chrysler employed Ronney Householder as a racing liaison. He was a former Indy driver and a longtime associate who had appeared in Firestone advertising prior to the war and that may well have played a role in this opportunity.

Chrysler Engineering maintained the engines, and the A311 reached its apex of fame when the company opened up its new test track facility in Chelsea, Michigan, in the summer of 1954. Four top drivers were on

The A311 engine helped spearhead the factory-based performance efforts of the Hemi engine for racing. After being rescinded from Indy competition, Chrysler built these specialty engines for Firestone's tire test program. (Photo Courtesy Chrysler Group LLC)

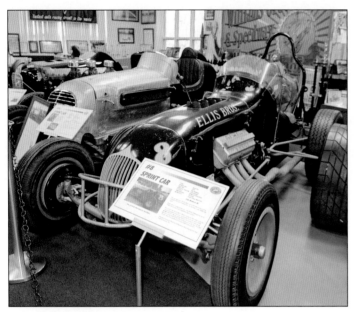

The Ellis Brothers, like other competitors, found success running a Hemi engine in sprint car competition; in this case, the Dodge Red Ram. Here, the car is at the Eastern Museum of Motor Racing in York Springs, Pennsylvania.

hand, three of them with competitive Indy 500–bred Offenhauser roadsters and Sam Hanks in the A311 Firestone test car, which was built and maintained by another Householder associate, Ray Nichels of Indiana. The world closed-course record stood at 148.17 mph at the time and was decades old. All four cars broke it that day at Chelsea, with Hanks going fastest at an amazing 182.554 in the A311, a new record that stood for a number of years. Hemi power broke it again in the next decade or so.

Power for the Masses

For the hot rodders and postwar America, 1955 was a watershed year. Many point out that the small-block Chevy arrived on the scene, but more important for Chrysler fans was the new Chrysler C300. It was the result of ongoing development of the Hemi V-8 engine, which had now become a Chrysler mainstay and had also been added in various smaller displacements to both the DeSoto (in 1952 as the Firedome) and Dodge (in 1954 as the Red Ram) model lines.

In 1952, 35-year-old Robert Rodger was promoted to chief engineer of Chrysler Division, overseeing the Chrysler and Imperial lines. Also serving as head of Chrysler's Product Planning Group, Rodger had come up with a concept to put the street-performance version of the 331 Hemi, which now made an actual 300 hp, between the fenders of a New Yorker. Aided by designer Virgil Exner, Chrysler added an Italian Ghia-styled nose from the Imperial as well as curbside and creature

comforts, and sold the new-for-1955 model as a performance car.

The Chrysler C300, named for its horsepower number, was a big hit on the showroom floors, even among those who could not afford it. This car was akin to some of the legendary prewar machines such as Duesenberg and Cord that had been sold based on a good top speed as well as the body design. The theme that Rodger hit upon was, in actuality, the muscle car: a street car whose primary reason for being was to promote performance in a stylized body design.

The idea was not lost on hot rodders, who had already been using versions of Hemi FirePower in street rods, drag cars, land-speed machines, and race boats. The new C300's biggest fan, however, was likely an older gentleman from Wisconsin who owned the Mercury outboard boat engine company. Elmer Carl Kiekhaefer had already seen the possibilities of Chrysler Hemi engineering with past efforts in the 1952 and 1953 Carrera Panamericana Mexican road races. After running Chrysler New Yorkers in 1954, he bought, built, and campaigned a string of new C300s in both NASCAR and AAA stock car racing for 1955. With big-name drivers, he dominated that year with multiple cars, his own engine lab work, and enclosed car haulers.

Backed by Mercury Outboards, Frank Mundy won the final AAA stock car season title. The organization left the business of sanctioning races after that season when a racing accident in Le Mans, France, killed dozens that year. Meanwhile, Tim Flock, a noted driver in southeastern

This photo of the 1955 AAA champion, signed personally by driver Frank Mundy, is in the Chris Economaki Collection at the Eastern Museum of Motor Racing in Pennsylvania. Mundy, driving for Carl Keikhaefer's team, was that sanction's final stock car champion. (Photo Courtesy Eastern Museum of Motor Racing Collection/Uncredited Personal Image)

Don Garlits' re-creation of the first dragster into which he installed a Hemi is simply named First Time Out. It was a forerunner to his legendary string of touring Swamp Rat cars. The heavy 354-ci Chrysler engine ruined the frame while being flat-towed for the first time. The frame had formerly hosted a fuel-burning Ford flathead.

circle-track racing, did likewise with Mercury Outboard–backed Chrysler products in the NASCAR Grand National standings.

Kiekhaefer also hired other drivers, including Herb Thomas, "Speedy" Thompson, and Tim's brother Fonty, who also won events in his cars. There was one other racer who was finding success with Chrysler power on the growing NASCAR circuit, a less well-heeled racer from the piedmont of North Carolina: Lee Petty.

Petty had run straight-6 Plymouths since 1949 because of their durability, but switched to a Dodge Coronet in 1953 when the first 241-inch Red Ram Hemi Dodge appeared. He won his first NASCAR season crown the following year, running both Dodges and Chryslers. The Petty crew went on to become a big part of the next generation of the Hemi, although this heritage was established early on.

The legendary Emory Cook-piloted Cook & Bedwell dragster is also preserved at Garlits' facility in Ocala, Florida. After Cook gave Don some rapidly dictated speed secrets, Garlits came back to beat the vaunted car at the 1957 World Series of Drag Racing in Cordova, Illinois, that same weekend. Cook's spectacular performances at Lions Drag Strip in early 1957, repeatedly topping 160 mph, led the NHRA to actually ban nitromethane for several years.

Meanwhile, a young hot rodder out of Florida had gone to a late-model salvage yard outside Tampa to buy an overhead-valve V-8 Cadillac or Olds engine for a car he was using to tow his primitive Ford flathead dragster. "As kids we thought nothing would ever replace the flathead; how could anything be better than that? But we knew they didn't have torque, either, so you wanted something that could tow," recalls Don Garlits today.

"The moonshiners wanted those Cadillac and Olds engines, too, so when I got to the yard, the owner Claude Majors told me someone had come in the day before and bought every one he had. Then he said, 'Donald, I've got just what you need,' and took me in the back. There was a 10,000-mile 1954 four-door Chrysler sedan with a Hemi in it. It had been rear-ended, but it was beautiful."

The plan was to swap the engine into a 1939 Ford daily driver; Don paid $450 for it and took it home. He quickly found out the car was fast on the street, and soon after, he made a very quick 114-mph run at the time trials held at MacDill Field. So Garlits decided to put this Hemi engine into his "rail job," a car he had built strictly for drag racing. The engine's weight bent and ruined the chassis during its first flat tow to Brooksville, Florida, but Garlits was undaunted. He quickly built another chassis, learned how to run the engine on ever-increasing amounts of nitromethane for fuel, and the rest is history.

The Hot Dodge D500

Although Plymouth never had a Hemi in the early days, Dodge had a racing package car that arrived in 1956: the D500. The D500 was announced in December 1955 as an available option on the Custom Royal and Coronet sedan model lines. Certainly spurred on by Kiekhaefer's success and his connections with Chrysler's executives, it was built to have a lighter body for circle-track racing and special features to legalize it as stock, such as Imperial-type brakes and suspension parts. A raised-deck 315-inch single WCFB carb version of Dodge's Super Red Ram Hemi

This 1956 Dodge D500-1 is a rare surviving example of this special NASCAR vehicle, which was created in very limited quantity as a package car for racing. The one here is basically unrestored, moderately re-lettered, and was very likely used in drag racing. Tim Dupont of Utah owns it.

The engine in the D500-1 featured a dual-inline Carter WCFB 4-barrel carburetor on the 315-inch Super Red Ram and heavy-duty suspension parts. This was the ultimate racing package from the factory in the first-generation Hemi era.

was under the hood. An even better upgrade, the D500-1, was released soon after, on January 12, 1956. It used two WCFB 4-barrels and boosted the power number from 260 to 276.

Kiekhaefer, now with Buck Baker as his primary driver, took home a second NASCAR season crown that year, using the new 354-inch 300B Chrysler and D500-1 Dodges. Ironically, at the end of that season, he realized he was promoting Chrysler more than Mercury Outboards (whose very name created its own confusion in the racing world), and he subsequently sold his circle-track equipment and concentrated on high-powered watercraft.

The 1956 Dodge set numerous records. A recent Korean War veteran, Arnie Beswick, out of Illinois, ran one successfully in drag racing. After the start of 1956, the initial D500 package was broadened to include other Custom Royal and Coronet bodies, including station wagons. Sales success then muddied the D500's heritage further still when the term was applied to larger, 325-inch models in 1957 that were much heavier than before. That same year, Chrysler bored out the Hemi V-8 to its legacy maximum size of 392 inches for the first time, installing it in the new 300C. However, by then, the clock was ticking for the first-gen Hemi engine.

Changes for Better or Worse

The manufacturing of the dual rocker shaft Hemi engine, with its heavy weight and complicated valve gear, was costly. In 1955, to replace the final straight 6-cylinder engines in its lineup, Chrysler introduced a new single rocker shaft V-8 engine, the Spitfire. This engine featured a polyspherical combustion chamber, with the exhaust valve upright and the intake canted, but both operating from the same rocker shaft. Quickly adapted to the smaller blocks in other lines, it became the Red Ram at Dodge (the Hemi was renamed Super Red Ram), and

The Hemi was bored out to 392 ci for 1957, and it could be found in the Chrysler 300C, which featured Virgil Exner's classic Forward Look vehicle styling. Robert D'Agostino of Delaware owns this rare survivor convertible.

Buried under the twin air cleaners of D'Agostino's 300C is a Hemi in its most potent street form. Many of these beautiful cars were scrapped as time went on, often by racers who simply needed their scarce engines for more performance-oriented desires.

Plymouth's first V-8, the Hy-Fire. In 1956, Plymouth created the basis for what became the A-engine design, coupling the existing poly-head design with a new smaller block configuration.

Meanwhile, the company engineers were busy developing a fresh big-block design that became referred to as the B series. Although the Hemi efficiency and performance were indisputable, testing showed negligible differences between the poly configuration and the inline wedge chambers already used by other auto companies. The wedge design was also lighter and less expensive to manufacture than the poly version, a fact not lost in the argument.

This new engine first showed up in 1958 in 350- and 361-inch sizes. With a deck height of 9.98 inches, as measured from the crank centerline, it became the LB, or simply B, engine. Chief Engineer Robert Rarey directed the simultaneous development of a higher-decked (10.725) design, which became the RB (raised-B) engine. The inherent design benefits and cost savings quickly proved themselves, and production of the first-generation Hemi ended just as it had begun when the 1958 model year concluded, as the sole province of the Chrysler/Imperial line.

Meanwhile, Back in Detroit

Hot rodding had become a national pastime; even the cover of *Life* magazine said so. For young college graduates with this interest, looking for a job at one of the Big Three was a given.

For instance, one was a legal scholar, Elton "Al" Eckstrand, who, after being disappointed by opportunities at the FBI and General Motors, bravely made a personal appointment to see E. C. Quinn, then president of Chrysler. He was given five minutes at the corporate headquarters.

With his application signed off by Quinn himself, Eckstrand went on to work for the company until 1960. He was better known as Al when the suit came off and the racing gloves went on. Like many others at the time, he was a street racer, but also drove cars on the beach at Daytona for the Pure Oil time trials and started drag racing at the strips that had begun to spring up in the Detroit area. Eckstrand's high-echelon connections allowed him audiences with executives that the engineering guys didn't have.

The next year, 1956, the company was interviewing a young Penn State physics graduate to possibly work in the engine lab. Tom Hoover was deciding whether he would land at Chrysler or pursue a career over at Pratt & Whitney. The roar from a dyno cell made his decision. It was a freshly built A311 race mill under load. He was told by his guide, "That's a Firestone engine; special stuff," according to an account in Dave Rockwell's book, *We Were the Ramchargers*. Hoover immediately decided that Chrysler was his place.

Lunchrooms and a Labor of Love

Rockwell, who worked as part of the Ramchargers team even though he was not an engineer, noted that too great an interest in performance and racing could possibly "vaporize a promising career" for a young engineer at Chrysler in those days. Kindred performance-loving spirits often gathered in the corporate lunchroom. Hoover met guys like himself, among them Tom Coddington, Mike Buckel, Jim Thornton, and Wayne Erickson, plus others. They appreciated everyone else's efforts and talents, even if they worked in separate parts of the

Members of the Ramchargers were at one of the NHRA's Hot Rod Reunions in Bowling Green, Kentucky, to be honored for their efforts in racing. A replica of the High & Mighty 1949 Plymouth is at left; team members are in the truck.

Accelerating during exhibition runs at the Bowling Green race, the original Plymouth built by the Ramchargers in 1959 was noted for several important innovations in the sport.

engineering labs in Highland Park. In keeping with the times, they decided to form a car club, the Ramchargers.

The Ramchargers became one of the most feared teams in drag racing. Starting with their personal cars, they first experimented with a variety of ideas against competitors on Woodward Avenue. When the NHRA Nationals landed at the new Detroit Dragway for two years, 1959 and 1960, they built and documented an engineering exercise, taking advantage of the A311 engine science on a 354-inch Dodge truck block in a 1949 Plymouth coupe; it was eventually called *High & Mighty.*

The car, running on gas in the Chevrolet-populated class of C/Altered, demonstrated how their creative minds worked when ideas congealed. It featured the first tunnel-ram-type intake, tuned single-pipe headers with bell ends, a scientifically analyzed center of gravity, wheelbase adjustments, and other tweaks never before seen in dragdom. However, when the NHRA rewrote the rules for 1961, it ended the *High & Mighty*'s legacy in competition with a pencil stroke.

So, for 1961 racing, the team decided to see what could be done to put the company's newer products into NHRA competition. This came through Dodge thanks to the efforts of Frank Wiley, who had just become the director of public relations for Dodge and Dodge Truck. The ungainly 1961 B-Body Dart, powered by a 413-ci RB wedge engine, became the weapon of the moment. Quite interestingly, a .060 overbore on this RB block gave it a displacement of 426 ci. More important at the time were the changes to the ram manifolds that had become part of Chrysler performance cars, all of which were large, heavy vehicles (except the Valiant, which optionally used a ram-tuned slant-6 layout developed by Tom Hoover).

Ram Tuning for Torque and Power

The ram-tuning effect played a significant role in the technology that ended up in the 426 Hemi drag racing

package and in Chrysler's noted bathtub NASCAR intake. Balanced velocity of a singular air/fuel charge between the intake runner opening at the intake manifold's plenum area and the valve was the goal. The idea was to cram the air into the cylinder by its resonance and air speed; think of pressure backing up against the intake valve to rush into the cylinder as soon as the valve opens. By dividing the desired RPM level by 84,000 (a number derived from other air-speed calculations), a very specific length for the intake runner could be mandated for ram tuning. The lower the RPM desired, the longer the runner length.

These effects had first been observed during the work on the A311, but Hoover and others in the engine lab had begun to apply the principle for passing-gear acceleration at 3,000 to 3,500 rpm by ram-tuning intake manifold runner length. These became part of the production car option releases for 1960 on B- and RB-type engines. However, that RPM meant having carburetors literally

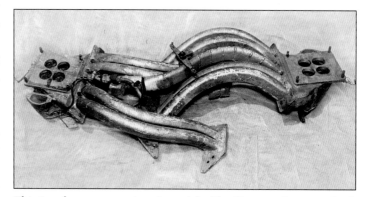

This is a long-ram setup (provided by Kramer Automotive). It is an early hand-fabricated version for testing, possibly during the beginnings of the ram induction program.

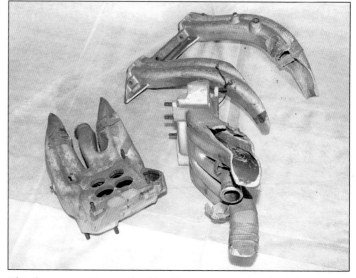

This long-ram (provided by Kramer Automotive) is a cutaway set modified by removing plenum area separations, which in turn allowed for the ram effect to occur at greater RPM levels.

draped over the opposing valve covers to achieve the ram effect on a 30-inch runner.

For the 1961 Dart to be used in racing, the team cut a set of manifolds apart with careful precision and reworked the twin runner's wall separation inside, creating an actual per-cylinder runner length of just 11 inches to move that ram-tuning effect into the 5,000- to 6,000-rpm range. Ram tuning was worth 5 to 20 hp based on how much tuning could be done to the exhaust as well.

The first place the new stocker ran was testing at Detroit in early August, but it made its mark in the Optional/Super Stock category at the 1961 NHRA Nationals at Indianapolis Raceway Park. Eckstrand marched through the field, a single Dodge (and Chrysler product) among the Ford, Chevy, and Pontiac competitors in the top 50 stockers racing for Mr. Stock Eliminator. Beating Dave Strickler and Mickey Thompson landed the Dodge in the semi-finals against Dyno Don Nicholson. Against Dyno Don's 409 Chevy, shifting problems with Chrysler's underdeveloped 3-speed manual transmission ended the team's race day.

As the team prepared to leave, the NHRA asked the Ramchargers to run a match race against Nicholson, who had just beaten the Arnie Beswick car in the final round. Eckstrand won the match convincingly, which gave Frank Wiley a lot of magazine ink. Nicholson later admitted to (the late) Jim Thornton that agreeing to that one match race was one of the dumbest things he ever did. Hoover, meanwhile, contends that it was the most important drag race in the history of Chrysler racing.

Regardless, with Ramcharger carb specialist and deal negotiator Dan Mancini working with track operators, the team was paid to run match races for the first time. Late that same year, Tom Hoover left the engine lab to become the company's new race coordinator for Chrysler Engineering.

The Way Things Were

Change was in the wind nationwide as the 1960s approached. For the manufacturers of passenger cars, the reality of political intervention reared its head. Congress had begun an investigation into the marketing of performance in relation to public safety after a tragic accident at the 1955 24 Hours of Le Mans killed more than 80 people, as well as smaller but dramatic racing fatalities in the United States. On June 7, 1957, a committee from the American Manufacturers Association (AMA) announced that it was recommending that all members, including Chrysler, Ford, and General Motors, cease advertising power and race prowess, cease promoting races as part of corporate policy, and other terminations. The AMA resolution was a paper tiger for men such as Semon "Bunkie" Knudsen at Pontiac, who just wanted to sell cars and figured he could still get pieces to racers one way or another.

For Bill France and NASCAR, who were already feeling the effects of advantageous factory involvement after the Mercury Outboard team's C300/D500-1 efforts, the AMA decision was first considered a blessing. However, the powers that be in Highland Park knew Kiekhaefer's NASCAR effort was canceled and concluded that fewer visible gains would be possible. Like General Motors and Ford, they also agreed to the AMA's recommendation. However, time proved this agreement could not withstand the pressure of the coming performance era.

Ray Nichels (standing) and Paul Goldsmith with the Firestone tire test car, after the early Hemi project had disappeared. In this image from 1959 it appears to have received a Pontiac engine. Little did the duo realize when this image was taken that they proponents of the Race Hemi during the 1960s. (Copyright CR Racing 0501065, Ray Mann Photograph)

For those who wanted to race, whether drag cars, hot rods, land-speed cars, or boats, the familiar engine had its plugs running through the valve covers. This competitor is from the 1961 NHRA Nationals. (Photo Courtesy Ray Mann Archive, quartermilestones.com)

CHAPTER TWO

January 1963-February 1964
The Dawn of a Legend
The 426 Elephant Engine

Sound carries in winter, and in those cold days of early 1964 in Highland Park, Michigan, what echoed down the nearby residential streets from the dynamometers at Chrysler Engineering's brain trust was something else.

This was a deep, threatening roar resounding from the company's well-known crucible of technology, designed to reset the ideas about Chrysler Corporation vehicles more than any prior advance had. To this day, engineers associated with the evolution, as those first 426 Hemi race engines came to life, recall it as a sound never equaled in their memory.

As mentioned previously, before the 1950s ended, the Hemi engine, in its original form, had proven itself over and over, but had fallen victim to changes in perceived economies. During its chrysalis, which lasted from 1958 until early 1963, many other changes occurred in the world and at Chrysler.

From a racing perspective, the AMA agreement of 1957 to not promote products via competition was quietly being put away by most Detroit manufacturers. The depictions of automobiles in popular culture, advances in engineering and styling, and perhaps most important, the construction of the huge paved Grand National racecourse in Daytona Beach, meant you needed horsepower to be "in with the in crowd."

Chrysler had gone through a good deal of upper-level managerial upheaval, even scandal, during this time, with a former external auditor, Lynn Townsend, ascending from comptroller to the position of president in the middle of 1961. Townsend was noted as being fiscally

The 426 Hemi prototype engine as finalized in circle track form was photographed for release to the media, possibly before the problems were solved. Chrysler was now ready to make racing history. (Photo Courtesy Chrysler Group LLC)

In 1964, respect for the owner of a new Race Hemi engine in drag trim was immediately established when the hood was lifted. Longtime racer Bob Reed told me that the first event he ever saw a Hemi run during a southern match race, his father turned to him and said, "Boy, you gonna have to sell all this 409 stuff, 'cause we ain't gonna outrun nobody."

conservative, but he also had two teenage sons. They let their dad know that Chrysler products were not making many inroads, either in power or appeal, among the younger people who were cruising the byways of Detroit and elsewhere. By that fall, the new president set up a new racing development group. In October 1961, Tom Hoover became the first race engineering coordinator for the company.

Ramchargers Influence

The first order of business was taking what the Ramchargers had learned already in their 1961 NHRA Nationals foray into late-model drag racing, subsequently developing the Maximum Performance 413 engine (known as the Max Wedge) car packages around the new 1962 models.

So, events leading up to the Hemi's formal debut were actually quite fluid. Thanks primarily to the ongoing race development efforts of the Ramchargers, the Max Wedge went through a number of quick iterations in that short time. After being offered at 413 ci in 1962, it was pushed out to 426 ci to meet the latest Automobile Competition Committee of the United States (ACCUS) 7-liter (max 427.17-ci) limit the following year. It was then developed even further with advances in manifold, cylinder head, and valvetrain design.

All of this happened over the course of approximately 28 months. The final version, known as the Stage III, arrived for racing at almost the same time the dynamometers at Highland Park were first testing the new 426 Hemi. The environment in which the Hemi was developed was not static. And it was full of well-educated, enthusiastic, race-seasoned engineers who wanted nothing more than to see Chrysler succeed.

And yet members of the original Ramchargers team, which included college-educated engineers at various disciplines within the company, were not professional

Tom Hoover and his cohorts at Chrysler Engineering had taken the things learned through almost a decade of street performance, racing efforts, and product development to create the first Max Wedge engines and package cars around the 413-ci RB engine, seen here with a cross-ram intake and free-flowing exhaust. It was this experience that helped launch the new 426 Hemi in less than one calendar year. This example is part of the Englehart Collection.

racers. They were hot rodders with schooling, work discipline, and camaraderie. All of them were expected to be on the job five days a week doing mostly non-racing-related engineering work, arriving at 8 am on Monday regardless of if they had just towed their race car all night from who knows where.

These weekend jaunts could take them out on Friday right after work, towing throughout the Northeast or Midwest for multiple events, and back into Detroit long after midnight on Sunday. Work on equipment happened on weeknights. This successful effort was achieved along with a remarkably high rate of team members staying married; it's a tribute to the wives, who deserve credit for allowing it to go on as long as it did.

Had it only been about winning on the quarter-mile, Townsend could not have been happier with what was

The rear view of a 1962 Plymouth, on the eve of Hemi development, and as the Max Wedge era began to show signs of being a serious threat. Although styling issues were going to leave a bit to be desired early on, power had become an important facet of Chrysler's market presence as a result. This example is part of the Englehart Collection.

Buck Baker stands beside his Chrysler Newport at Daytona in 1961. Styling on the early 1960s model line was done by committee, and the results during those tumultuous times were unfortunate. (Copyright CR Racing 0701063, Ray Mann Photograph)

already accomplished by 1964. During the Max Wedge era, Hoover and the crew developed first-rate equipment, and after verifying the engine's utility first-hand on the track, put that information and parts into the hands of racers, who in turn put Chrysler products into the winner's circle across America with regularity. The team itself had won both major NHRA events in 1963 in Stock Eliminator.

A lot of the success was achieved because of the development of better peripheral components, especially with Chrysler's new 3-speed Torqueflite transmission, which did not have an equal at that time. Of course, during 1962, Ford was still ramping up its efforts, and General Motors was dominating in the experimental ranks in drag racing. However, things on that front changed quite rapidly at the start of 1963.

AMA Resolution Fallout

On January 21, 1963, GM President John Gordon and Chairman/CEO Frederic Donner notified the presidents of their corporate divisions that General Motors would indeed continue to honor the original AMA resolution of 1957. This directly affected the racing programs of the Pontiac and Chevrolet Divisions, now headed by Pete Estes and Bunkie Knudsen, respectively. Estes quickly terminated his contracts, including a major backing of Ray Nichels' operation in Indiana.

Nevertheless, Knudsen's guys ran the Daytona 500 with the canted-valve big-block engine that later became the Chevrolet Rat Motor in 396 and larger formats. A publicity blackout gave it a more notable name: Mystery Motor. Associates under Knudsen managed to keep a handful of NASCAR and drag racers busy through the 1963 season, but any help was going to be given solely as research and development support, without any formal associations. Meanwhile, with the racing focus now past, Estes' chief engineer, John DeLorean, helped spearhead Pontiac's newest street toy, the GTO.

As this scenario unfolded, Ford recognized that it

was perfect timing for its efforts and heavily funded programs in all forms of auto competition, taking on the moniker Total Performance. This was based around not only NASCAR and drag racing, but also a very serious, exotic, and expensive effort in sports car, open-wheel Indy car, and Formula 1 racing. Millions of Ford dollars went into racing during that decade.

If corporate "outsider" Lynn Townsend had not been president of Chrysler, it is possible that Ford would have ended up with little focused competition in almost every form of domestic auto racing (except drag racing) after General Motors pulled out. But Townsend was president, and his Chrysler team also saw that General Motors' sudden and almost complete withdrawal made success a real possibility.

The Executive Board Weighs In

Although work was already ongoing with a better-evolved circle-track effort for the RB engine, particularly with the Petty family (who had enjoyed support from Plymouth since 1959), it was not enough. Townsend reportedly called for an executive board meeting soon after the running of the 1963 Daytona 500, where the Max Wedge Plymouth, driven by Richard Petty, had finished sixth behind five Ford entries. Townsend wanted a program to take home the top accolades at Daytona 500.

Beyond Petty, a number of Chrysler campaigners running in NASCAR also used the wedge engine, but the engine design had endemic difficulties when considering the requirements of extended, high-RPM running. The wedge combustion chamber design, with its pair of inline valves set closely together and semi-shrouded by the chamber's shape, was not optimal for high-RPM cross-flow breathing. Nor were the head ports (intake or exhaust) conducive to efficiencies for a long run. Add in the necessity for better bottom-end durability, and success was going to require either a very steep redesign or all-new design, and the only practical alternative was to withdraw from factory circle-track efforts entirely.

Race Coordinator Tom Hoover later recalled how things progressed very soon after that gathering of the

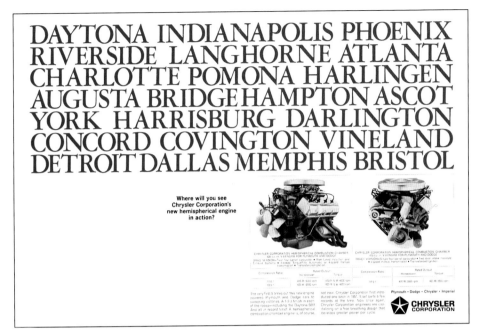

DAYTONA INDIANAPOLIS PHOENIX RIVERSIDE LANGHORNE ATLANTA CHARLOTTE POMONA HARLINGEN AUGUSTA BRIDGEHAMPTON ASCOT YORK HARRISBURG DARLINGTON CONCORD COVINGTON VINELAND DETROIT DALLAS MEMPHIS BRISTOL

Where will you see Chrysler Corporation's new hemispherical engine in action?

This double-page advertisement showed photos of the new 426 Hemi engine and listed well-known race-tracks where the engine competed. (Photo Courtesy Chrysler Group LLC)

executive board, "The meeting that launched the 426 Hemi as a new idea was in a little conference room on the second or third floor of the main engineering building on Oakland Avenue in Highland Park, not in a hallway as is sometimes thought.

"It was called by Bill Rodgers, who was Bob Rodgers' brother. Bill was the assistant vice president of engineering, so when the word came down from Townsend that he wanted to win the 1964 Daytona 500, Bill called the meeting; he started it and then left. So it was Robert J. Cahill, Willem Weertman, Don Moore, and myself; all engineering people. Don was the second-in-command of the A311 program and had been my boss in the engine lab before the whole race program got started."

The men agreed that the original Hemi design did not need much improvement. With their backgrounds, they were also aware that this would be a big step forward if it could be redesigned to fit the existing block. Their consensus was to propose adopting a new Hemi head using the same basic designs that the company's past engineers had developed and refined onto a strengthened version of the RB block, retaining that engine's crankcase and displacement dimensions (4.80-inch bore center, 4.25-inch bore, 3.75-inch stroke) for the sake of cost and time.

After some initial design considerations and with approval from the engine group up through Chief Engineer Robert Rarey, racing group executive Jack Charipar talked to the executive board about this effort. Tom Hoover accompanied him, carrying the A311 engine blueprints. The meeting went quickly and smoothly, ending with Townsend looking at them with just two words: "Do it." The decision was finalized on paper soon afterward.

Assistant Chief Engineer Willem Weertman, who worked directly beneath Rarey, assigned Frank Bialk, a talented development draftsman, to the job. Bialk, who worked in the Advance Engine Group (that is, prior to release for actual production) under Bob Dent, was to do the initial layout for a new hemispherical head; it was March 28, 1963, and the engine was given the designation A864.

To say this adaptation was a simple translation of old technology to an existing block is incorrect. Bialk's parameters were to retain the 58.5-degree difference in the angle between the intake and exhaust valve locations and to find a way to add a fifth head bolt (that was already used in the RB block) to the new head for better cylinder head retention and sealing. In addition, he was asked to make the engine installable on the assembly line, where the unibody shell of the car is lowered over the engine and associated K-frame-based suspension components. Even though it was a team effort and Bialk's creative genius is not to be denied, Hoover's insight helped make some of this more quickly feasible.

Better Heads

The challenge began with the valves centered in the combustion chamber, which now possibly included a very long exhaust rocker arm. Weertman humorously called this "the pump handle." There was also an issue with its pushrod location, now running through a main bead for the head gasket. Hoover suggested simply rotating the entire valve layout on its center toward the intake side. This, in turn, maintained the original 58.5-degree split, and it brought the exhaust valve location to a more upright position, allowing for a shorter exhaust rocker arm and resolving the pushrod problem.

Bialk laid it out, and by modifying the shape of the outer edge of the valve cover, clearance for the assembly line drop (with minor changes) was also achieved. Although this tightened the intake valve-to-piston location on the lower edge of the combustion chamber somewhat, Bialk found room for a huge 2.25-inch intake valve and 1.94-inch exhaust valve in the new locations despite

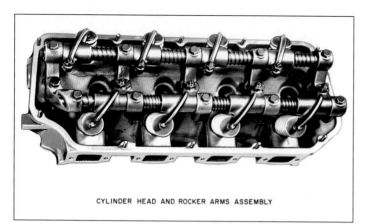

CYLINDER HEAD AND ROCKER ARMS ASSEMBLY

The angled offset of the engine's rocker arms. Had the valves not been rotated off the bore centerline toward the intake manifold, the lower row of exhaust rockers would have been much longer, making assembly installation very difficult, if not impossible. (Photo Courtesy Chrysler Group LLC)

a spherical radius of just 2.42 inches (4.84-inch circumference) for the combustion chamber. As previously noted, the Hemi chamber was actually spherical in depth, not a true 180-degree hemisphere; imagine one-third of a ball as opposed to the full half dome.

As with the early double-rocker Hemi, each head used twin steel shafts milled for oil movement to support four rocker arms apiece. The arm's arches were angled across each shaft for clearance with one another, and light coil springs separated and centered them from the shaft supports. In turn, those five shaft supports were not cast into the head, but instead premachined from iron, positioned with dowels, and each held in place with one head bolt. The forged malleable steel rockers utilized bronze bushings to prevent galling, and they were actuated from the camshaft using hollow pushrods with hardened steel end caps and mechanical tappets made from steel extrusions with iron heads.

This arrangement worked, but even at this point, the engineers involved understood that valvetrain weight and geometry needed to be as durable as possible. In time, the heavy, complex arrangement created some challenges as engine RPM levels increased.

The valves, based on the reworked combustion chamber as measured from the bore centerline, had a 35-degree angle on the intake side and a 23-degree angle on the exhaust side. Stem diameter for intake and exhaust was .309 and .308 inch, respectively, and used a high-RPM valvespring featuring inner and outer coils separated by a spiral dampener. Steel retainers and valve locks held it all together.

Final valve-lash adjustments were made using an adjusting screw/lock nut arrangement on the pushrod

side of the rocker arm. Carried over from the early Hemi, the unique spark plug was located close to the center of the chamber, offset to one side between the two valves. Each wire was routed through a removable tube inserted in the valve cover.

The fifth head bolt was its own problem. The RB/Max Wedge used five head bolts (the early Hemi had used four), but a normally spaced and fitted fifth bolt needed to go directly through the center of the Hemi's intake runner. Bialk pondered this issue for a while and then came up with the idea of attaching this fastener through a boss cast into the tappet (or lifter) valley. Milled open, a stud that threaded into the head directly below the intake runner ran through the boss and was torqued down via a nut at the base of the boss.

"The A311 experience was all based on that 58.5-degree difference in valve angle; that drove the whole thing," remembers Hoover. "The A311 was one hell of a program, and frankly, that kind of thing rarely happened around Detroit. Bill Weertman considered Frank Bialk's major contribution to the design how he attached the head to the cylinder block and solved the issue of the fifth head bolt. Bill thought it was the big deal, but I felt the 10-degree inboard tilt of the valvetrain was it.

"What the tilt did was solve two other serious problems. First, we were really concerned by the long exhaust rocker arm being able to run high-valve-gear speeds. I mean, Garlits and those guys were spinning the old 392s at 7,000 rpm. We did not want to use an exhaust rocker

This is a ported 1964 Hemi segment (provided by Kramer Automotive). This view shows the rotation of the valve positioning toward the intake side to shorten the exhaust rocker arm, and the threaded area beneath the intake port for the fifth head bolt (later a stud) to come up through the tappet valley. Harry Weslake designed the mild-contour rise on the lower port surfaces to help facilitate better airflow and port velocity. This was critical to the initial design. Weslake also gave input for the design of the final Stage III MW port that same summer of 1963.

any longer than the 392. But if we had not moved it, the other problem was that the exhaust pushrod was positioned right through the head gasket bead. Sealing would have been a real problem.

"There was another benefit we understood pretty quickly. That change also improved the shape of the intake port. For decades, that port on the 426 Hemi was the standard by which the whole industry judged their intake port flow performance."

The head was not fully completed yet. Creating performance-oriented port runners was now paramount, but the one thing not available was time. Chief Engineer of Vehicle Performance Planning Bob Cahill's connections with racing designers in Europe were called upon. Sir Harry Weslake, based in England and knighted for his work on the Rolls-Royce airplane engine during World War II, came onboard as an outside contractor. The exhaust side of the head was now constrained by the valve's angle and head dimensions, resulting in a dogleg bend.

Hoover chuckles, "We knew that exhaust port needed all the help it could get, and only a world-class flow expert of Weslake's stature could understand how to fix it. Sir Harry worked a lot on that exhaust port, but actually could find very little wrong with the intake port. Bialk got that right the first time.

"One thing that Sir Harry was concerned about was the engine's lack of swirl; swirl is basically the effect of how the incoming charge goes down into the engine bore. It needs velocity coming out of the port and around the valve, and, done properly, turns within the cylinder to improve the mixing and reduce cylinder pressure. If your incoming charge is also increasing pressure while the piston is moving toward top dead center, you are fighting yourself; it is pushing against the crank."

Bottom-End Modifications

Next, work turned to the bottom end. One major difference between the early Hemi block and its wedge replacement was the lower skirt. The wedge used a deep skirt, a 3-inch vertical lower edge that allowed the main caps supporting the crank to be further supported within the sides of the block itself. For the RB-based Hemi engine, engineers added cross bolting through the block's skirts to further strengthen it; these were added to Bialk's redesigned mains number 2, 3, and 4 using larger 3/8-inch cap bolts. This was a critical change in terms of bottom-end durability.

A 1966 SAE paper coauthored by Weertman and Robert J. Lechner on the Hemi noted that the vertical separating load (measured at top dead center) on the main supports at 7,200 rpm was more than 18,000 pounds. The

The piston's shape fit into the combustion chamber. Not often considered was the sheer piston weight required to raise the engine's compression ratio in the deep, 4.84-inch-circumference spherical chamber. (Photo Courtesy Chrysler Group LLC)

cross bolts greatly stabilized this effect. The early Hemi block using nitromethane did not have skirts so a similar solution was reached. A milled steel aftermarket girdle was added that did basically the same thing. It was positioned between the block and oil pan, but this did not fix any inherent casting deficiencies in the block casting itself.

The reciprocating hardware was almost all new as well, as Bill Weertman recounts in his excellent book, *Chrysler Engines 1922–1998*. Starting from the bottom end, the forged crankshaft was dimensionally similar to the RB version. But it was also shot-peened, machined, lapped for smoother journal surfaces, and finally nitrided or tuftrided by heat-treating the machined surfaces with ammonia to further harden them. The NASCAR versions used aircraft-grade 4340 alloy steel (for greater tensile strength), while the drag race crank was made from a slightly less costly 1046 carbon steel formula. Both proved to be more than adequate.

Onto this long arm went new connecting rods that featured a beefier I-beam design and strengthening in a number of areas, plus large 7/16-20 rod bolts (increased in 1966). The arm used a non-floating tool steel wrist pin in the rod with the pistons moving on a .0007- to .0014-inch interference clearance on the pin bore. The new piston was made from a large aluminum extrusion, impacted during formation to give a thickness of .305 to the piston head, which in turn was then machined for valve reliefs. To achieve the desired 12.5:1 compression coupled with the .020 head gasket, the piston protruded out of the bore by .755; minimum piston-to-valve clearance was set at .070. A three-ring layout was chosen for piston sealing and oil control. All of this rode on tri-metal bearings.

During the initial dyno work, rod designs were slightly modified, but the real issues showed up in the piston and block (which I discuss shortly).

This cutaway of an early 331-ci Hemi from 1954 resides in the Garlits Engine Room. Note the very thin lower walls of the block casting and the lack of skirting at the pan rail. Nevertheless, this was the de facto engine for nitromethane applications by 1964.

This 1966 cutaway Street Hemi resides in the Garlits Engine Room. It shows that the skirting issue was amply addressed when the early RB-series wedge design was finalized. For the Hemi, cross bolts went through the sides of the skirt and into the crank-supporting main caps for stability. Note also the thick cylinder walls.

A mechanical tappet camshaft and a double-roller-timing chain layout synchronized cam events to the crank. For NASCAR racing, cam timing was finally settled at 312/312/88 (intake/exhaust/overlap), while the drag racing cam was initially at 300/300/76, with lift at .520 inch. During the latter part of 1963 and early 1964, these cams were in simultaneous development; a .540-lift version was eventually introduced and used in the 1965 A990 engine. Of course, the aftermarket was involved almost from the beginning as well.

That left the externals. The ignition was set up using a black Prestolite transistorized box for greater spark accuracy, with the dual-point distributor mounted at the same front location that the wedge used. This required some minor adaptation to intake manifolding based on its angled positioning. The intermediate shaft was geared to work off the cam and also turn the oil pump, which was redesigned for greater volume and mounted on the driver's side of the block. A group of pan and pickup configurations based on the given racing environment was also developed.

Finishing it off, engineer Forbes Bunting created a dual-plane intake design in keeping with NASCAR's single 4-barrel rule, which first used a Holley vacuum-secondary model with the NASCAR-mandated maximum $1^{11}/_{16}$ x $1^{11}/_{16}$ bore layout. Working with Hoover, he simultaneously reworked the existing Max Wedge ram intake for the Hemi engine to mount two offset 4-barrel Carter carbs.

Dyno Testing

With plans finalized, the company's American Foundry in Indianapolis produced the initial blocks while the first heads were cast, complete with Weslake's port developments, at the Campbell Wyant Cannon foundry in Michigan. These parts were sent to the Trenton, Michigan, engine plant for machining and then to Highland Park for final assembly. Hoover jokingly told author Dave Rockwell that it was the engineering equivalent of the D-Day invasion of Normandy. Weertman and his crew rode herd over the supply chain to ensure that all of the pieces were on hand.

Virtually everyone inside and out understood the nature of the challenge in terms of timing for the early 1964 debut and contributed to the effort. The first new 426 Hemi engine began assembly late in November, and the moment of truth for the effort came on December 6, 1963, when the initial engine was fired up on one of the smaller dyno cells at Chrysler Engineering.

Pulling on the dyno handle, the hope was to surpass the Max Wedge's maximum power number of about 490 horses. According to engineer and engine builder Steve Baker in Anthony Young's epic book *Hemi*, Assistant Chief Engineer Ev Moeller was in charge of the engine's dyno development and among those watching as the first elephant began to roar. The needle on the Amplidyne dyno (now preserved in the Walter P. Chrysler Museum in Auburn Hills, Michigan) only went to a 400-hp measurement. Using slide rules to calculate the amount above that, the engine attained 425 horses at just 4,800 rpm.

Moeller gave the okay to keep going so that the operator would not get in trouble if the dyno broke under

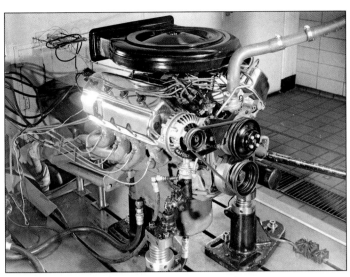

A replicated version of the early 1964 Hemi first being tested on an Amplidyne 400-hp dynamometer is on display at the Walter P. Chrysler Museum in Auburn Hills, Michigan. (Photo Courtesy Chrysler Group LLC)

the strain. According to Mike Buckel, the engine put out 530 hp on that first run and exceeded 550 in subsequent pulls. Dyno operator and Golden Commandos team member Troy Simonsen also verified that the first 426 Hemi was indeed run on one of the smaller units because of time constraints.

"The dynamometers on which the race Hemis were normally tested at Highland Park were water-cooled, eddy-current GE models," remembers Hoover. "The water ran over the armature to cool it and fell to the floor.

Forrest Pitcock, who drove the Golden Commandos race car on occasion when not operating a dyno for Chrysler in Highland Park, replicates that first A864 Hemi pull at the display now found in the basement of the Walter P. Chrysler Museum. In this image, Pitcock's son Scott serves as his assistant.

The first A864 I saw run was in room 12. I remember because it was a fresh engine and they were checking the valve-gear oiling; the rocker covers were off and smoke and oil was all over the place.

"Now, for some reason, I was not at the cell when the first Hemi was tested. I think Buckel was there. The big difference was that the Amplidyne had a lot of copper wire wound around the poles of the armature, meaning it was speed limited. Get it moving too fast, and the copper windings on the armature could get thrown off; a bad idea. Ev [Moeller] really took a risk if he ran that first Hemi on an Amplidyne. If something had broken, someone would have been in a lot of trouble.

"We also had room 7 set up as a load cell with an inertia wheel. You would start at, say, 3,000 rpm and bring it up to 7,000 rpm, then figure out the elapsed time number by the time it took to move the wheel. It was nothing but a gigantic flywheel on very good bearings, the equivalent of a 3,600-pound vehicle with a 4.10 axle and no wheelslip. Mike Buckel and Forrest Pitcock did the most significant work in load testing with the inertia wheel. They did the only work within engineering on high-nitromethane content; they made 1,350 hp from a normally aspirated 426."

Unfortunately, the joy was short-lived. As fresh engines were brought on line, a number of piston failures occurred in rapid succession. According to Jim Thornton (quoted in Rockwell's book), these were the result of high-RPM heat stresses on the piston, causing the pin to loosen in the piston skirt, which in turn caused the piston to fail with extremely damaging consequences. The piston was reengineered to move the pin location up farther, add more material in the crack-prone areas, and reduce pin-piston clearance. However, valuable time was lost.

"The biggest problem I remember with the initial engines was with the piston pins," agrees Tom Hoover. "They didn't break; they wanted to move sideways. We went to a larger pin; I think from 1.03 to 1.09. And the retention clips that held the pins in place, we reworked those as well."

Once these issues were resolved, testing in earnest began. They replicated the severe race conditions of a 500-mile race by moving the engine through a variety of RPM changes over the course of several hours. (This was the sound mentioned at the start of this chapter.)

Track Testing Disaster

The real crisis emerged late in January. The law of unintended consequences came into play. The cylinder blocks were cracking vertically along the right bore bank, opposite of the redesigned piston pin pier. The angle of movement of the piston on the rod end during the rod's rotation cycle is called piston cam. Now, thrust from that hefty 867-gram piston was exerting enough pressure under long-running conditions to stress the cylinder walls in that area to crack them.

Ray Nichels' associate, Paul Goldsmith, performed the first track test from January 14 to January 21 at the Goodyear test track in San Angelo, Texas. It had showed promise but resulted in two engine failures despite warm-up and careful prep. Steve Baker wrote an internal memo dated January 27 as a follow-up to the weeklong effort. It records that the first engine, after two days of set-up and a number of warm-up laps, failed after just one full-throttle lap. A Nichels Engineering–built A864 Grand National Hemi engine was installed next, and, after chasing ignition issues, also went just one wide-open-throttle (WOT) lap before it, too, failed.

Back in Detroit, the endurance test engines also showed problems. Larry Adams, a racing engineer, went to Bill Weertman's office the day after Baker's report was released with a frank assessment that the new Hemi block itself would not last 500 miles, period. The piston had just been redesigned, so that solution was immediately ruled out. Moreover, it was now January 28; the Daytona 500 was only 26 days away.

Core Stress

Because the cast-in cylinder bores are surrounded by water passages for cooling, Weertman and Adams looked at the failures and determined that perhaps the cylinder walls could be made thicker and have some additional metal added to their exterior during the coring process. A block is cast from multiple forms, or cores, made of chemically bound wet sand, supports, and other materials. The group of cores for a cylinder block are first made in molds, dried, and then fitted together to create an overall structure of passages. The cavities are then filled during the molten metal pour, taking into account shrinkage and material changes.

"The core is made up of complex shapes made of sand, with a sort of glue holding it all together," explains Tom Hoover. "The exact mix was usually a carefully guarded secret at each foundry. The final tooling for the cores would have been made of stainless steel, but for an experimental piece, we used plastic to make the cores. To modify those core castings, you might use a putty knife to gently scrape some of the sand off, but you wanted your best good-old-boy hands doing that. Not just anyone could do it right, and they carefully recorded whatever they changed so it could be repeated."

This meant that the hoped-for solution entailed shaving away some of the casting sand from the premolded water jacket core so that more molten metal filled that area during the pouring. Templates to do this were specified, and Chrysler foundry liaison Louie Taylor and pattern maker Earl Pinches flew from Detroit to Indianapolis with the directive. Time was critical.

They attempted the changes, but the fragile sand cores did not hold together to make pouring possible. Another day lost, Taylor frantically called Weertman, and Bill was immediately on a flight to Indiana. Looking at what had been done, he realized that the change required some more finesse. They had solved the thickness issue, but now could not pour a block. The three men worked for several hours on gently file-changing fresh-cast water jacket cores (both sides) in those areas for another attempt. Because of the size of the melt, they modified enough to cast 12 blocks and made templates for future use.

They left to try to get a couple hours sleep at a hotel. Soon after the final castings emerged from the modified cores, the foundry called Weertman to tell him the whole run was scrap because of large, voided areas where the hot metal had not filled in.

A. J. Foyt is at Indianapolis Raceway Park in one of Norm Nelson's wedge-powered Plymouths in the spring of 1963. Already competitive in wedge form on short tracks such as IRP, the following years found Chrysler dominating everywhere with the new engine. (Copyright CR Racing 0501011, Ray Mann Photograph)

"You use an oven-type fixture to dry the cores once they are cast," states Hoover. "If, due to the rush to save the program, the cores were not completely dry, any moisture would flash to vapor and make a void in the casting. Once the casting is done, you have to wash all the sand out of it; the core assembly is ruined doing that. You have to mold another group of cores each time."

Another set of cores were created, scraped, prepped, set up, and poured. The core process itself took about three hours, and the engineers eventually worked around the clock with a group of cooperative foundry employees. On February 3, as the race teams rolled toward Daytona to formally enter Speedweeks competition for the Daytona 500, the first good blocks emerged from the process. Weertman examined them and approved the run, but told them not to ship to the Trenton plant for machining yet.

During the January dyno testing effort, factory metallurgists from the company's stress lab had analyzed the new block structure as well. They had electronically measured the strain levels inside the casting during a full weekend of dyno testing. With the loads created by its heavy reciprocating parts, the redesigned RB Hemi block was subjected to internal conditions not seen before, and weakness was found in the normally stable bulkheads. A resulting recommendation was a furnace stress-relieving process, accomplished by rebaking and then slowly cooling the fresh castings prior to machining, all of which added time to the process.

"The problem was, those first blocks had enough stress built into them that they almost cracked just sitting there," recalls Hoover. "Metallurgy is involved, but the heating and cooling was also vital. Add in design issues, such as avoiding sharp corners and things that can induce cracking under the load by the reciprocating assembly, and there were problems. The solution was heat treating."

Meanwhile, Bill France's Daytona Speedway had begun to come alive for the 1964 year. Driver Paul Goldsmith had already seen what the engine could do, as he had test-driven 180 mph in Nichels' Plymouth in Texas the month before. In early 1963, with Pontiac's support gone, circle-track friend Ronney Householder hired Nichels. He had taken on the additional responsibility at Householder's request to become Chrysler's primary race component distribution point. The factory had also picked up other former GM teams during 1963, such as those of Ray Fox and Cotton Owens, as well as continuing support of the already-established Petty Enterprises.

By the time Weertman and his team had received those machined blocks back at Highland Park and begun another big series of endurance RPM testing on the

redesigned version, the beachfront racetrack was open. Prerace inspection began on February 4, so a number of teams had the earlier, but weaker, renditions of the engine to use for qualifying, with Householder giving orders to not fully show their hand.

In Conclusion

"The story has been floating around about the problems with the block," says Hoover. "But it really was Bill Weertman, in the middle of the night, who saved the whole Daytona Beach effort. He made the cylinder walls thicker and, thanks to advice from some of the old hands at the foundry there, made it happen. He is one of my heroes; he was a very disciplined person. Just look at his book on Chrysler engines. It was a gargantuan task to put all that on paper. He did it."

As an aside, following several days of testing in California using cross-ram Hemi drag engines built by Nichels Engineering from early castings, the company had already given up on any attempt to get an A/Factory Experimental 426 Hemi drag package into action at the NHRA Winternationals that month. Despite development work on a drag version of the engine that had been ongoing at the same time as the circle-track configuration, it showed little improvement over the Stage III Max Wedge at the track. It was quietly dropped and the Stage III wedge was run at the early 1964 events. Besides, everybody was now focused on winning the 1964 Daytona 500.

This colored cross-sectional execution of the new Hemi helped introduce it to the public once the engine was released. The Hemi wrote history in terms of engine technology as well as racing. (Photo Courtesy Chrysler Group LLC)

CHAPTER THREE

1964
Seven Liters of Elephant

NHRA and NASCAR Domination

The world of racing changed when the checkered flag ended the 1964 Daytona 500. The follow-up dyno work on the February 3 castings proved that the fixes initiated by Bill Weertman had worked and Chrysler was no longer simply playing games.

The manufacturer came to win. As the Indianapolis foundry cast more good Hemi blocks during the first two weeks of February 1964, everybody knew they were cutting it very close and the race date for the Daytona 500 was just around the corner.

Although those better engines were fastidiously fitted together by engine builders such as Baker in Highland Park, Daytona's sports car races and Continental races came and went. Suddenly it was February 21, two days before the 500, and time to finalize starting positions. In the meantime, the teams receiving the latest engines actually drove from Daytona to Detroit and back nonstop; the company didn't want to risk flying the powerplants to Florida in one group. As the weekend began, engineer Bob Lechner and a friend drove to Florida in a pickup truck with four additional backup builds as a final precaution.

As per NASCAR rules that year, there had already been two short pole-position races in the very first week to determine the starting row. On February 6, Paul Goldsmith was in a Nichels entry and Richard Petty in the blue 43. Both Plymouths showed what was coming, even if they had the less-durable engines. On practice laps, they clocked 174.91 and 174.42, respectively, barely resetting a long-standing 173-mph unblown Daytona track lap record by Dick Rathmann in a United States Auto Club (USAC) Champ Car in 1959. In a Daytona newspaper article published the next day, even the 1963 winner (and Ford driver) DeWayne "Tiny" Lund had to admit, "That Mayflower billygoat of Petty sure did fly."

The Plymouth pair then sealed the deal on February 8 when Goldsmith won the first 50-miler (20 laps) for the pole and Petty won the second one for the other front-row seat, both with speeds averaging more than

Bud and Barbara Faubel in the Honker Hemi Dodge, the very first assembly line–Hemi Dodge, now owned by collectors Don and Mary Lee Fezell. Although Bud did not score his first big national win until the following year, the Hemi turned the racing world upside down right from the beginning.

170 mph. In addition to now leading the pack for the Daytona 500, these victories also put them in the first spots for the two 40-lap (100-mile) qualifying races held on February 21 to determine the remaining starting positions for the 500.

Of course, as soon as the pole runs were over, the cat was out of the bag. Ronney Householder was all smiles, noting to the press that the new hemispherical performance engine was capable of 500 hp. Although not mass produced, Chrysler released 110 or so lightweight drag racing specials fitted with the Hemi, plus a handful of steel-nosed examples before the end of the 1964 model run. This satisfied Bill France's idea of a production (versus experimental) engine.

All through Speedweeks, the teams were instructed not to run the engine flat out, as the factory did not want to give anybody an undue reason to complain before the big show. After all, General Motors was now out of racing (the manufacturer had won every Daytona pole from 1960 to 1963) and Ford had assumed it would have little trouble dominating with the latest Total Performance wedge engine, also new, even if the big Marauders and Galaxies were giving up some size to the 116-inch-wheelbase unibody Belvederes and Dodges.

However, even without going flat out, the eight Chrysler Hemi cars managed to take the seven top spots, plus tenth (#5 Jim Paschal), during the February 21 qualifiers, and both events were won by Dodges (Junior Johnson and Bobby Isaac). The 1964 Daytona 500 Hemi teams included two cars from Nichels Engineering (#25 Paul Goldsmith's Plymouth on the pole and #26 Bobby Isaac's Dodge in fourth), two Plymouths from Petty Enterprises (#43 Richard Petty in second and #41 Buck Baker in 5th), two Dodges from Cotton Owens (#6 David Pearson in seventh and #5 Jim Paschal in tenth), one Dodge from Ray Fox (third-place #3 Junior Johnson), and one Plymouth from Burton & Robinson (#54 Jimmy Pardue in

sixth). There were a handful of other Chrysler campaigners as well, but only these aforementioned teams had the new Hemi powerplant.

"I was there, but not for the race," recalls Tom Hoover. "I sweated out all the fresh engines coming down, even the ones Lechner brought with his buddy, and was there to see them win the qualifiers. I stayed as long as I could until I just barely made it to Pomona; the problem was, the races were on the same day. But by then I figured, 'If they can't win the race now, there's nothing I can do about it!' I did get to go back down for the Firecracker race [NASCAR Grand National race at Daytona] in July."

The better engines, some being driven from Michigan as all this happened, were soon needed. Johnson won the first 100-mile qualifying races on Friday but reported falling oil pressure. A post-race inspection showed that the block bulkhead had split along the oil galley from the cam clear down to the main bearing support. There was little hope for the original block configuration to go the distance of 500 hard miles.

Had the engineering team at Chrysler not chosen to do the extreme-duty endurance testing a month earlier, the Hemi might have been nothing more than a footnote to folly in the history of the Daytona 500, regardless of its horsepower potential. As we know, it is winners who make history.

Race Day: February 23, 1964

February 23, 1964, dawned crisply cool in Daytona, with a record-size crowd on hand for the finale. Both Richard Petty and Paul Goldsmith were using blocks that had been cast on February 10. They were stress-relieved, machined, and built into race engines; broken in on the Highland Park dyno rooms; and then trucked to Florida during the previous couple of days.

Petty was upholding the family business, and his father Lee chewed on a big cigar as the race lined up to start. Lee was now a multiple-time Grand National series champion. He had won the first paved race at Daytona and then been sidelined by a gravely injurious wreck during the 1961 qualifying for the race. He and son Maurice were serving

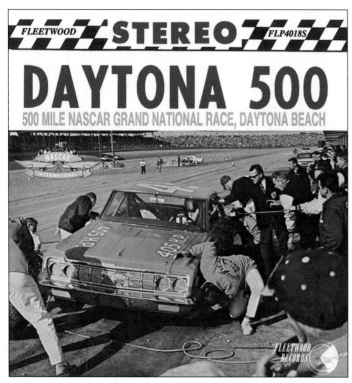

The Daytona 500 was a big enough deal that a record of the sounds and announcing of the event was released. This is a collector's item today.

From the beginning, circle-track racing required parts that didn't look much like those used on the street or dragstrip. This pair of large-capacity oil pans from the 1960s was provided by Kramer Automotive. The dry sumps had not yet been developed.

as co-crew chiefs on the team effort, with young Dale Inman heading up the pit crew.

One primary reason for the Petty operation's success was an intense attention to detail. With long years of experience in NASCAR racing, the Randleman, North Carolina–based team left little to chance and nothing on the table. Car prep was secret, the equipment was top notch, and Richard was fearless. In five prior seasons, he had won many events and posted two runner-up finishes in the yearlong Grand National points chase. The team made the wise choice as the day unfolded to change tires on every pit stop and was prepared with stacks already marked for each corner of #43.

Goldsmith, who had been running both stockers and Indy Champ USAC cars for several seasons, was spearheading Nichels' effort. Although the Pettys kept things close to the vest, Nichels had been assigned to do a good deal of chassis and technological car development by Householder and then relay those results to the factory for its overall effort and progress in the sport. As a result, Nichels Engineering's little shop in Highland, Indiana (close to Chicago), had quickly become a factory for parts and race cars for Chrysler competitors in NASCAR, USAC, and other sanctions. Plans for expansion in nearby Griffith were already being made.

According to researcher Bill LaDow, who interviewed Nichels extensively prior to his passing in 2005, the shop

had been developing chassis, suspension, and durability pieces throughout 1963 for Chrysler's circle-track assault. This depth of involvement was the reason Goldsmith was chosen to run the tire tests at the Goodyear track in San Angelo before the engine's release. Suspension engineer and Ramchargers team driver Jim Thornton had even ridden shotgun on one of the runs in Texas as Goldsmith chased the 180-mph barrier. The back tires lifting momentarily from the racing surface occasionally reportedly left backtracking skid marks as a testament to Hemi power and Goldsmith's nerve. Now, on a Sunday with all hands on deck, the 1964 Daytona 500 began with Chrysler officials keeping their fingers crossed.

Weertman, Lechner, and others were in the grandstands and were greatly concerned when Goldsmith, who led just one lap before Petty drove around him and took the top spot, made an unscheduled stop in the opening laps, as did some of the other front-runners. Had

Highly modified vented valve covers also were used in circle-track applications. These (provided by Kramer Automotive) allowed pressure and heat to be removed from the crankcase. They date to the 1964–1965 era.

Richard Petty takes a run around Bobby Johns en route to his 1964 win at the Daytona 500, beginning his quest for his first season-long NASCAR crown. (Copyright CR Racing 0601062, Ray Mann Photograph)

the engine failed? No, the problem was windblown paper debris from the stands blocking the radiator and causing overheating. During the first quarter of the race, Petty ended up making an extended stop when Buck Baker ran out of gas in the team's #41 entry, and both Plymouths rolled into the Petty pit areas at the same time.

In those days, one crew serviced both cars, and by the time it was over, Richard had fallen to fifteenth place. It was at this point that he decided to let the Hemi really go. Within 10 laps, clocking speeds on the backstretch well in excess of 180 mph, he retook the lead on lap 42. He never relinquished the top spot again that day, leading 184 of the event's 200 laps on the 2.5-mile circuit. And he was all by himself on the lead lap when the checkers fell.

Behind him came Purdue and Goldsmith to give Plymouth a 1-2-3 sweep. The Dodges of Cotton Owens/Jim Paschal and Ray Fox/Junior Johnson finished in fifth and ninth, respectively. Baker was twelfth, Isaac was fifteenth (having run out of fuel). The only car that didn't finish was Pearson, who blew a tire on lap 52 and totaled the whole side of Owens' #6 Dodge riding along the front stretch wall.

According to *Motor Trend*'s reporting of the race in May 1964, Ford was already developing the new 427 SOHC (single-overhead cam) and immediately asked NASCAR to make it legal. Bill France took a wait-and-see approach to that, but Ford knew it had some work to do, regardless of publicity bravado to the contrary.

Soon afterward, a humorous Chrysler pin was created and given away at Chrysler headquarters that stated "Total What?" in the same type style Ford used. The company had no intention of letting up on the pressure. The Hemi was a considerable force in stock car racing that year, and was also making history in the quarter-mile.

Hemi Quarter Horses

With Daytona behind them, the Ramchargers were able to take another look at the Hemi drag engine. As mentioned, the only real difference between the track engine and the drag engine in 1964 was the crank material, the camshaft, and the intake manifold. The drag engine program was also listed in confidential and inner-office correspondence as A864. In fact, you had to specify a separate circuit package (likely distributed through Nichels) to get the circle-track pieces. Although even some engineers have used the A990 nomenclature to refer to all cross-ram drag packages in 1964 as well as 1965, the A990 is actually the aluminum-head engine that was developed in the summer of 1964 and released in the 1965 car packages.

After the January test using a pair of 3861-S Carter carbs, the company consulted with Holley about the dual 4-barrel carb package for the ram manifold. Gary Congdon, a Ramchargers team member who worked with Holley, recommended using 770-cfm vacuum-secondary R3116A models and rotating each carburetor 180 degrees from its normal mounting. This placed the paired primary-inlet locations of the Holley to the outboard side of the manifold opening with the secondary openings both located inboard. The dynamic of fuel mixture movement through the plenum under real-world load conditions with this little change made a huge difference in performance and quickly proved itself on the track. One

These new tubular exhaust headers for the Hemi (provided by Kramer Automotive) were a vast improvement in both weight and flow compared to the cast-iron Max Wedge versions. Used in both circuit and drag applications, this set is in basic NOS condition with the crossover pipe to balance exhaust pulses. The two ends meet at a Y-junction and feed into a single muffler.

The drag cars ended up with a pair of 311 6-series 4160 Holley carbs mounted with the secondary bowls facing each other; the linkage rotated on a stud between them. This early race-used intake (provided by Kramer Automotive) has the plugs to access the removed intake bolts; the top did not come off.

of the engineers sheepishly admitted years later that the Carter carburetor specialist had already recommended this on the AFBs previously used, but that change was rejected at first because of the complexity of the throttle linkage needed for the Holley models.

Mounted in the new manner, it worked well. As a result, the new Hemi drag engine had Holleys on the ram intake, with the secondary float bowls facing each other, and a somewhat complicated center-mounted bell-crank linkage making it all work. The manifold was a one-piece aluminum casting, featuring carb openings covered by milled carburetor plates with square-bore $1^{11}\!/_{16}$-inch primary and secondary openings. The intake top was not designed to be removed. Cast-in bosses for threaded plugs were added to access the intake manifold bolts inside the plenum. The linkage unit was mounted to a raised boss in the center of the intake's top surface.

A864 Drag Packages

Under NHRA rules for 1964, a minimum of 50 units was needed to make the package legal for Super Stock. Both the Dodge and Plymouth models had received a serious redesign that year, considered much more stylish than the first Max Wedge entries. Because many teams already had 1964-model drag cars with the Max Wedge, some of the early Hemi engines went into those bodies. These cars ran in Factory Experimental until the actual run of Hemi Super Stock cars, built beginning in late April, were approved by the NHRA.

One of the first Hemis to make a formal appearance in drag racing competition was Melrose Missile VI. The year-old car is seen here at Bakersfield's March Meet in California in 1965 under the tutelage of Cecil Yother. The win painted on the side (at the 1964 Winternationals) was the final big NHRA Max Wedge victory in Mr. Top Stock Eliminator, when Tommy Grove was driving. (Photo Courtesy Charles Milikin, Jr.)

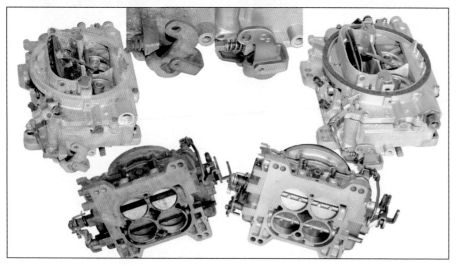

Here is a pair of nearly identical Carter AFB cross-ram carbs (both provided by Kramer Automotive): a 3705 for the Max Wedge (left) and a 3861 for the Hemi (right). Note the difference in linkage arms. Other changes were internal. According to paperwork found by Greg Lane, when Holleys were selected, already-released Hemi Carter carb sets were returned to Chrysler. These were later used on the steel hardtops built that summer.

George Nesbitt was an original Hemi car buyer in 1964. However, he and a partner later took the Hemi out of the Plymouth body and used the engine in a gasser. The body was sold and disappeared, and that partner later bought him out. Some years ago, Nesbitt was able to buy the original engine back, rebuild it, and create a tribute hardtop Hemi around it.

At that time, the Hemi was only available as a racing package, the NHRA-legal versions being lightweight sedans. For the street, the factory was still offering the single 4-barrel 426S wedge that featured smaller ports and better curbside manners than the Max Wedge. However, that summer, after the lightweights had been created, a very small run of hardtop models (35 Dodges and 35 Plymouths) with all-steel bodies, except the aluminum hood scoop used on Hemi vehicles, were built.

These 70 cars used the 3861-type Carter carbs, not the Holley versions. Tom Hoover surmises these may have been built to get rid of extra A864 pieces because they were not needed on the new A990 aluminum-head cars being readied for 1965. There is also some evidence suggesting these were created to fill outstanding orders for race cars from earlier in the model year. Contrary to popular belief, it is very unlikely that any of these late-built examples were sold specifically for circle-track use.

In the Greg Lane paper collection is an inner-office letter announcing that, on August 20, the A864 drag racing program was officially superseded by the new A990 aluminum-head package, which was used for the 1965 model run. A864 Hemi parts not being carried over were now obsolete. I cover the A990 design changes in Chapter 4, although the engine changes for it had already been finalized by August 28, 1964.

Maxed-Out Technology

Before looking at the actual 1964 Hemi car packages for drag racing, a review of their predecessors is in order. The 1964 Hemi drag cars were a combination of new horsepower plus the discoveries of the Max Wedge era. Two areas in particular seem to have come to real fruition with those A864 package cars: weight saving and wheelbase changes.

Weight Saving

Chrysler had come a long way since the 1962 steel-bodied 413-ci Max Wedges first arrived. In the process of becoming competitive, Jim Thornton developed methods of stamping aluminum parts, and some of them became part of the 1963 Stage I cars in February. The midseason Stage II race car package released in June of that year also utilized the panels. Coupled with moving the factory battery to the trunk area, there was a big difference in weight balance. In late 1963, the final Max Wedge combination was released with even more of the exotic pieces on 1964-model vehicle designs. The 1964 A864 Hemi drag package was actually the finale for the aluminum-panel effort in Super Stock, as major rules changes were enacted by the NHRA at the end of the 1964 season.

Hemi package cars were based on the sedan B-Body, the Savoy for Plymouth, and the 330 base model for Dodge; these units weighed less than the sportier hardtop editions. As with the final Max Wedge package, the cars received an aluminum diet of front bumper supports (previously aluminum in the Max Wedge; the Hemi car bumper was now thin-gauge steel), front fenders, hood with level-top scoop, radiator air shroud, and hood-lock vertical support brace. Added to this on the Hemi cars were aluminum doors swinging on aluminum hinges, with the use of plexiglass side windows and thin lightweight Corning glass in the rear; these doors had both vent windows and passenger car window mechanisms. The threaded aluminum tie-down pins placed in the four corners replaced the hood hinges.

Al Eckstand had this former Max Wedge 1964 Plymouth with a primered nose running in the A/FX category at the NHRA Nationals. A number of the earlier 1964 model package cars were re-engined with Hemi power. (Photo Courtesy Kramer Automotive Film/Print Library)

Most telling, both models were fitted with a grille that was an anodized polished stamping. Engineers redesigned the grille by mating two grilles to create a version with only a single headlight at each fender.

Inside, the cars used carpeting without jute backing, no sound deadener or undercoating, no dash padding, and no silencer pads, just as the 1964 Max Wedge package had. Except for the Hemi changes, the seats were the lightest available units, mounted on aluminum supports. In a March 24 letter to NHRA's Jack Hart written by A. W. Steckling, the special car manager of product planning, it was referred to as a "business coupe." The rear seat was removed entirely and replaced with carpet and a light filler panel.

Using multipiece welded tubular exhaust headers in place of the Max Wedge's cast-iron versions reduced weight even more. This in turn was coupled to an H-type pipe arrangement with bolt-attached cutoff plates, using a singular pipe leading from a Y-junction rearward over the differential housing, and then feeding the pipe into a single large transverse-mounted muffler located directly ahead of the back bumper.

In addition to moving the battery to the trunk, the battery selected was a 95-pound version from the truck parts book. This was mounted in a steel tray close to the passenger-side rear wheelhouse for better traction.

Wheelbase Changes

Aiding weight-saving measures were wheelbase changes. This development began innocently enough, as the Ramchargers wanted to come into alignment with the 1-inch difference between the Dodge and Plymouth production models for 1963. That, in turn, led to moving both front and rear wheels forward slightly while maintaining the legal wheelbase and taking into account a 1-inch production variance allowed by the NHRA.

Ramchargers Tom Hoover (left) and Tom Coddington (right) at the All-Hemi Reunion in Ohio in 2007 posed with the 2-percent Ramchargers A/FX car, showing the wheelbase changes that help spur on the more radical changes in 1965. This car is part of Mike Guffey's collection.

In late 1963, Jim Thornton and other members decided to take the wheelbase relocation for a Ramchargers Factory Experimental project even further for the 1964 season. This entailed using special upper control arms and torsion bars to move the front K-member and wheels forward 4 inches. Then they moved the rear axle forward 5 inches via its spring mounting points. This was all still within the 2-percent amount of variation from the stock wheel-to-wheel distance required by FX rules.

Four of these cars were built from Max Wedge race car packages in late 1963. For Dodge, it was the Ramchargers and the new Dave Strickler/Bill "Grumpy" Jenkins duo; for Plymouth it was *Melrose Missile* driven by Tommy Grove and the Golden Commandos. Al Eckstrand was driving during the aborted Hemi FX testing in California that January.

Running the 1964s

For 1964, the company was as aggressive on the dragstrips as it was in NASCAR. After all, the GM ban had not been a loss to Chrysler. Once available, Dodge quickly signed Bill Jenkins and Dave Strickler, who had previously been a thorn in everyone's side in hot factory-associated Chevrolets. Soon after the GM announcement, Hayden Proffitt, another former GM stalwart, moved into a Plymouth for 1963. He and the *Melrose Missile* entry from Northern California upheld Plymouth's West Coast honors.

Dodge had a new Detroit team (formerly with Plymouth) based out of Dick Branstner's fabrication shop. Ramcharger member and transmission expert Roger Lindamood was the driver, retaining his *Color Me Gone* car moniker. Dick Landy also moved from Plymouth to Dodge for the new season. Finally, the Ramchargers had an inner-factory rivalry made up of Chrysler employees in Plymouths, who called themselves the Golden Commandos, as well as Al Eckstrand, the former corporate lawyer who now ran Plymouths as "The Lawman."

Chrysler made the formal announcement for the 1964 Hemi package cars in March. The Dodge model was given the moniker 426 Hemi-Charger and the Plymouth was denoted as the 426 Super Commando, although valve cover decals still stated Ramcharger and Super Stock respectively. In print, the sedan bodies are often misidentified as sportier Dodge Coronet or Polara models, or Plymouth Sport Fury or Belvedere models.

With plans for the lightening package finalized, it was time to procure parts and assemble enough examples of each brand to become legal for Super Stock. A flurry of internal paperwork from February through April shows a very fluid situation with ongoing engine development occurring. J. W. Hurst of Chrysler Marine & Industrial finally sent a memo on April 3 stating that any further changes to the A864 drag package would prevent an estimated build start date of April 27 for the new packages (NHRA wanted any 1964 Super Stock package fully authorized by June 15 to prevent problems in tech at Indy). According to Jim Schild and the extensive research done by Darrell Davis, the majority of the lightweight Hemi race cars were created in mid-May. Bud Faubel of *Honker* Dodge fame received the first production example.

Although the initial valve cover clearance issue regarding lowering the body over the engine/K-frame assembly was fixed in the design stage, there was still a challenge in the assembly-line environment with shock tower clearance. Because of the offset of the wide engine in relation to the passenger-side shock tower, something needed to be done to allow the valve cover to be removed without unbolting and jacking up the engine.

The solution was two-fold: Reverse (or invert from the brake-facing side) the stamped shock mount support to move the shock's stud away from the valve cover lip, and cut a rectangular hole just above the frame rail in the tower for clearance. Some of the first cars delivered were not changed this way, but the vast majority were.

Driveline Options

The cars could be optioned with either the 3-speed Torqueflite or the just-released A833 New Process 4-speed, which had first become available that model year. Its drawback was a very high 2.66 first-gear ratio, making it difficult to launch the car on 7-inch tires without wheel spin. Like the Stage III Max Wedge 1964-model race cars, the Hemi used a 4.56 Sure-Grip gearset in an 8¾ housing that was actually the slightly narrower 1963 width (53.25 inches versus 1964 OEM 54.25 inches), likely to facilitate tire clearance. The spring mounting points allowed the rear axle to be set 1 inch farther forward as well. Brakes were drums on all four corners.

As mentioned, Hemi cars began appearing on the nation's dragstrips in late spring, first as Factory Experimentals and later, with verification of production, as regular Super Stockers, outpacing both the Max Wedges and facing down the threat that had been created by the Ford Thunderbolt. This was a lightened Fairlane with a 427-ci wedge for power, and although the Fairlanes held down the fort in Super Stock (eventually giving Gas Rhonda the points-cumulative 1964 NHRA World Championship), the Hemis ruled S/SA from the moment they arrived.

Meanwhile, work continued on FX development, culminating in what appears to be basically the car that Al Eckstrand received in early summer 1964. Eckstrand took delivery of a Hemi sedan from the Alexander Broth-

ers (the four FX cars were also sedans) that featured a rearranged wheelbase greater than that seen before. Eckstrand had formerly driven for the Ramchargers team, a relationship that had ended somewhat poorly in early 1963, but he knew everyone at Chrysler from President Lynn Townsend down. He used those connections to get both funding for his *Lawman* team cars and receive the latest equipment being developed. It landed him in the driver's seat of the *Golden Commandos* car in 1965 as well, and he was a talented driver.

He told me that he was simply instructed to pick up the car and use it. He ran this car as *Outlaw Lawman*, a match racer, during the summer and fall of 1964 with minor success, recalling that, as a lawyer by trade, he was uncomfortable because sanctioning authorities could dispute its legality. He also remembered receiving a very early set of prototype injectors created for the 426 Hemi in August of that year from Stuart Hilborn personally. Testing with these was very minimal due to Eckstrand's other non-racing responsibilities, and he was quietly reprimanded by friends in high places to remove them immediately.

Hilborn injection was an economical way to achieve maximum fuel balance and distribution. Mechanical fuel injectors for a Hemi were something Tom Hoover had begun pursuing in early 1964, despite the fact that they were not legal in Factory Experimental. A set was ordered that spring for dyno testing. He became particularly focused on this when word came down that Ford's SOHC engine was indeed becoming a reality for 1965 drag racing and was in the smallish, just-released Mustang

Al "the Lawman" Eckstrand received this Plymouth in the middle of 1964, and is posing with it in the Los Angeles Coliseum before embarking on a summer tour. This car was likely referred to in a July 31 letter to the NHRA, but it is believed to have not been allowed to run in FX competition by the sanctioning body. (Photo Courtesy Eckstrand PR Archive)

BIG DADDY'S FIRST 426 HEMI EFFORTS IN TOP FUEL

Don Garlits' first attempt to use the 426 in a blown-fuel rail was in Swamp Rat VIII; he has replicated this car and is using it at static Cacklefest events. It is seen here at the Garlits museum in 2014.

With a 92-percent dose of nitromethane crammed into the cylinders via the supercharger, Don Garlits has re-created the sights and sounds of 1960s fuel racing in Swamp Rat VIII, the car in which he ran a 426 Hemi.

Of course, the kings of drag racing were the fuel dragsters, which at this time (1964) were just breaking into the 200-mph range after a ban for several years by the NHRA. For many competitors, the early 392-ci engine was the weapon of choice for supercharged nitromethane consumption, and the potential performances were often tragically better than the safety available at the time. Many drivers were hurt and killed in the slingshot design. The engine was mounted directly in front of the driver where fire was a grave concern, not to mention traction and stopping issues on poorly built tracks.

In all fairness, safety problems were endemic to all motorsports in this time period, so danger came with the territory. Starting in 1964, the new 426 Hemi engine was developed in both a new dragster the Ramchargers built and by the most famous dragster driver of that era.

Already being referred to as "Big Daddy" at the ripe old age of 33, Don Garlits had maintained a working relationship with Frank Wylie and Dodge for a number of years, running Max Wedge Super Stock cars in 1962 and 1963. Even with parts at a premium, Garlits agreed to help develop the 426 engine for supercharged competition, while still racing his 392-ci *Swamp Rat* fuel dragster. This effort began in early 1965, and Garlits and his crew built *Swamp Rat VIII* to support the engine's progress. Its first notable success actually came in its debut, when driver Connie Swingle took the runner-up spot at a special consolation race for non-qualifiers during the 1965 March Meet at Bakersfield, California. Garlits himself won the 64-

car main event over another Garlits entry driven by Marvin Schwartz, both with early 392-ci power.

The following week, Garlits received a call from Wylie, who informed him, "Don, we are not making 392s anymore." Garlits was going to have to be the pilot of the 426 machine from now on. Garlits had recently bought shop property down the street from Dick Branstner Enterprises in Troy, Michigan, and had just moved his family from Florida, so losing his Dodge deal at that moment would have been pretty serious. Ironically, due to the weather and unrelated family needs, the Garlits family ended up in Michigan for only a year before returning to the Sunshine State in 1966.

Swingle's effort notwithstanding, at midyear, the car was front-halved for length and became *Swamp Rat X*. The only car Garlits ever painted entirely red, it struggled through the 1965 and 1966 seasons as Don worked on it, and his usual string of detractors (sometimes including NHRA boss Wally Parks) were again suggesting that he was washed up.

"I tried everything I could think of," he says, recounting the parts he changed. "The one thing I never did, though, was put spark lead into it. . . ."

For Big Daddy, it all came to a head in the summer months of 1966 when a race promoter stiffed him out of his money, at gunpoint, for underperforming when speeds over 200 had been advertised. Even though he had won the event, his best speed had been a frustrating 192 mph. With his reputation on the line, he was determined to simply blow up the 426-ci engine on his next run. It was a match race in Rockford, Illinois, scheduled for the following day, and he just let his Dodge deal go.

The supercharged environment was always a pass/fail situation when major changes were made. If it wouldn't run, try something else and hope it doesn't break. So Garlits decided to advance the ignition timing despite warnings from crewman Bob Taffe and others. He added 10 degrees of spark advance, from 34 to 44.

"At the time, I figured that would kill it," Garlits recounts now. "This much spark lead would have normally split the sides of an old 392 apart. Instead, the 426 humped down

the track to a blistering 213-mph pass with no damage. There was no water in the pan, the bearings looked great, and it was like a light went off. Man, I've been jacking with this thing for a year and a half. I took that mag and twisted it!"

He bumped the timing to an-unheard-of 50 degrees on the next pass, and the car responded with a clean 219-mph speed that was the fastest unofficial time for any fuel dragster to date. Both he and Emory Cook drove this car during the next year or so, and the culmination of the effort was Don Garlits' famous win at the 1967 U.S. Nationals, when he clocked a 6.77 in the final and shaved off his beard on the starting line.

The engine's first U.S. Nationals title and one of the biggest wins for Garlits in his lengthy career happened at Indy in 1967, when he went 6.77 in the final. He shaved his beard on the starting line before getting into the winner's circle with NHRA founder Wally Parks. (Photo Courtesy Ray Mann Archive, quartermilestones.com)

body. He relayed his concern in an internal memo to Ev Moeller dated July 10, noting the change to injection was a necessity on the match race trail for 1965. Hoover wrote a follow-up to Bob Lechner on August 17 asking for horsepower estimations with injectors for the A864 drag exhibition engine.

Soon after Eckstrand's unauthorized attempts, Ramcharger Tom Coddington, whose day job was in fuel systems and design, worked closely with Hilborn on a much more refined set of injectors. These were first tested the following January using the even more altered 110-inch-wheelbase 1965 mule car 558. The scope of this experimentation was fairly thorough according to Rockwell's noted Ramchargers book, but Coddington's vital role in pump and fuel circuit development cannot be understated. Without his work, things could have turned very differently the following season.

Specifications for the Eckstrand *Outlaw* and other

mid-1964 Hemi FXers were sent via airmail to the NHRA in a letter from Dale Reeker dated July 31, 1964. These included most of what had been submitted for the Winternationals, plus a fiberglass front bumper, one-piece door glass with no vent windows, plexiglass windshield, and several aluminum pieces, as well as the Holley 4150 carb (PN 2532095).

The latter item was a notable change. This was the recently released Holley 3-barrel with a 960-cfm airflow with its one-piece $1^{11}/_{16}$ x .5–inch secondary plate. According to at least one period report, this unit is reported to have been on the A. J. Foyt–driven Ray Nichels' #47 Dodge that took a win at the Firecracker 400 at Daytona on July 4. Handwritten on this NHRA document are the words "gas and altered only." Eckstrand raced at Indy in A/FX using his 1964 wedge body with a Hemi hastily installed, instead; though not verified, *Outlaw* was likely in B/Altered if present.

NASCAR 1964 Revisited

For the Hemi, the 1964 racing season in NASCAR, from the beginning of the season until the political gales of October, is worth recalling. Yes, Richard Petty won the season crown and did so with consistency. But by statistical evidence, Ned Jarrett in the Bondy Long Ford did more; he won more races (15 to 9), had more top finishes, and won more poles. This was due in no small part to an exotic lightweight valvetrain that Ford released soon after the company's Daytona drubbing, a change that allowed the 427-inch Ford wedge engines to safely spin up to 7,000 rpm.

But Petty had led on the most laps and had run 700 more miles than Jarrett that season, who missed two races in a brutal 62-race schedule. After Daytona, Petty put on his short-track game, running either #43 or #41, and winning at venues including the .333-mile in Harris, North Carolina (a one-time event); Huntington, West Virginia; and Spartanburg, South Carolina. There were also second- and third-place finishes at the longer, big track events: Atlanta, Charlotte, and Darlington. Crew chief Dale Inman seemed to have had little trouble figuring out how to keep the Hemi happy. Petty, as did all the other teams, suffered a handful of engine-related DNFs that year.

The tour was the longest in NASCAR's post–beach era history, and Petty was loyal to the fans and the points system. The only one of the 1964 events he did not compete in was the second qualifier for the Daytona 500, in which he was not eligible to run anyway. In July, Lee Petty, still recovering from his 1961 injuries, drove 28 laps in two events: Old Bridge, New Jersey, and Watkins Glen, New York. That finished off the career that had begun in 1949, doing so in the Hemi-powered #41.

For the guys out of Nichels' growing shop, NASCAR was not a real focus, at least not enough to run a season-long points chase. At the time, Goldsmith and Nichels divided their loyalties between stock and open-wheel racing. Nichels' stock car drivers throughout the era read like a who's who: A. J. Foyt, Troy Ruttman, Charlie Glotzbach, Bobby Isaac, and others.

Most were in the saddle no more than three times a season, and Foyt won the summer Firecracker 400 event at Daytona after abruptly leaving Ford. Young Bobby Isaac won the team's only other 1964 title with his victory in Daytona qualifying, and he was runner-up to Foyt at Daytona that summer. With racing veterans such as Joe Leonard, Len Sutten, and others on the USAC and Automobile Racing Club of America (ARCA) tours, there was always an overall Midwestern race focus for Nichels Engineering.

Cotton Owens and his driver David Pearson ran hard enough in the 1964 season to finish behind Petty and Jarrett. Only he and Petty did the whole race tour. Pearson won eight events that season, while Cotton drove twice, to win at Richmond and place second in Hillsboro, Virginia. As with the elder Petty, these were the last two events in a career that had started in 1950 and ended with Hemi power.

Also in the NASCAR top-ten that year was Jimmy Pardue, a ten-year racing veteran who ran 50 events and finished fifth in the points despite not winning a single race. Pardue was killed at a Charlotte tire test following the Hillsboro race in September.

Jim Paschal finished seventh as a Chrysler contract driver; he raced the first half of the year with Owens and then ran for Petty Enterprises. He won the World 600 at Charlotte in his first ride out of Randleman in #41.

The other top-ten driver was Buck Baker, who ironically had vacated the Petty family seat. After a start with both Pontiacs and Petty, Baker ran #3 Dodges for Ray Fox and a handful of Hemi Plymouths for one-year team owner David Walker. Incidentally, Walker also used Buck's

The 62-race 1964 Grand National tour included a stop at Lincoln Speedway in New Oxford, Pennsylvania, that summer. In this photo by Len King, young Richard Petty is with #41 at this event; the Petty family ran several numbers on their cars that season, and Richard was not always #43. (Photo Courtesy Len King Photographic Collection, Eastern Museum of Motor Racing)

David Pearson finished third in points in 1964 after being the only Hemi DNF at the Daytona 500 when he had a tire failure. (Copyright CR Racing 0304071, Ray Mann Photograph)

Jimmy Pardue died testing tires in this Burton-Robinson Plymouth late in the 1964 season. The event winner at New Oxford was David Pearson. This photo is also by track photographer Len King. (Photo Courtesy Len King Photographic Collection, Eastern Museum of Motor Racing)

son Buddy, Tiny Lund, Lonnie "LeeRoy" Yarbrough, and Marshall Sargent as drivers of his #89 entries before the end of the season.

To summarize the Grand National season, the Chrysler Hemi held its own, but was up against a lot of talent in the Ford ranks: Jarrett, Billy Wade, Freddy Lorenzen, and others. These seasoned teams plus the higher-RPM valvetrain kept things fairly even. Final 1964 stats show 30 wins for Ford, 14 for Dodge, 12 for Plymouth, 5 for Mercury, and noted black racer Wendell Scott's lone victory at Jacksonville (his only career win, and the only winning Chevy). Ford won the NASCAR manufacturers' cup, plus the season titles in the USAC, ARCA, and IMSA series; the Hemi won hearts and the history books.

Summer Drags On

The summer of 1964 saw the drag Hemi quickly brought up to speed. On June 15, Bob Cahill sent the NHRA a list of 55 Dodge owners and 57 Plymouth owners to ensure Super Stock legality, and this homologation was confirmed in writing by NHRA Executive Director Jack Hart to Chrysler Engineering's Bob Rodger on July 1. With more than 100 examples running nationwide, drivers and tuners who followed the information available on the cars also put them into the winner's circle and record books.

One of them was young Hank Taylor of Texas, whose well-heeled father had a friendly rivalry with a local Pontiac dealership owner who happened to be racer Don Gay's father. Taylor received a new 1964 Max Wedge Plymouth hand-delivered by Hayden Proffitt and followed that up with a Hemi version in late spring. Taylor toured that summer with mechanic H. L. Shahan calling the shots and became a 15-year-old media sensation in drag racing with several strong event finishes.

Perhaps the most serious competitors outside of the Ramchargers on the Dodge side were the Stickler/Jenkins juggernaut on the East Coast and Dick Landy out West. The Pennsylvania team lost no time moving from its Z11 409-ci Chevy to the Hemi, and ran in both Super Stock legal trim and with the 2-percent FX car built at the start of the 1964 season, both now Hemi-powered. The team was colorfully featured in an early issue of a new magazine, *Super Stock & Drag Illustrated*, and backed up its efforts with excellent performances. It culminated in a racing tour of England against Ronnie Sox' Mercury under the auspices of the NHRA late in the year.

Meanwhile, Landy's substantial mechanical prowess garnered him a lot of West Coast press visibility. Blessed with all-American football-player looks and noted for an unlit cigar clenched between his teeth, Dandy Dick epitomized what Dodge wanted as a race hero during its 50th anniversary year. A big feature on his reworked 330 sedan in *Hot Rod* magazine in early 1965 gave credence to his vital role in the coming ultra-stock revolution. Landy had his own dyno shop in Sherman Oaks, California, and had

Following a season of record setting and high visibility, including a class win at Indy, Dave Strickler launches his A/FX entry on the tarmac of an English airstrip. It was during a late-1964 drag racing exhibition hosted by the NHRA at several locations in Great Britain. (Photo Courtesy Lynn Wineland Archive, quartermilestones.com)

Tommy Grove and Melrose Missile VI *posted runner-up honors in A/FX to Dave Strickler during eliminations at Indy. Both cars have survived and are under restoration. (Photo Courtesy Kramer Automotive Film/Print Library)*

No longer a teenager but still enjoying life, Hank Taylor poses with the Hemi Plymouth in which he toured in 1964. This was at the Flatlander Fling, a one-weekend Hemi reunion held in Nebraska in 2009. Today, noted collector Len Grimsley owns this car, as well as Hank's 1964 Max Wedge car.

gone so far as to develop a complicated set of 180-degree headers similar to those used on some open-wheel cars to increase exhaust efficiency.

In late 1964, the factory gave Landy leeway to pursue a program of more radical change. This included a forward-placed straight front axle originally found in the A100 pickup and a multi-adjustable rear axle placement that allowed him to shorten the wheelbase substantially. Longtime car owner Pete Haldiman lays claim to the idea that this vehicle was the first true Funny Car, although the term had not yet been coined.

Perhaps a note is in order on straight front axle configurations. In an August 4 letter written to NHRA's Wally Parks by Dodge's public relations rep Frank Wiley, the argument was laid out for the use of this axle because the diminutive A100 camper and pickup registered as passenger cars, not trucks. Wiley noted that Billy Jacobs of Georgia and Jack Sharkey of Chicago had both gone this route to install Hemi engines into Darts, and it was much safer in the event of wheelstands to keep the front wheels in proper alignment.

A follow-up telegram on October 6 from Wiley to Jack Hart notes that this must have been okayed, as Connecticut racer Bill Flynn was running this unit in his A/Modified Production Dodge the following weekend, and Landy's rebuilding was close behind. By then, however, Jim "B. B." Thornton was already at the drawing boards for the coming 1965 late-model stockers, which used the K-frame/torsion bar package.

Beyond development work, Thornton had been busy that summer, as he and fellow Ramcharger Mike Buckel now shared driving duties on the team's two cars, an S/S and the A/FX model. The FX car, with its 2-percent wheelbase change, had set both ends of the NHRA national record at 11.22 seconds at 125.17 mph. These records were set the very first time it raced with a Hemi on April 26, 1964. And it had posted an 11.01 by the end of May.

The Big Go

Testing was ongoing, but as August wound down, it was time for the ride out to Indy for the Nationals. The weekend before, the Golden Commandos had scored a

Late in the year, Dick Landy created an even more radical FX conversion with a straight front axle from the A100 compact pickup truck, as well as an adjustable rear axle location. Pete and Renee Haldiman now own the car.

One of the most important cars in the history of drag racing, Landy's 1964 Automotive Research Dodge is considered to be the catalyst for what became known as a Funny Car in 1965. The straight axle was legal as a factory experimental part because the A100 truck actually registered as a passenger car on paper.

Roger Lindamood attained immediate fame when he took home Mr. Stock Eliminator honors at the 1964 NHRA Nationals in Indianapolis. Jim Thornton lost traction for an instant off the starting line and the Ramchargers had to settle for a runner-up finish. Their car reset NHRA's Super Stock speed record to more than 130 mph later that day. (Photo Courtesy Ray Mann Archive, quartermilestones.com)

big win at Detroit Dragway's independent championship match when dyno operator Forrest Pitcock drove away from Don Nicholson's 427 Comet in a final round that paid a big $1,320 ($1.00 a foot) to win. By then, both the FX Comets and Hemi cars were down in the 10-second zone under the proper conditions.

Chrysler Hemi door slammers flooded in for NHRA's Labor Day weekend bash. The S/SA class had the largest number at 39 entries, followed by a handful of Hemi door cars against the S/S Thunderbolts in the 51-example stick class. Thornton took the class title over the Commandos in the automatics, while Butch Leal upheld Ford's honor in a Thunderbolt for the manuals.

Monday's final 16-car Top Stock field was for the two class winners and the next 14 fastest cars; that was Leal and 15 Hemi cars. Leal then fell in the first round to Thornton, who proceeded to march his way toward the final, beating Pitcock and Faubel.

Meanwhile, Roger Lindamood, who had actually been driving the *Ramchargers* FX car that record-setting day in April at Detroit, was on his game in *Color Me Gone*. He beat Faubel's second car driven by Dick Housey in round one, Bob Harrop in round two, and Dick Landy in the semifinals.

With announcer Jon Lundberg working the huge crowd on the mic, Lindamood jumped to lead the pack and held on to win when Thornton briefly lost traction, 11.31 to 11.47. But once again, that was not the end of the day. The Ramchargers had already announced this was the team's final year in the Stock ranks so they could refocus on experimental cars. They came out on a Monday afternoon single after the final to hammer the S/SA record down to 11.20 at an unreal 130.06 mph. It was the first car to legally surpass that speed barrier.

The team lowered the NHRA record to an 11.13 in October, and Thornton even clocked times in the 10.90s against FX cars at a Cecil County, Maryland, factory bash that fall.

At Indianapolis Raceway Park, three of the 2-percent factory cars and Eckstrand's hastily changed wedge were in A/FX, where Dave Strickler, who had broken a transmission in his S/S car, emerged the winner in a field mainly full of 427 Comets. He beat Grove's *Melrose Missile* in an all-Hemi A/FX final. Fred Cutler also had a destroked NASCAR Hemi in a 1964 station wagon to win B/FX. Bill Flynn did not have a Hemi yet, so he moved his Dodge Max Wedge into A/Modified Production and won his class as well.

According to the 1964 NHRA entry list printed before the event, a handful of faster cars had Hemi engines. The first real 426 Hemi crate offering to the public was not until 1965, so there are recorded instances of people removing Hemi engines from brand-new Super Stocks in 1964 and 1965 to place them into other altered and gas bodies.

Late in 1964 at Cecil County, at one of its final appearances, the Ramchargers Super Stock car in match race trim actually clocked runs in the 10.90s, unheard of even for A/FX at the start of the season. This rare twilight photo dated October 1964 may be from the same big Super Stock race. (Photo Courtesy Kramer Automotive Film/Print Library)

The A925 Diversion

Drag racing was never the sole focus of the Hemi's task, although that's where it established its greatest overall legacy in motorsports. For Ford, there was no time to lose, and work on an overhead cam engine went full-tilt after Daytona. The Ford SOHC, or Cammer, was created to take advantage of hemispherical combustion chamber technology and eliminate issues with valvetrain speed by placing a single camshaft inside of each cylinder head. With no associated loss through the pushrod geometry, the design allowed greater RPM potential, and early reports trickling out stated it was capable of 550 or more horsepower with little problem.

A 1966 SAE paper by Ford engineers verified that those numbers were actually higher. Jack Charipar was the first to confirm the engine's rapid development, and, heady with the Daytona visibility, Chrysler's executive board approved funds for work to begin on a viable alternative in the summer of 1964.

A single-overhead cam still needed rockers to actuate both intake and exhaust valves; the next step was to use a pair of overhead cams, each dedicated to one function. The double-overhead cam design offers even better high-RPM valvetrain stability, simpler cam design, and allows for four valves per cylinder because pushrods and rockers are eliminated. Ironically, a DOHC conversion on an early Hemi by Bob Gillelan had been on the cover of *Motor Trend* in August 1957, but designer Frank Bilek was tasked with something a little more complicated.

The commitment of initial funding for the A925 program proved that it was a serious effort. By June of 1964, the first A990 aluminum heads had been cast for dyno development. It can be assumed that some of the core work was used to cast the prototype aluminum heads for the new DOHC engine, which remained basically unchanged in the reciprocating assembly. At this stage of development, valvetrain testing was the sole focus. According to Bill Weertman's written recollections, there were some initial problems with cam stability.

Meanwhile, Bialk was hedging his bets with a second design that would also have 32 valves, but would use a pair of camshafts in the tappet valley that ran off a timing gear in the conventional cam location. Although it was a compromise, it would go into development only if NASCAR outlawed overhead cam designs. The DOHC was probably under development for only a couple of months in the autumn of 1964.

According to research by DOHC engine owner John Mahoney, all development formally ended in January 1965. A running example was never constructed. A set of heads and valvetrain gear were mounted on a block,

which was operated through the belt drive to replicate the RPM possibilities via an electric engine.

As the speculation increased about the SOHC being completed that fall, Ronney Householder was dispatched to personally give Bill France a photo of this test engine, which had become known around the engineering department as the "doomsday machine." There was reportedly more to this than simply making a statement. The cost of developing another race engine in its entirety was not lost on the bean counters. The A925 would have likely cost millions to bring online, and no doubt Ford would have doubled-down as well. France took one look at the photo and made a decision that changed the course of racing history.

The War of Words

On October 19, 1964, Bill France was ready to announce a major rules revision for the 1965 season. He supposedly stated that the primary push for these changes was to get the independent GM loyalists back. In January 1965, new rule changes in engine legality, vehicle size, and car weight went into effect for NASCAR. Dodge and Plymouth experienced the negative effects of most of these changes fresh off their 1964 championship season.

Of course, the thing that most Chrysler enthusiasts today note about this announcement is that the Hemi engine was ruled ineligible to race, as was the Ford 427 high-riser engine design. Both were deemed competition powerplants and not available through common passenger-vehicle channels. As noted previously in this chapter, the Hemi had been released in small numbers

Legendary driver A. J. Foyt, wheeling the #47 1964 Dodge of Ray Nichels, ran just two Grand National events in 1964, winning the Firecracker 400 at Daytona, and failing to finish at Charlotte. Foyt ran Nichels' #29 Dodge to back-to-back wins at the Indianapolis Fairgrounds and Langhorne, Pennsylvania, in September as well. (Copyright CR Racing 1410003, Ray Mann Photograph)

for drag racing. Although an additional batch of approximately 70 steel-nose production-weight Hemi cars were built, they were not street oriented in 1964. Still, there was more to the rules changes and more to the story than meets the eye.

Chrysler and Ford were pushing the edge of the performance envelope. Horsepower and speed were rapidly rising. NASCAR stars "Lil Joe" Weatherly was killed and Glenn "Fireball" Roberts fatally injured during the first half of the season (at Riverside and Charlotte, respectively). In addition, the untimely death of Plymouth driver Jimmy Pardue during tire testing on September 22 at Charlotte may well have played a role in the October announcement of rule changes.

From a pure business perspective, France saw two things evolving simultaneously. First was the escalation of horsepower among participating manufacturers, limiting the options for independents that did not have connections or financing for the better components, which were under constant development at this time. This, in turn, had kept GM racers out of the Grand National picture almost entirely since the start of 1964, and France, as he stated in the October 19 press release, wanted to change that.

The second factor could well have been safety. Upon seeing the Ford SOHC and Householder's picture of the A925 "doomsday" DOHC Chrysler engine, France perhaps recognized the potential for even more spilled blood in a year in which people had witnessed death on live television at the start of the Indy 500 (Eddie Sachs and Dave MacDonald). A number of racers announced after the fast and wreck-strewn Firecracker 400 that they might not be back as drivers. Only Junior Johnson made good on the threat; the fear was very real. France ultimately chose to try to set the clock back 12 months by restricting the Hemis and high-risers. He likely felt that doing so would slow the cars following the record speeds of the 1964 season.

Even more difficult for Chrysler to fathom than losing the Hemi was an associated change that limited cars at superspeedway-type tracks, such as Daytona, Darlington, Atlanta, and Charlotte, to full-size models of 119 inches or more, and the new minimum weight for all entries. So not only was the Hemi banned outright, but also now Chrysler drivers were forced to race with wedge-powered big cars on the superspeedways and ballasted wedge-powered midsize cars on other tracks. During 1964, Chrysler used its 1964 B-Body designs at its stated shipping weight for all events.

Not considered by NASCAR at that moment was that Ford and GM engine development had already held a dominant position compared to the Max Wedge engine, regardless of the body it was in, and especially in the highly visible superspeedway environment. Ford could easily go back to its refined late-1963 version of the 427, especially with the aforementioned high-RPM valve gear, and the racing-styled Galaxie and Marauder fastback designs. Chrysler, however, could not simply switch back to the 426 wedge in the C-Body cars and expect to be competitive. Former Indy car driver Householder, who was old-school when it came to racing, had no intention of giving in; the war of words escalated quickly, even on the day of the announcement.

France had stated publically he hoped that USAC, the popular Midwest sanctioning body for both open-wheel and stock cars, would accept his new rules as written.

Instead, Harry Banks, who was the competition director at USAC, found out what was happening in NASCAR

The #5 Plymouth of Herb Shannon from Peoria, Illinois. Seen at Indianapolis Raceway Park, Shannon was a USAC-only stock car racer, with a highest finish of sixth at the DuQuoin State Fairgrounds that year. Nichels' racers were often backed by dealer organizations at noted events. (Copyright CR Racing 1102017, Ray Mann Photograph)

Len Sutton is seen here at IRP in the #29 1964 Dodge, yet another Ray Nichels car. From Portland, Oregon, this was Sutton's final full year in USAC stock cars, finishing second at Milwaukee and third at Langhorne. He retired in 1965 after friend Mel Kenyon suffered severe burns at Langhorne, Pennsylvania, that year. (Copyright CR Racing 1102020, Ray Mann Photograph)

THE RAMCHARGERS RAIL

Perhaps the Ramchargers team didn't have the seat-of-the-pants dragster experience of Don Garlits, but it did have the benefit of analytical engineering. And the team also had Dan Knapp, a skilled craftsman at the group's shop in Ferndale. Knapp had been very successful in the Top Gas class before the nitro ban ended. When he found out that the Hemi dyno block 004 was going to be scrapped, he took it home, sleeved it up, and began building a new dragster for the powerplant, deciding it would be on fuel.

Although the Ramchargers team was busy with its pair of Hemi door-car entries in the summer of 1964, the possibilities of supercharged nitro racing were intriguing. Knapp fabricated a lot of the components himself. The team tested on methanol, with Knapp's former driver Don Westerdale at the throttle; they poured in 50 percent for the first time at a big event at Detroit Dragway the week before the 1964 Indy Nationals. The car won on Saturday and was runner-up on Sunday, running as quick as 7.90 at 189 mph in its first competitive appearance.

The following weekend, it ran 7.95 to make the field at the 1964 Nationals, but fell to parts problems. Winner Garlits ran 7.75 to take the title later that weekend in his 392-ci car. This first Ram's rail met its end in October when substitute driver Ray DeNoble off-roaded it at speed at Milan, Michigan. Yet the engine had been successful enough that Frank Wylie released funds for the team to get a new 150-inch state-of-the-art chassis from Woody Gilmore of California.

The team refined the 426 Hemi engine combination for 1965. The team towed one to Bristol in June 1965, having just realized intuitively that more spark lead might be possible due to the inherent deep-skirt bottom end of the 426 Hemi block. Westerdale, whose day job was a foreman at Ford's Rouge River plant, was again the pilot, and he could only duck with the magneto turned to 50 degrees. Instead, he cranked off a 7.78 at 192.00, the best run yet on the car.

The team stepped it up: 55 degrees in round one yielded 7.60 on a shut-off, 60 degrees in round two was 7.51 at 204.44 Low ET of the race, and a shut-off at 65 degrees when Westerdale red-lit against the Ford SOHC entry of Connie Kalitta. Boosted to 70-percent nitro and 60 degrees of advance, the car almost won the AHRA Summer Nationals in Gary, Indiana, soon afterward, turning the event's best time, 7.89 and 207.84, before breaking a rod in the finals against Art Malone.

The team took the NHRA AA/FD record at a points race at York in July, resetting the number to 7.47. The group's best number fell to a blistering 7.31 against Chris "the Greek" Karamesines at Detroit Dragway in mid-August 1965, though the car was now consuming a lot of parts.

The team chose to park the altered-wheelbase door car over Labor Day in 1965; all effort was focused on the dragster at Indy. Making an opening qualifying run

The Ramchargers dragster finished its active racing career with an explosive victory at the AHRA World Finals at Tulsa, Oklahoma, in the fall of 1969. Leroy Goldstein drove the team's race car during the 1969–1971 era. (Photo Courtesy Ray Mann Archive, quartermilestones. com)

Under extreme loads of fuel, the team also found the weakest links in the engine's hardware as members made record-setting runs. This view of an engine swap was typical of many racers at the annual Nationals. (Photo Courtesy Pit Slides Archive, quartermilestones.com)

on Friday, Westerdale hit 7.507 and 210.00, .15 quicker and 6 mph faster than the previous top qualifiers on hand, Connie Kalitta's SOHC beast and Don Prudhomme in Roland Leong's *Hawaiian*. However, they lost to Prudhomme in the second round of class on Sunday, having backed off their big tune-up.

Then, during Monday's finals, the team lost the engine in round two. Despite heroic efforts to repair it, the rail did not make it down the track in round three. Adding to the ignominy of it, Keith Black tuned the 392-ci in the Leong-Prudhomme's *Hawaiian* to a 7.505 in the final, taking Low ET as well.

Still, 1965 culminated for the Ramchargers by winning NASCAR's Championship at Dragway 42 in West Salem, Ohio, where the team again met the Prudhomme-driven *Hawaiian*, the most notorious car in the nation at the time. In a cash-rich final (the drag racing division of NASCAR paid far better than any of the other sanctioning bodies at the time), and when it counted, Westerdale won the first season title for the 426 Hemi in a Top Fuel program.

During 1966 and 1967, the Ramchargers pushed the envelope of performance through experimentation, qualifying tops at Indy three years in a row. Chuck Kurzowa took over driving the car and then Leroy "the Israeli Rocket" Goldstein, who made it a season title winner just before the team moved into the Funny Car ranks.

Two things became very evident in the fuel ranks over those first three seasons. First, when properly built and tuned, the 426 Hemi could take a lot of abuse, and the aftermarket, already tooled up for 392-ci parts, quickly came up with solutions and options for the new engine as development continued.

Second, the advent of street versions of the Hemi engine in 1966 meant blocks, heads, and other peripherals were as close as your local Mopar dealer. No longer did the few still-available Imperials or Chrysler 300s have to provide fuel engine parts.

It was a somewhat slow transition, but the 426 Race Hemi dominated professional drag racing within a decade.

---

prior to the formal announcement. Seizing an opportunity, Banks issued his own statement that same October day: "We feel that changing specifications without adequate prior notice works a hardship on our personnel and on the manufacturers." USAC rules went unchanged for 1965, with any adjustments to be made beginning in 1966, a point Householder made repeatedly for any serious rules adaptation.

Chrysler-Plymouth Vice President Bob Anderson responded to France in the press the next day: "Racing had always prided itself on being progressive. Here we are now, backing up. Any engine takes a couple of years of experimentation to develop its full potential. I cannot speak for the corporation, but we certainly will go over the rules closely in Detroit. It could mean we won't be at Daytona."

Leo Beebe at Ford also issued a statement that day, October 20, saying not only did the company applaud NASCAR's decision, but also noted tersely that Ford would not run two types of cars and would not race in the USAC series in 1965 if the NASCAR rules were not adopted.

It did not take long for Householder to summarize Chrysler's position two days after that. On October 23, he didn't mince words: "There is a very definite possibility that factory-sponsored Plymouths and Dodges will be withdrawn from NASCAR competition in 1965. I don't want to undermine anybody or create a problem, but

the new rules NASCAR announced put us out of business down South." He noted that the Fury and Polara were strictly for the luxury/big car market, unbalanced in design for racing and styled solely for street purposes. "Aerodynamically, we would be dead."

On October 28, five days after his first statement and nine days after France had made the first announcement, Householder called his bluff and rubbed his nose in it. "The new rules are not consistent with racing's tradition of bringing the best and newest engineering equipment to the racetrack," he said. "We also believe the rules will work to the disadvantage of many car owners, race drivers, and crews, and track owners. The effect of the new NASCAR rules will be to arbitrarily eliminate from NASCAR the finest performance cars on the 1964 circuit, including that of the Grand National champion."

The factory rep ended by saying, "We have no alternative but to withdraw from NASCAR-sanctioned events and concentrate our efforts in USAC, IMCA, NHRA, AHRA, SCCA, and other sanctioned events in 1965."

France still didn't budge, and it became more personal: "If the Chrysler Corporation feels its standard 426-ci automobiles are not competitive with comparable-size cars of other American manufacturers, then I would be the last to criticize Chrysler on its withdrawal from NASCAR racing."

That same day, Banks played USAC's hand from the other corner at Ford. "The machines that ran in 1964 are just as competitive today as they were then, so we see no justification for any manufacturer to withdraw from USAC racing," he commented.

On October 31, when Ray Fox' Chrysler contract expired, it was not renewed for 1965, sending Buck Baker and LeeRoy Yarbrough to independently owned Plymouths. Fox eventually ended up trying to run Chevrolets in 1965. The Cotton Owens team (backed by the Carolina Dodge Dealers) was reassigned to run USAC in 1965.

Householder had already shipped Richard Petty a Barracuda shell to use for a drag race project, and drag racing was eventually his focus in 1965. Ray Nichels, in the midst of building a huge new shop, remained the clearinghouse for the non-drag racing Hemi programs, and his close relationship with Householder was his one saving grace at the uncertain moment.

The first two weeks in November found France trying to defend his position, his track owners hoping it was a bluff. A final salvo issued by the National Chrysler-Plymouth Dealer Council asked France personally to reconsider. It was for naught, and the 1965 Grand National series began with only a handful of independent Chrysler entries on hand.

Two months later in February, France used the 1965 Daytona 500 to announce NASCAR's rules package for 1966, which was to categorize vehicles into three groups: Group 1 for full-size models at 119-inch wheelbase and ACCUS 7-liter engines (429.999), Group 2 for midsize models at 116-inch wheelbase and a 405-ci displacement, and Group 3 for the new compact or pony cars at 5-liter (305-ci) displacement.

Although it is often stated that Chrysler boycotted the series for the entire season, it actually loosened up in late June of 1965 when Banks and France agreed to a set of new rules immediately, though too late for Chrysler to attempt any repeat of the championship.

By then, the factory was noting in 1966 model previews that a street version of the Hemi was part of the engine lineup. The new Group 1 and 2 rules were enacted as a part of the NASCAR/USAC rules configuration at midseason, even though the big C-Body cars remained part of the equation on the longer tracks until the end of the year. Also, and more important, the minimum weight requirement was suspended and replaced with a cubic inch-to-weight measurement of 9.36 pounds.

Unfortunately, frustration with sanctioning bodies was not limited to circle-track racing. Late in the year, the NHRA announced its 1965 rules package as well, and with the desire to keep current-year GM cars competitive, those included steel-only bodies for Stock Eliminator. Previous packages featuring aluminum or fiberglass pieces would be legal for Modified Production, but otherwise would no longer be able to race in NHRA's door-car classes. The lightweight GM vehicles of 1963, the fiberglass-nosed Ford Galaxies and Thunderbolt Fairlanes, and the 1964 Hemi cars and their aluminum-paneled Max Wedge predecessors from 1963 to 1964 were all out.

Ironically (or fortuitously), the exploding popularity of match racing meant that an owner or racer could now simply suspend legality and go all out into what was now known as "run whacha brung" drag stockers. Although new Hemi Super Stocks were on the drawing board, even the factory agreed to go all out. As a result, 1965 was a year to remember.

Although Dave Strickler struck out on his own with a Dodge deal for 1965 and had an altered-wheelbase Coronet, he started the season at Pomona racing his Super Stocker in A/Modified Production because the NHRA had outlawed non-steel body panels for stock-class cars that year. (Photo Courtesy Lynn Wineland Archive, quartermilestones.com)

CHAPTER FOUR

1965
Fuel, Freaks and the Factory
The Hemi Rules the Quarter-Mile

Indicated on documents as Car 558, the just-completed chassis was mounted on a surface plate in the confines of the structures lab in the Chrysler engineering department at Highland Park for photography.

In bare metal and with a tubular safety structure built inside, the uncloaked unibody looked stark. It was at the end of 1964, and Chrysler's brain trust of racing-minded engineers, some of them members of the Ramchargers and Golden Commandos teams, were about to turn the sport of drag racing on its head, forever. Once covered in fresh sheet metal and fiberglass, 558 became a car.

The redesign of the Plymouth Belvedere had not been overly dramatic between 1964 and 1965. But this example was different, its wheelbase radically rearranged toward the front. The effort was to be a serious one, but if there was one thing that defined the introduction of the second-generation Chrysler Hemi package to the masses in drag racing, it was the Funny Car revolution.

With the announcement of Ronney Householder's plan to boycott the Grand National series for the following season, suddenly funds were available to get the engine integrated into drag racing at all levels. Foremost, this effort included factory-assisted experimental projects, Super Stock–legal package cars, and supercharged engine development. The latter soon took on additional significance because of Ford's desire to put its also-outlawed SOHC engine into the nitromethane environment. The fact that drag racing had steadily evolved as a major motorsport, with promotional possibilities in a lot of locales that did not have late-model circle-track racing, was not lost on Chrysler's management.

Of all the things that took place in Race Hemi history between 1964 and 1969 from a drag racing standpoint, none took on the historical significance of the altered-wheelbase program, both from a visibility standpoint and from the perspective of later history. As mentioned previously, the Ramchargers team had taken advantage of wheelbase restructuring in late 1963 when

The Golden Commandos Plymouth piloted by Al Eckstrand and Landy's Dodge raced in the final round of the Super Stock Nationals on August 7, 1965, perhaps the high-water mark of the factory's 1965 experimental program. The Ramchargers Dodge clocked its unheard-of 8.91 at Cecil County the same evening. Seen here at the All-Hemi Reunion in 2007, Mike Guffey owns the Plymouth and was also responsible for helping preserve the Dodge, now owned by Nick Smith.

Although not legal for AFX, two of the factory altereds raced each other during the downtime between rounds at NHRA's Winternationals. This is Butch Leal's new Plymouth; Dick Landy was his competition. (Photo Courtesy Lynn Wineland Archive, quartermilestones.com)

Rob Schatz is in his 1965 Performance King hardtop Plymouth tribute. It has been radically altered to a 110-inch wheelbase. Chrysler did this for factory teams in 1965. Schatz is one of many who have re-created the package for nostalgia racing.

A. J. Casini in the Bob George A990 sedan still has the as-built Super Stock 115-inch wheelbase, which was slightly less than the 116-inch passenger car specification.

readying four cars for the 1964 Factory Experimental (FX) category, using the NHRA's allowable 2-percent formula.

As designed, Chrysler's multiframed unibody construction allowed some opportunity for adjustment, but the more serious FX-type cars required special factory parts, such as suspension supports, special body pieces, and any process that could help move weight from the front to the back. Wanting to stay with a standard-size car, once the A925 DOHC engine program was curtailed, the engineers took the wheelbase possibilities to the extreme.

To maximize traction and launch performance, the chassis was heavily modified. The engine weight was in a fixed position. The vehicle's construction and sanctioning body rules limited how far it could be moved backward. By simply moving the wheelbase forward, some of that weight could be transferred rearward, where less of it was on the front and the back tires could take advantage of added traction through the effects of transfer.

Various experiments in drag racing had proven that this was advantageous, as cars in the altered categories often had their front axles extended beyond the vehicle nose. Indeed, this was most extreme in slingshot rail dragsters, where the light front suspension and bicycle-size tires were moved far forward and the driver was directly behind the engine, with the seat pocket actually straddling or behind the rear axle.

For production-line cars, it was a little more difficult to execute such changes for making the most of weight transfer while still appearing stock. Regardless, in the fall of 1964, experiments of wheelbase relocation by Chrysler continued to their logical end. The efforts in late 1964 by Dick Landy and Bill Flynn to adopt a semi-adjustable Dodge straight front axle to the B-Body Dodge platform as a possible FX-legal change had proven to have merit, but that layout was not attractive for a showcase factory effort. Because Ramcharger Jim Thornton's specialty was in the suspension lab, he came up with a fresh design on

the upcoming 1965 models working with product planning department member Dale Reeker.

First, special upper control arms and longer torsion bars were developed that allowed the K-frame and front wheels to be moved forward a full 10 inches. This placed the wheel opening just behind the front bumper and required replacement fiberglass front fenders with a forward-placed opening.

Next, the rear wheels were moved as far forward as possible, 15 inches, to the area beneath the rear quarter window. This was done by simply cutting out the rear unibody frame and floor, removing part of the floorpan section ahead of it, and simply moving the whole suspension/axle substructure forward inside the body to relocate the axle housing. The wheel opening and fenders were segmented and then patch-welded back together to form the new body opening.

The somewhat hard-edged styling of the 1965 B-series body helped keep the cars semi-legitimate visually, but there was no doubt, now with a 110-inch wheelbase, that it was radically changed from its OEM appearance. The project was approved all the way to Chief Engineer of Product Planning Bob Rodger, who simply shook his head and stated he wondered where it would end.

The Team Effort and Amblewagon

Once approved for construction, the prototype Plymouth was carefully built in the structures lab. Its changes were documented and it was finished offsite at the company's Woodward Garage by Dan Knapp, Dan Mancini, and Roger Lindamood. This was the engineering department's own private little lab and research facility, located near its namesake avenue.

Now knowing what was needed, the next step was finding a subcontractor to do the conversions and construction, which had to be done fairly quickly. Using the sporty hardtop body, this prototype included the body and wheelbase changes, fiberglass part installation, and reassembly. Amblewagon, a conversion company located in Troy that created customized vehicles such as ambulances, received the bodies and parts to do the work using a confidential Race Car-A/FX Dragster manual that Chrysler's structures lab had created while building the prototype. Coordinator Dale Reeker oversaw and led the Chrysler engineers on location.

"Regarding the Amblewagon conversions, those cars did not get modified K-frames; the K-frame was the standard design," recalls Tom Hoover, even though versions in stainless steel offered weight savings. "The beauty of the car design was that those front longitudinals went straight forward; you could actually move that thing up 10 inches provided you had new welded-in nuts to attach the K-member to. All you had to do then was make special torsion bars.

"What was special about the front suspension of those Amblewagon cars was the fabricated upper control arm. It was not modified; one of the aftermarket companies fabricated those from tubing. Jim Thornton designed that; it needed the 10-inch offset due to the way it was mounted to the unibody, and it was pretty special. The rest of that stuff, though, was the standard design."

At Reeker's request, Dick Landy was asked to find a company that did acid dipping in aerospace-rich Southern California with a tank large enough to drop an entire unibody vehicle shell into. He selected AeroChem. He once recounted that this was the largest job the firm had ever done on standard sheet metal at that time. The first car was dropped in during daylight hours and produced a large, visible green cloud. In deference to the neighbors and authorities, the rest of them were done at night.

It also took some effort to determine how much time in the tank was enough. As a result, some of the cars were lighter and less structurally sound than others. Indeed, the Dodge body slated for Bill Flynn was reportedly so unusable it did not come back. He began the season in a regular 1965 Hemi Super Stock that was turned into a fully altered sedan by Branstner Enterprises under factory direction that spring.

It then was necessary to assemble a group of drivers and teams to pilot the cars. To start the season, Amblewagon and other teams, in one form or another, built 11 cars. Seven were fully changed over to begin with, and four others were modified with semi-stock wheelbases and ultimately re-created. This also included the undipped mule car that started it all and Flynn's aforementioned late delivery.

The Ramchargers' single car, driven alternately by factory engineers Thornton and Buckel, led the charge for Dodge, in addition to five other drivers: Dandy Dick Landy; 1964 Nationals champ Roger Lindamood of Detroit with Dick Branstner; Bud Faubel from Pennsylvania; Dave Strickler (now with Bill Stiles) of York, Pennsylvania; Bobby Harrop of New Jersey running under the auspices of the Philadelphia Region Dodge Dealers; and Flynn from New England.

For Plymouth, the factory team of the Golden Commandos joined forces with lawyer Al Eckstrand for the

Ronnie Sox's Paper Tiger *in the sunset at Cecil County, site of several important performances. The Sox & Martin team was one of the premier players in the Plymouth ranks during the muscle car era. (Photo Courtesy Charles Milikin, Jr.)*

Bill Flynn's Dodge was the only one of the original group constructed entirely from an A990 base, being converted at Dick Branstner's shop under factory direction. This track, York U.S. 30, was the site of the huge 1965 Super Stock Nationals. (Photo Courtesy Kramer Automotive Film/Print Library)

For all the drivers involved in the 1965 altered-wheelbase program and devoted to Mopar racing, the vehicles were career highlights and fondly remembered. This is Lee Smith with his car at the York U.S. 30 reunion; until recently, it was part of the Greg and Kathy Mosley collection.

new year, using the test mule and a new car. Lee Smith from Moline, Illinois, received an altered Plymouth, which ran out of Learner Sales & Service, one of the largest Imperial dealers in the country. Tommy Grove, winner of the 1964 NHRA Winter Nationals continued in the *Melrose Missile* entry of Charlie DiBari's Melrose Motors dealership, and young Butch "The California Flash" Leal (formerly of the Ford factory team) was now onboard for the season. But the real news for Plymouth's program in 1965 was hiring Ronnie Sox and Buddy Martin away from Mercury.

The Boys From Burlington

Ronnie Sox and Buddy Martin had proven their competence during the prior three seasons racing for Chevrolet and then Mercury. Sox, the son of a gas station operator in North Carolina, was gifted at shifting transmissions. Martin was a former railroad employee who found his calling in the business end of motorsports. Professional and personable, the duo were extremely successful in whatever they campaigned and were joined by talented mechanic Jake King during mid-1964. Lured away by some non-racing amenities that Mercury did not agree to, this team became Chrysler's most prolific drag racing winners in stock-type cars in the following decade. This was despite the fact that King's first response to seeing a new Hemi was reportedly, "What is that thing?"

NHRA completed its rules revisions for 1965 at the start of January. NHRA's Wally Parks and National Director Jack Hart flew to Detroit, saw the prototype Plymouth, and said, "Uh-huh; no." The rules for A/FX in 1965 were

basically unchanged: weight-to-cubic inches ratio of 0 to 8.99, minimum weight of 3,200 pounds, and 2-percent maximum change from production wheelbase, with NHRA approval needed before acceptance. The NHRA dryly informed Chrysler these new cars would immediately end up in the Altered division among the prewar coupes. As a result, the cars then being readied for reassembly were not legal for FX racing in 1965.

Perhaps it had been hoped that more leeway would be granted for the new cars, but it is more likely that Chrysler had already recognized that the company's match racing efforts would be more visible than the handful of NHRA FX-legal races. Regardless of that, the rival American Hot Rod Association (AHRA) run by Jim Tice and NASCAR's new Drag Racing Division were both amenable to the new cars as highlight acts, so Chrysler remained committed to the program. Also in the mix was the reality of Ford's SOHC, which had been approved by the NHRA for FX and was now in short-wheelbase Mustangs and Comets. As in NASCAR, Chrysler had no intention of showing up just to get its lunch eaten. The fight was on.

Four already acid-dipped bodies were ready to make a showing at the NHRA season-opening Winternationals in Pomona, California. Not yet converted to full altered status, these were readied in semi-stock wheelbase form for highly visible teams to race there in A/FX. For Dodge, these were *Ramchargers* and *Color Me Gone,* while *Golden Commandos* and *Melrose Missile* represented Plymouth. The Ramchargers took apart a new Super Stock package car for some of the components and completed the dipped body in the team's Ferndale shop. Other teams may have done likewise.

Because of FX rules that required the submission and approval of all unique parts by the NHRA, these four cars

Going into the NHRA Winternationals at Pomona, the A/FX class was run as Mr. Factory Stock. As a result, four of the cars slated for conversions to full match racers were set up in 2-percent legal form instead. This is Ramchargers with Jim Thornton driving. Mike Buckel drove this car at the AHRA event a week earlier. (Photo Courtesy Lynn Wineland Archive, quartermilestones.com)

featured some components that were never used again. When the event concluded, the cars went back to their respective team shops for full conversion, as did the others that Amblewagon had built. The Commandos reportedly started again from scratch because their FX car was so weak from the acid-dipping process. The car had been delivered with the roof detached.

In mid-January, the 558 mule was taken to California for testing, similar to what had occurred in 1964. Chrysler often rented a regional track prior to big races for this purpose. Ramcharger Tom Coddington did the data work as Thornton drove the car at Carlsbad Raceway during this private factory tune-up session. The primary focus was not simply the vehicle structure, but ongoing developments with Stu Hilborn on the new fuel injection layout, which was already showing promise.

The A990s Show Up Too

For the engineers, the work in the fall of 1964 had been divided between the new exhibition program and a new 1965 Super Stock car. Once the NHRA had announced the new rules in Stock, Chrysler ended up being the only company to create cars for 1965 (an all-steel body, produced in a minimum of 100 units). They actually became some of the class' most successful entries. Mike Buckel recounted that this package, coded the R01 Plymouth and W01 Dodge on paper but most frequently referred to as the A990 package based on the Hemi engine, was Jim Thornton's finest hour as an engineer.

Indeed, never lacking in ingenuity, Thornton had found ways to stamp body panels and supports from a thinner-gauge metal. There was no factory acid dipping

The Logiudice car was part of the 50th anniversary display at Carlisle's Chrysler event in 2014. Here you can see its transverse-mounted muffler.

on these cars, although racers certainly did so. Coupled with deletions, component changes, and careful balance, the end result was a vehicle structure and engine combination that weighed a mere 3,125 pounds. The NHRA minimum weight was 3,400, so most of the extra 225 pounds needed went into the area behind the rear wheels.

Both cars were two-seat business coupe sedans riding on slightly tightened 115-inch wheelbases, without backseats, with a roll bar, and with the battery in the trunk. Both used a 4.56 final gear 8¾ differential; the only order option was transmission choice (A833 4-speed or A727 automatic) and exterior color. Moreover, production was a full engineering department release based on assembly-line creation, not simply a modified or subcontracted deal as others used. This strategy kept not just the spirit of the law but the exact requirements the NHRA used for determining eligibility.

This particular A990 Plymouth is owned by Joe Logiudice and is considered one of the most original in existence. Showing just 217 miles and never raced on the track, it had been purchased originally as a street racer by a young man in Connecticut.

This is how the Logiudice trunk may have looked as delivered. It included a large truck battery, a set of race plugs, a special transmission hub, and a hood plate with air horns to replace the air cleaner.

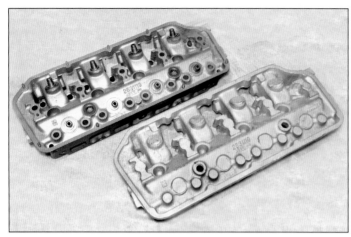

At the bottom is a machined 1965 A990 aluminum head casting and on top is an unmilled head courtesy Kramer Automotive. After dyno tests were done, the castings were given some reinforcement in certain areas to prevent stress-related cracks. These heads used a slightly smaller intake valve than did the steel-headed A864 version.

This view shows the same two heads from the combustion chamber side; note how close the final intake location is on the built-up head (top), which has been deck-milled .030.

Aluminum heads (such as these provided by Kramer Automotive) required the use of seat inserts, which was why the intake valve measured 2.23 instead of 2.25 inches. Bronze-wall valveguides and inserts below the springs to prevent galling of the aluminum were also mandated by the change.

The Hemi's A990 configuration was the culmination of an effort that began soon after the 1964 Daytona 500. Race coordinator Tom Hoover was eager to have a set of prototype aluminum heads cast; this happened in July. Development on them had been successful. After some minor changes to the castings for rigidity, they were approved for the engine with no changes to ports or combustion chamber. Intake valve size was reduced very slightly from 2.25 to 2.23 inches to accommodate the valveseat inserts, and cam timing events took advantage of the ongoing dyno work, with .540 lift and 312/312/88 specs.

For 1965, the tubular headers were mildly changed, again feeding into a single pipe and transverse-mounted muffler. One real difference from the A864 package was that the cross ram was magnesium instead of aluminum, and it still hosted a pair of R3116 Holley carbs.

According to research by Jim Schild, the 101 Plymouths were built in late 1964, while the Dodges were delayed by labor strikes; 35 had been built by the winter races and the remainder during the rest of that spring. Based on the reality of the Plymouth versions, the NHRA issued a waiver to let the Dodges race until the full quantity were built and delivered.

1965 AHRA and NHRA Winter Events

When the AHRA season opened on January 29, 1965, at Beeline Dragway near Phoenix, Arizona, seven entries were ready for a class Jim Tice's crew designated Ultra Stock. The Golden Commandos raced the 558 mule car, driven by team member and dyno operator Forrest Pitcock. It was equipped with Hilborn injectors; all other entries were carbureted.

Sox & Martin's new car was so light it was damaged during transit and was hastily repaired at a local dealership. But Sox went to the top of the charts with a 10.74 in qualifying before bending the car again. The team cleverly named it *The Paper Tiger*. Butch Leal, Dick Landy, Bud Faubel, Bobby Harrop, and Lee Smith also made this event in their new fully altered cars, but Leal and Landy both had to withdraw before class eliminations with manual transmission woes.

Also on hand as part of the AHRA modified-wheelbase Super/Stock class were the four new NHRA-legal A/FX

cars: Lindamood's *Color Me Gone* and the Ramchargers *Candymatic* (with Mike Buckel driving), *Melrose Missile* of Grove/DiBari and the Eckstrand-driven *Golden Commandos* car, plus Strickler in his 1964 aluminum-nosed Super Stock car that was now running in NHRA Modified Production trim (his new car was still being worked on).

S/S-1 was for AHRA stock-wheelbase, steel-bodied Formula 1 Super Stockers (equivalent to NHRA's Super Stockers but with any width tire allowed inside the wheel well) with new 1965 Plymouths of Bill Jenkins/ Doc Burgess, Dick Housey/Ted Spehar, and class winner Joe Smith/Fenner Tubbs as highlights. After qualifying on Friday, the 16 fastest cars from six classes (three for sticks, three for automatics) were run off on Saturday for a Mr. Stock Eliminator class crown. The damage to Leal, Landy, and Phil Bonner's sole Ford entry, a 427-ci Falcon, led to three more S/S-1 legal replacements in the program.

When the smoke had cleared, Bud Faubel's altered U/S *Honker* Dodge took home $1,000 in prizes and money.

Faubel had been an awarded fighter pilot and occasional NASCAR driver before getting on the straight and narrow in the early 1960s. He had actually driven his Amblewagon-built car from Detroit to Chambersburg, Pennsylvania, on the Pennsylvania Turnpike in cold weather. He later recalled that this helped him understand the value of heat cycling a cylinder block, something Tom Hoover had also been contemplating.

Faubel raced during the 1965 season with this car and others. He ran a 10.96 to win the Mr. Stock Eliminator crown during Saturday's class runoffs title over Eckstrand's identical 10.96 in the Commandos' S/S car. Mike Buckel took the Ramchargers' NHRA-A/FX–legal S/S machine to a handicap victory in the overall Top Stock Eliminator on Sunday over Del Blades in a D/S Chevy.

A week later, the four A/FX-legal cars raced Ford's new fastback Mustangs and Comets with SOHC power at the NHRA Winternationals in Pomona, California, which was run in one day because of bad weather. The results were unimpressive, with only Tommy Grove going to the semifinals. He had accepted a deal from Ford prior to the event, so it was his last ride in *Melrose Missile*. Charlie DiBari's noted car and backing then went to mechanically minded racer Cecil Yother for the remainder of the season and beyond.

Tommy Grove drove the Melrose Missile 2-percent Plymouth for the last time at Pomona, as he had recently signed on to drive for Ford. New driver Cecil Yother likely changed this car into full-altered status at the dealership. (Photo Courtesy Lynn Wineland Archive, quartermilestones.com)

Photographer Lynn Wineland captured the Lindamood/ Branstner Dodge during the one-day-only rain-shortened 1965 NHRA Winternationals. This latest Color Me Gone entry was a prominent competitor that season. (Photo Courtesy Lynn Wineland Archive, quartermilestones.com)

If the A990 scoop was made functional, the owner could install the pair of air horns and the scoop-sealing plate stored in the trunk. This plate would have been bolted to the bottom of the hood.

Two new fastback Mustangs, specially equipped with SOHC engines by Ford subcontractor Holman-Moody, ran off for the Factory Stock crown (which was basically the A/FX class eliminator at this event); Bill Lawton won. A *Super Stock & Drag Illustrated* magazine analysis noted that the new Mustangs did not meet the letter of the law in NHRA Factory Experimental. They were actually altered by 2.18 percent. As they say, "the show must go on," and with the Chrysler factory out of A/FX for all practical purposes for the rest of 1965, the Mustangs and Comets owned the class that season.

For the Top Stock crown at Pomona, former Dodge tuner Bill Jenkins took his turn in the driver's seat and won in a new A990 Plymouth called *Black Arrow*.

Because no other factory was involved in 1965, Super Stock was an all-Mopar affair, with 15 Plymouths and Bill

The engine in the Logiudice car was an A990. All of the peripheral items are still with the car, including a chrome oval-shape air cleaner (shown) in case the car did not make use of the hood scoop.

Bill Jenkins with the winner's flag after taking Top Stock at the NHRA Winternationals. With permission from owner Doc Burgess, Jenkins modified this car to match race that summer and won the A/MP class title at Indy with it. (Photo Courtesy Lynn Wineland Archive, quartermilestones.com)

A NOTE ON B/FX AND C/FX

Fred Cutler, the son of a Chrysler management employee, began 1965 with his 1964 B/FX class (9.00 to 12.99 pounds per cubic inch) Dodge station wagon using a destroked 383-ci Race Hemi engine. He later installed the same combination into a modified 1965 Super Stock body he called *The Road Runner*. He did well with this combination in both body designs despite a big-buck effort by Ford in the B/FX class.

In C/FX, with its 13.00 weight break, no Hemi could have worked unless installed in a full-size truck. Dave Koffel of Ohio, a metallurgist and former gas-class racer, built his own altered-wheelbase Plymouth from a wreck with factory help that spring, and he still had the 1965 Super Stock body that had provided the engine for his match race project.

After the factory-supported Cobra-powered C/FX

Galaxie of Bill Hoefer won Junior Stock at the first NHRA Springnationals, Koffel installed a "worked" 273-ci LA-series engine in the A990 body that July. With factory direction, the car set records soon afterward and won C/FX class at Indy unopposed with this combination. Koffel eventually came to work for Chrysler.

A handful of Chrysler independents ran in legal A/FX trim because the factory had submitted paperwork for the changes. This included minor wheelbase changes and fiberglass parts and, most important, bigger rear tires. These were especially evident in the South, where legal Super Stock racing was not the big deal, but match racing was. Although competitors including Shirl Greer, Herb McCandless, and Bill Shirey won a handful of rounds that year, the big event titles inevitably went to the well-heeled Ford racers.

Flynn's Dodge. Jenkins beat Hank Taylor, D. R. Spence, and Bill Shirey before meeting up with the new team of Dick Housey and Ted Spehar out of Detroit. With Spehar's carefully built engine, Housey had covered the other A990 cars by almost .2 during the factory test at Carlsbad, but Jenkins won on a small holeshot. He was about to embark on a highly visible career behind the wheel, although this was his last season with a Hemi.

Exhibitionists

The altered-wheelbase Chryslers might have been outlawed at NHRA events in FX, but as exhibition cars, they were welcome. Butch Leal and Dick Landy took their repaired cars to a couple of side-by-side exhibition runs during the downtime between rounds on Sunday afternoon at the NHRA Winternationals. But perhaps they made a bigger splash at Bakersfield, California, during the legendary March Meet less than two months later, along with other Chrysler factory teams. Landy won with a 10.26 on carbs and gas, which was the quickest time yet for these cars.

Between AHRA's Phoenix event and this race the name Funny Car seems to have gained widespread familiarity. It has been said that Mercury rep Fran Hernandez was the first to use the Funny Car title derisively to describe the cars he was forbidding his drivers to compete against. Other apocryphal stories have track announcers inventing this name as the cars came to the starting line at those early events. Regardless of who started it, in early 1965 Funny Car meant the newest radical 1965 Plym-

This Dodge helped establish Dick Landy's reputation, especially after he toured the East all summer. Landy won several big events, ran some great times, and finished by taking the crown in a well-publicized West Coast match race series that fall. He is seen here at Bakersfield, before the injectors were added. (Photo Courtesy Charles Milikin, Jr.)

ouths and Dodges, and the teams running them easily found paying match races regardless of their locale.

Adding to that notoriety was the phenomenon of wheelstanding. Landy had begun to catapult into even more fame when he showed up at Lions Drag Strip in Long Beach, California, for a photo session and did what became quickly referred to as moonshots: high wheelstands that put the back bumper almost to or even on the pavement. Photographs of that day ended up in many periodicals, and the promoters began to clamor for the same antics out of all Chrysler drivers in these cars.

However, a lot of money was invested in the special cars and their support that year, and the action of returning the front end of the car to earth too hard had a dramatic and detrimental effect on parts, such as suspensions

Even today, there is a fascination with the altered-wheelbase program. Here are Rob Schatz in his Performance King Plymouth and Dan Householder in the Hemi Madness Plymouth, after a flag start at the annual Nostalgia Nationals at Beaver Springs Dragway in Pennsylvania. (Photo Courtesy John Stunkard)

and transmissions. The repair bills were extensive, as the factory teams paid for all of the parts that the sponsored teams broke. Multiple engines, transmissions, differentials, and suspension parts, as well as salaries and travel expense accounts all added up to this being the highest budget drag racing effort by Chrysler to that time by far.

Finally, in May, engineer Dale Reeker sent all the teams a terse telegram telling them to cease wheelstanding. The die was cast, however, and "accidental" occurrences continued. Moreover, for those who were racing their own home-built cars and not sending Chrysler a bill for parts, doing a moonshot was an easy way to get exposure.

Now known alternatively as a Funny Car, Ultra Stock, Unlimited Stock, Match Bash, or Experimental Stock, the outrageous machines became a major part of popular drag racing during those first six months. Upon seeing the Chryslers in January, Ford reps actually forbade their sponsored drivers to race against them and, other than Bonner's one-off 427-ci Falcon, boycotted the AHRA event. They finally relented by June, and the race between all parties quickly accelerated to see who could go faster, via parts and radical wheelbase modification. As a result, many non-Mopar Funny Cars appeared soon after.

Thunder Valley Opens

That change of heart was also just in time for the first NHRA Spring Nationals scheduled for early June at Larry Carrier's new dragstrip in Bristol, Tennessee. Adjacent to his circle track and tucked between a pair of echo-producing hills, it was officially called Bristol International Raceway and immediately afterward unofficially known as Thunder Valley. In addition to FX classes, Carrier and the NHRA scheduled a Match Bash class with agreed-upon rules just for the altered-wheelbase cars. Dave Strickler won that race in his Dodge. Other late-model cars were on hand in the Altered classes, and a handful of 1965 Hemi Super Stocks with legal changes ran against the Mustangs and Comets in the A/FX class.

By this event, Dave Koffel and other independent racers had also arrived on the scene with cars they had built themselves, some with factory help, some without.

For all-out efforts, Plaza offered fiberglass parts. Chrysler released blueprints to select independent racers such as Koffel, and some entries made use of a straight front axle.

Reflecting on the old Southern match race adage, "run whatcha brung and bring all you got," that first race

York U.S. 30 Dragway in Pennsylvania was the site of several notable contests in 1965. Dave Strickler's car is seen there early in 1965; he later won the one-time-only Match Bash class race at the 1965 NHRA Springnationals. (Photo Courtesy Kramer Automotive Film/Print Library)

Homebuilt and changed FX cars cropped up early in 1965. Shirl Greer is in front of the dealership in Kingsport, Tennessee, with his almost-new Dodge. It has been changed to A/FX legal trim with a fiberglass nose, big tires, and 2-percent wheelbase change (note rear wheel location). (Shirl Greer Old Champ Archive, Courtesy Brian Greer)

at Bristol gave a lot of people a chance to show off in front of a crowd, even if the high-visibility cars ended up in the altered classes following the Match Bash class race. In fact, many legal Mopar and Ford FX and S/S entries were radically modified following this race, including a second car that the Sox & Martin team had just received from Plymouth. Many of the previous year's package cars, no longer legal because of the NHRA's all-steel body rule, were also converted into Match Bash trim to get in on the action.

Faster on Fuel

Meanwhile, fuel formulations and fuel injection systems were being developed. Hilborn, using the testing information generated by Coddington and Chrysler in January and late March, created very specific tube lengths and throttle bore diameters for optimal ram effect. These were available in two heights: a short version for manual-transmission cars and a taller one for lower-RPM launching automatics. The company also now offered complete injector packages that were set up specifically for the factory altered program, with return and idle circuits that Coddington had engineered. Released in April, these proved to be a major advance, as Sox made the first non-supercharged door-car pass into the 9-second zone at York, Pennsylvania, with a 9.98 on gasoline on April 24.

The Ramchargers, their car now converted to fully altered status, followed that on May 1 with a 9.83 effort against Sox at York. Because the lengths precluded them from being underhood, it now appeared that the engines were literally sprouting out through the hood scoop as if uncontainable. This look only added to the powerplant's growing notoriety.

Nitrated gasoline had been used to some effect in the past in match racing (legal FX was always a carbureted gas-only proposition), but the factory also began releasing information to its racers on using blends of nitromethane and alcohol with the new Hilborn parts. The result was an amazing number of performance advancements in the following months. According to Mike Buckel in Rockwell's *Ramchargers* book, this method first began during late 1964 on the *Little Red Wagon* experimental during its FX phase at 20-percent nitro, but the truck used only methanol later.

The Ramchargers team took its typical analytical approach to all of this, finally settling on healthy blueprinted Tom Hoover engines at either the 426 standard or a stroker-crank (472-ci) combination in the Dodge for match racing. Group members continued to figure out optimal fuel use and vehicle adaptations, experimenting with small loads of 30 percent or so when necessary.

"I built just one 4.10 stroker Hemi for that car, and it only ran a few times," admits Hoover. "That was an engine for high nitro content that Dan Mancini, Tom Coddington, and I put together. The rest of the time we

Factory experiments in fuel injection were ongoing throughout the early months of 1965. Various lengths were based on launch RPM speeds, shift points, and the sonic effect of air/fuel moving in the overall runner length between the bell opening and valve. The tall set was once on the Melrose Missile Plymouth. The other set is for a 4-speed application; the rearmost air bells are trimmed for clearance. Both sets were provided by Kramer Automotive.

Also used with the new injection units at the time was this separator plate, hand-fabricated to provide support of the opened-up fiberglass hood. Braces were added to the injector tubes to hold it in place. Other than the examples that went directly to the factory teams in 1965, these parts were not commonly released. This example was provided by Kramer Automotive.

used the 426 engine. It made more torque, but the power was about the same. We first raced Roger Lindamood with it and he knew that something was funny and commented about it accordingly. When we ran the big number at Cecil County, it was with the 426, though.

"You know, with nitro, you really didn't need a stroker. You get a lot more heat and friction. Once you get the engine to a high enough speed, you are making less power because of it. And you could break stuff easier."

The car was touring fairly regularly, so the team was getting paid exhibition money while the testing continued. Racing in July against Pete Seaton's new Chevelle, Buckel rolled the Dodge on a pass at Detroit Dragway. He was unharmed and the damage was more cosmetic than serious.

"In those days, the rims were about 4 inches wide, and with 4 pounds of air in the tires," says Hoover. "And I'll tell you, once it started walking away, it was over. You could hit the brakes, give it power; it didn't matter. It was gone. The engine had 24-inch pipes on it that night, and even upside down, it kept running for a little while because of the nitro and the hot parts. So it sucked in all kinds of garbage. Mancini and I pulled all kinds of grass, muck, you name it, out of it when we took it apart!"

The team hurriedly repaired the car, but it missed a huge race put on by *Super Stock & Drag Illustrated* magazine on August 7 to go to a prescheduled event at Cecil County Drag-O-Way in Bayview, Maryland. Thornton, using the biggest load of fuel yet (50 percent) pushed the primer-painted Ramchargers *Candymatic* into the 8-second zone with an 8.91 lap in sea-level air conditions. The team had already run a couple of passes in the 9.1 range prior to the accident, but this run, a full second faster than Sox's pass just three months prior, and 2 seconds quicker than the 10.91 FX best at Pomona at the start of the season, was a watershed mark for stock-bodied drag racing.

The Ramchargers ran match races with a healthy dose of fuel and occasionally a 472-ci engine. Seen here against Hubert Platt at Aquasco Raceway in Maryland, Candymatic was one of the most feared entries in the nation by this time. Unfortunately, this historic car was later disassembled for its parts and scrapped. (Photo Courtesy Kramer Automotive Film/Print Library)

The Woodstock of Drag Racing

That same night the team also missed a landmark event at York, Pennsylvania. Now considered by many to be the Woodstock of drag racing, that one-day show, the Super Stock Nationals, brought virtually every other major name in match bash racing to one venue. The magazine's publicity and match bash racing's huge popularity in the Northeast led tens of thousands to show up at the county airport for the event. As the crowds became more unmanageable, the promoters eventually gave up charging admission.

Most of the factory teams from Ford and Chrysler were on hand, as was a contingent of independent GM drivers, racing in a number of classes divided by fuel and weight. The heavy hitters were in an Unlimited category, burning nitromethane, while gas classes consisted of both altered and stockers, again based on weight, engine size, and fuel method (injected or carbureted).

As the event progressed past midnight, with fans standing on the apron of the track despite admonitions from announcer Jon Lundberg, the Unlimited class came down to Landy and Eckstrand, both on heavy levels of injected fuel. The lawyer took the title on a holeshot with a 9.67 to Landy's quicker 9.58.

Recounting the surreal experience years later, Eckstrand considered it the highlight of his career in American drag racing. On each run he could see nothing but people lined up on the edges of the track until the Commandos' car launched and they disappeared. Through the nitro fumes, goggles, and firemask, he caught a glimpse of the stars as the car did a high wheelstand. Then it returned to earth to roar side-by-side with its competitor. Without guardrails between the exhibition and the audience, liability was never far from the Lawman's mind, but the people almost magically parted as the pair of cars continued toward the finish line. Being the winner each time allowed him to summarize it by simply saying, "It was great!"

"We were the best two cars in the country that night, and nobody can ever take that away from either of us," he told me in an interview for *Mopar Muscle* magazine. "It was my last big drag race win. I retired at the end of the season." He moved to England soon afterward.

Bobby Harrop's *Flying Carpet* Dodge took home the bigger title of Mr. Top Stock in the early morning hours, running as quick as 9.32 on nitro in the process. This event and others like it in the East that summer helped set the stage for a multiweek West Coast Match Bash tour that ran from California to Washington State and back later in the season. Again, publicity played a role in exposing the series to immense crowds at every venue,

Bobby Harrop of New Jersey shut down the biggest names in the sport when he won the heads-up title at the Super Stock Nationals, running as quick as 9.32. This car was destroyed at the Cecil County Drag-O-Way season opener the following spring, and Bobby ran the ex-Ramchargers car for a time in 1966 as a result. (Photo Courtesy Kramer Automotive Film/Print Library)

culminating in a race in October at Lions Drag Strip in Long Beach, perhaps the premier facility in that state at the time.

Lions manager C. J. "Pappy" Hart had already seen that the crowd liked the cars at a Ford-laden AHRA national event that summer, but he pulled out all of the stops here, playing calliope music and including exhibition acts as part of the show. The series title, based on cash winnings, went to Landy, and he won the Unlimited Class titles as well as Lions Overall Eliminator race by beating Ronnie Sox in a handicap final. That was a major event, but Lions' biggest move onto the Funny Car map happened a week later when Gary Dyer showed up in the Grand-Spaulding Dodge to race Don Gay's Pontiac GTO in a four-way match race that included them, Hayden Proffitt's Comet, and Tom McEwen's *Hemi 'Cuda*.

Mr. Norm Grand-Spaulding Storm

Norm Krause's dealership in Chicago was in a small location at the corner of Grand and Spaulding on the city's southwest side, but aggressive marketing and able management made Mr. Norm's the largest seller of Dodge performance cars in the world. Gary Dyer had come onboard as Norm's racing coordinator.

"My role with Grand-Spaulding Dodge was to run the racing program, and a partnership was formed with them," recalls Gary today. "They supplied Mopar parts for the operation, but most of the operating capital was covered by match racing. I was driving a 1964 427 AFX Comet for the Chicagoland Lincoln Mercury Dealers and was at Indy when Norm and driver Pat Minick had a falling out; Pat gave me the okay to talk with Norm about teaming up with Grand-Spaulding. It was my idea to build a blown A990 car to not compete against any of the dealership's customers."

So for 1965, Grand-Spaulding Dodge had built a supercharged stock-bodied Hemi sedan from one of the 11 A990 Dodges it had ordered and received to sell. At midseason, when Roger Lindamood and Dick Branstner found their factory *Color Me Gone* money gone due to differences they had with Chrysler's racing bosses (plus publicized undeterred wheelies), the Dyer/Norm team bought that acid-dipped factory-altered Dodge to replace the home-built match racer.

"After running the A990 car, I told Norm we needed to get a lighter car with better weight transfer. We secured the *Color Me Gone* Dodge because it was 300 to 400 pounds lighter," says Dyer. Jim O'Connor drove his car for Norm at the York Super Stock Magazine Nationals in injected format. But once the supercharged combination was added to it from the A990 car and with Gary Dyer tuning and driving, it garnered greater notoriety in the annals of drag racing.

Dyer's original nemesis in the blown stocker ranks had been Arnie "the Farmer" Beswick, who had become a GM stalwart after his days in a Dodge D500-1 in 1956. Now racing primarily Pontiacs (as well as having a part-year Mercury FX deal in 1965 that ended at midseason, also amid factory controversy), Beswick was self-funded and ran a tight operation. In 1964, he had put together a nitro-snorting supercharged 1964 GTO and often raced the *Mr. Norms* entry with it. He continued with this car in 1965, but had a protégée waiting impatiently in the wings.

Don Gay was a teenager from Texas whose father ran a very successful Pontiac dealership near Houston. Already experienced at drag racing in the SS and FX classes prior to the GM racing ban of 1963, the two Pontiac racers knew each other, and Beswick helped Gay build his own supercharged 1965 GTO that spring, no expense spared. Gay took Norm's trouncing of Beswick personally.

In this publicity photo, the first Mr. Norms blown Dodge sedan is in action during a spring race in 1965. Gary Dyer suggested building the package to keep the dealership from racing its own customers. (Photo Courtesy Mr. Norm, Gary Dyer Collection)

Throughout the summer of 1965, Gay and Norm baited each other in a series of adjective-laden ads that ran in *Drag News* and *Drag World*, two weekly racing papers. The rivalry culminated in a widely heralded match race at Union Grove, Wisconsin. Dyer won by default, leaving the question of superiority unresolved. Pappy Hart, knowing these two could bring in the crowds, booked them for a best-of-three on a Saturday night in front of 10,000 screaming SoCal fans.

Lions, noted for honest clocks and unbelievable atmospheric conditions, was the final salvo for the factory altered-wheelbase program in 1965. The sport had seen a huge amount of transition in this one year directly as a result of the factory program. Although still unnamed due to its fluid status, the NHRA created XS (Experimental Stock) for early 1966 to find a formal category for these and other contraptions now being built almost continuously to race. However, when the factory returned to NASCAR for 1966, a good deal of the money that had been funneled into this program went with it. Only Sox and Landy were left as the only racers in the unlimited category who were actually sponsored. Several racers continued with deals for parts only; some with money still anted up by the dealers' associations.

As Dyer waited that night, Norm performed the classic match race ritual by sweeping long lines of dance-floor rosin, called "gold dust" in drag racing parlance, onto the racing surface for traction. The big supercharged engine came to life; this was the second run of the match. The Dodge and its young driver launched into the darkness, balls of flame cackling from beneath the floorboards. The crowd waited for the announcement.

It may have been like this: "Unbelievable! Gary Dyer just ran 8.63 at 163 mph, folks!"

Amazing and unquestioned, it was a fitting end to a true revolution. The type of car born out of that 558 project built in Highland Park in late 1964 was far more successful than anyone could have imagined. It was now honestly part of the sport, regardless of what its detractors thought.

Special Car Projects

The 426 Hemi engine helped establish Chrysler's reputation among the performance-minded public in other drag racing experimental programs in 1965. During that year, several other special car projects were in the works. These experimentals were built with some association with the factory or with sponsorship, and all would help write history. Most of them used the A-Body Dart and Barracuda body design.

Petty and Pearson in Straight-Line Racing

The NASCAR boycott proved serious and costly to those racers who had maintained a sponsored association with Chrysler, and the factory moved quickly to keep a couple of them in the limelight with 1965 model cars for drag racing. Plymouth still had newly crowned Grand National Champion Richard Petty, who had actually done some drag racing previously on a celebrity scale. In early October 1964, the Petty crew received a 1965 Barracuda body for Southern-style match racing and built it up using a carbureted Hemi engine mounted in the standard front location. They added the name *Outlawed* and *43 Jr.* to the sides, with a "If you can't beat them, OUTLAW them" bumper sticker and two offset tin scoops directing air to the carbs and cross-ram intake. The little car with its forward-mounted engine was running before the end of the year, and Petty raced it at the AHRA Arizona event in January in a special Super/Stock Experimental class.

Even with Petty's driving background, *43 Jr.* was a handful. On the last day of February 1965, Richard was racing Arnie Beswick's blown GTO at a little track in Dallas, Georgia,

Brian Kohlmann did extensive research to re-create the ex-Mr. Norm Dodge, *and eventually ran the car into the 7-second zone on nitromethane. He is seen here doing a fire burnout in the re-created car at George Ray's Wildcat* Outlaw *racetrack in Arkansas in 2001.*

when a breakage problem, never fully described, sent the car careening off the narrow surface into the trackside crowd. Several people were injured and a young boy was killed; Petty later admitted that he was devastated by the event.

That car was scrapped and the team built a second entry, which was also match raced and ran with the Hilborn fuel injectors in B/Altered at Bristol in June. Nobody was happier than Richard Petty to be back in NASCAR as things on that front thawed in early summer. After selling the second car to racer Eddie Ratcliff, Petty raced Freddy Lorenzen in Phil Bonner's A/FX Mustang at a drag match at Charlotte Motor Speedway as late as October 1965.

On the Dodge NASCAR side, Cotton Owens and David Pearson took to the strip in a Dodge Dart wagon called *The Cotton Picker*. Unlike the Petty machine, it featured a mid-mounted engine and Torqueflite combination. Although the car match-raced during the first half of the year, it never made any real waves with Pearson as pilot. Like Petty's car, it was fuel injected at Bristol, but only as an exhibition car. By then the team was back to circle-track racing, with Pearson running in USAC and returning to the Grand National series, as those issues were resolved. Bud Faubel ended up with the yellow wagon, and he raced it on several occasions during 1965, before his mechanic, George Weiler, bought it and turned into a match-racing car he called *Mr. Violent*.

Faubel's third project in 1965 was a twin-turbo beast built from an older 1964 *Honker* Dodge 330 with a 1965 Coronet A/FX fiberglass nose. Bob Keller, an aircraft engineer, suggested and directed it under the backing of Dodge, with assistance from the AiResearch Industrial Division of the Garrett Corporation. The work of these two aircraft-minded thinkers resulted in what may have

been one of the first turbocharger/intercooler installations on a drag car, and most certainly the first on the new Race Hemi design. The first lap on the car produced huge amounts of tire smoke and a 160-mph clocking.

However, the car was never actively developed because of the expense of the experiments. In the end, Mallicoat Brothers Racing of California took Hemi technology into the turbocharged environment later in the decade, doing so in the gasser ranks. Once sorted out, almost any twin-turbocharged combination was so successful it often ended up being outlawed in the forced-induction classes by the sanctioning bodies.

Don Garlits received factory help for a number of Darts in the era. In late 1964, a transmission explosion destroyed the first one on its maiden run. The second was Dick Branstner's old Dart Charger *Polka Dart*, which crashed during a match race at Detroit with Emory Cook as the driver. That was followed by a fiberglass roadster body on an old dragster chassis later in 1966, a car that the NHRA eventually outlawed.

Flying Fish

Plymouth also entered the mid-engine fray via two more Barracudas, from two very different sources. The first was a project sponsored by the Southern California Plymouth Dealers Association that put a supercharged Hemi on nitro into a layout similar in design to Don Garlits' failed experiment of late 1964. Transmission builders Don and Bob Spar of B&M Automotive built this car between late 1964 and early 1965. Inaugurated by Lou Baney, it was turned over to noted dragster pilot Tom "the Mongoose" McEwen. At the time, McEwen was running a 392-ci fuel dragster with Baney out of the Yeakel Plymouth franchise in Los Angeles.

Power for *Hemi 'Cuda* came from a blown 426 Hemi built by Dave Zueshel and backed by one of B&M's new Torkmaster fluid couplings. All of this was mounted in a box frame that also hosted the differential beneath the body. After an exhibition debut at Pomona, McEwen took it to Lions for testing and promptly tested the laws of aerodynamics instead, flipping and rolling the car at the top end of the track, but emerging uninjured. The dealer's association paid to have it rebuilt, and with a few aero adaptations, he ran the car on and off that season in exhibition and match race action. He clocked a great 8.88 at a fastest-for-1965 171-mph lap at Lions just moments before Dyer ran his 8.63. As McEwen shifted allegiances, the dealer's association turned the car over to driver Fred Goeske in 1966.

The second project was George Hurst's unconventional Plymouth Barracuda experimental car. It also used a mid-mounted injected Hemi and 4-speed transmission,

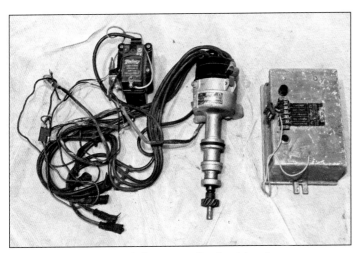

Although teams used the Prestolite ignition layout, many also experimented with aftermarket parts. This is a complex electronic ignition outfit (provided by Kramer Automotive) that was used on the Bud Faubel Honker that year.

Tom McEwen in Hemi 'Cuda *slows down from a fast run at the 1965 Winternationals. He eventually took this car to a fastest-ever 181 mph clocking at Lions the same night as the infamous Dyer-Gay match race. (Photo Courtesy Lynn Wineland Archive, quartermilestones.com)*

For 1966, tuner Bob Riggle took over from Bill Shrewsberry in the Hurst Hemi Under Glass. *He made a decade-long business of running the car before being sidelined by a devastating accident. He returned with several new versions of the car, including this one seen in action at St. Louis in 2004.*

with a 180-degree transfer box mounted to send the output to a differential that was installed upside down. Plymouth's PR man Sam Peacock agreed to help with money and parts, and the Woodward Garage crew was subcontracted to build it. This car was to be a testbed for a couple of suspension ideas Hurst was developing as well as a promotional exhibition car. With the big engine visible under the Barracuda's unique rear window, the car was called Hurst's *Hemi Under Glass*.

Former Mercury FX pilot Bill Shrewsberry was the first driver of the project, and it debuted at the NHRA Springnationals at Bristol in 1965. In brief testing beforehand, the car had shown a propensity to lift the nose. When Shrewsberry hit it in front of the crowd for the first time, the car actually stood up on its back bumper! He feathered it back to earth and was a bit unnerved. However, he came out and made a couple more passes to the delight of the crowd.

This car and its successors immediately became an enduring and popular attraction. Eventually, it was turned over to crewmember Bob Riggle for the 1966 season; he added a supercharger. In 1965, Shrewsberry was perhaps best known for taking his boss, George Hurst, for a bumper-bouncing ride in front of the crowd at the U.S. Nationals in Indianapolis late that summer.

Little Red Wagon

None of the projects that developed in those formative years as one-off designs had the impact of an A100 Dodge economy pickup truck that came from the Branstner/Howell/Lindamood shop at the factory's direction. Jack Shaeffer and Jim Collier of Detroit, who worked in the Dodge Truck factory, originally conceived and constructed the vehicle. It was an attempt at building an FX-class machine using a carbureted Hemi mounted behind the cab, coupled to a Torqueflite automatic and

a standard rear gear. It was not unheard of, as there had been a couple of larger Dodge pickups that had raced in the B/FX class during the Max Wedge era.

Little Red Wagon debuted in September with Jay Howell driving, but it often bounced around on the rear tires. That ended after sorting out the suspension with help from Jim Thornton, who designed a full subframe supporting the driveline and differential as one unit fitted into the standard vehicle frame. Howell, who was a pretty brave test driver, took the truck to Motor City Dragway near Detroit and hammered it. Up it went, and further testing quickly found that it was very light in the nose, and once up, it stayed up.

They called Super Stock standout Bill "Maverick" Golden from California to make a few runs in it. Maverick also saw the sky at each launch, but he saw the profit-making potential of a pickup truck that did wheelies down the dragstrip. He made a deal with Wylie for the truck instead of a 1965 drag car. He used the fuel injectors to keep the engine fed during the violent transitions and cut a square hole in the floor to see where he was going. *Little Red Wagon* commanded the same appearance money as some of the biggest dragster racers by the summer of 1965.

Indy Nationals and a Hemi World Title

The biggest event of any year was NHRA's Nationals at Indy, and 1965 was no exception. To make an appearance in Super Stock, several factory drivers received legal

Bill "Maverick" Golden racked up an impressive number of wins in Super Stock in 1963 and 1964, but never looked back when he was able to take over the controls of Little Red Wagon in late 1964. It was the top-booked car in 1965, earning as much money for its exhibitions as big-name fuel dragster pilots. (Photo Courtesy Lynn Wineland Archive, quartermilestones.com)

Few machines in any sort of motorsports racked up as many records as Little Red Wagon, virtually an institution for decades in the sport. It is seen here during one of Bill Golden's final driving appearances, at Pennsylvania's Maple Grove Raceway.

Fred Cutler ran his destroked Hemi engine in B/FX using this 1965 Dodge called The Road Runner. (Photo Courtesy Charles Milikin, Jr.)

Photographer Charles Milikin, Jr. was at the 1965 NHRA Nationals and took several important images of A990 cars that were not in Super Stock. This shows Bill "the Professor" Shirey running in A/FX trim, the only Chrysler in that class. (Photo Courtesy Charles Milikin, Jr.)

cars for the weekend. Butch Leal and Dave Strickler raced for the Super Stock stick title, with Leal repeating his 1964 win. Bob Harrop won over Jack Werst for the automatic title.

Other Hemis winning class crowns were Bill Jenkins' modified Doc Burgess–owned *Black Arrow* in A/Modified Production and Joe Aed with the ex-*Lawman* Aed-Housley Plymouth in C/Altered, while C/FX went to the A990 body with 273-ci power: a *Maloney Motors* Plymouth owned by Dave Koffel. The steel-nosed 1963 Plymouth Max Wedges of Don Grotheer and Ray Christian won AA/S and AA/SA, respectively. However, the Fords did win A/FX (Bill Shirey's Plymouth was the only non-Ford) and B/FX (Fred Cutler's 1965 destroked Dodge was runner-up) as well as Top Stock on Monday, which went to Bud Shellenberger's AA/S Galaxie. The A990 package proved itself less than two months later at the NHRA World Finals at Southwestern.

Bill Lawton of Rhode Island's Tasca Ford had an exceptional season. Driving the *Zimmy III* SOHC Mustang, he won Factory Stock at Pomona, won the gas crown at the Super Stock Nationals, and was in the thick of A/FX all season. He rode that momentum in Tulsa, Oklahoma.

After the yearly points debacles of 1964, the NHRA went to a race-off format to determine the winner, using a prequalified field of division finalists racing for a winner-take-all Top Stock crown. Ten entries were on hand for Top Stock: three A/FX Mustangs, three AA/SA 1963 Plymouths, the AAA/SA 1964 Galaxies of former Junior Stock World Champion Mike Schmidt and Bob Spears, and two 1965 S/S Plymouths raced by Arlen Vanke and Joe Smith.

Smith had been racing Plymouths out of the Fenner Tubbs franchise in Lubbock, Texas, for the past several seasons. He had been the Division 4 champ in 1964 and 1965 with Hemi power and he also repeated in 1966. Although, he had to be considered a dark horse in the Tulsa battle. He beat Don Grotheer and Ray Christian, the Indy class winners, and then singled in the semifinals to find Lawton in the other lane. Ford had offered new Mustangs to the class winners, so there was swag on the line. Before the hint of green, the Mustang launched and left a big red light at the starting line while Joe took a pleasant pass to 11.23, a new Ford, and a trip to Hawaii courtesy of the NHRA.

The year ended with current-model Hemis again on the NASCAR circuit, winning the NHRA Stock World Championship, setting a land-speed record (see sidebar "Flying Miles: A Look at Land Speed Efforts" in Chapter 6) and revolutionizing exhibition drag racing. There was really only one place left for the Hemi to conquer: the streets.

The C/Altered class was won by the ex-Lawman entry of Aed-Housley. Not often recalled is that a number of highly modified factory Ford team cars were placed into the B/Altered class at Indy in 1965. (Photo Courtesy Charles Milikin, Jr.)

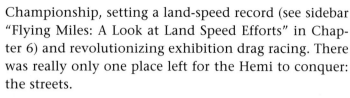

Joe Smith came out of Texas to give the Hemi its first World Championship in 1965, when he beat Bill Lawton at the first NHRA World Finals race in Tulsa, Oklahoma. He is seen here at the NHRA Nationals over Labor Day a month before. (Photo Courtesy Charles Milikin, Jr.)

Dave Strickler received a barely used A990 body from Ohio's Bob Lawless with help from Arlen Vanke. It was raced in this scheme for that weekend and then returned to Lawless, who had installed the Hemi from it into his prewar-style altered. (Photo Courtesy Ray Mann Archive, quartermilestones.com)

Found neglected in a Detroit alley by collector Chris Taddy, Paper Tiger Too was later purchased by Mike Guffey and subsequently restored by Erik Lindberg for Todd Werner. It is seen here at its debut at the All-Hemi Reunion.

The second altered-wheelbase car in the Sox & Martin stable was built from an A990 sedan after Ronnie drove it in Super Stock at the NHRA Springnationals in June of 1965. It was called Paper Tiger Too.

CHAPTER FIVE

1965
Circle Tracks and the Politics of Racing

NASCAR Bans and then Reinstates the Hemi

With Ronney Householder's decision to hold his ground on Bill France's rules change for 1965, it is sometimes assumed that Chrysler did not compete at all in NASCAR (or circle-track racing in general) that season.

Of course, the USAC series accepted the Hemi, but it was not anywhere as large as NASCAR's Daytona 500 in terms of exposure. The ARCA and IMCA (International Motor Contest Association) series also allowed the Hemi to run that year.

Daytona Doings and More for 1965

Actually, Hemi cars did race at Speedweeks on the banks of Daytona in 1965, just not in Grand National competition. One of the most notable instances occurred on a windy February 26, 1965, exhibition, two weeks after the 500. Heavily promoted by Dodge's PR guru Frank Wiley, a supercharged Dodge Coronet that Ray Fox had built reset the track's all-time speed record. Driver LeeRoy Yarbrough, who piloted Fox's 1965 Chevrolets, among other entries that year, took the 181.818 record despite a lack of traction, 45-degree temperatures, and strong crosswinds. He told the *Sarasota Times-Tribune*

that it was the "squirreliest ride" he'd ever had, as he felt the car go airborne, and was drifting sideways on all four wheels off the turns.

He made just three laps, setting the record on lap 2, before coming in on a premonition, only to find a 1/4-inch bolt had punctured a front tire. The title on the *Daytona Beach Morning Journal*'s story the next day was "Yarbrough Ran Scared." Even with the stock body, the Hemi had surpassed the closed-circuit world's record, set by drag racer Art Malone in a blown, open-wheel 392-ci Hemi winged Indy roadster called *Mad Dog VI* in 1961. Fortunately, the punctured tire featured a brand-new Goodyear innovation called the Lifesaver inner liner, which debuted at Speedweeks in 1965. Without it, had LeeRoy not listened to the voice in his head, he could have easily become another statistic in a year that again saw death on the race courses.

Although many thought there would be a follow-up effort, the Coronet never ran again. Its scooped,

On a cold, windy February 26, 1965, driver LeeRoy Yarbrough pushed this supercharged Coronet (built by Daytona-based car owner Ray Fox) into the history books. The three-lap record run reset the world's stock-bodied car closed-course record to 181.818. (Copyright CR Racing Memories 1410011, Ray Mann Photograph)

Fox (right) and Yarbrough pose with the car prior to the run. Yarbrough had hoped to re-attempt the effort, but that never occurred, and the car was converted back into a standard Grand National entry. (Copyright CR Racing Memories 1410010, Ray Mann Photograph)

The #25 Plymouth for the 1965 Continental race at Daytona was a project that Chrysler itself was involved with. Although few photos exist of this event, Chrysler Historical was able to locate this view of the car from the race paddock. (Photo Courtesy Chrysler Group LLC)

gold-striped hood is on display at the Fox family's Living Legends of Auto Racing Museum of Racing History in South Daytona, Florida. The car was converted back to a standard circle-track entry and was seen in the hands of independent campaigners before disappearing into history.

One of the more interesting efforts for Speedweeks was homologating the B-Bodies built for the drag racing program into FIA-sanctioned endurance competition for the 12-Hour Continental race. Thanks to research by author M. M. "Mike" Matone, the story of this effort came to light. Both Dodge and Plymouth were authorized to compete, with FIA approval coming on January 24 under Recognition Document 189 (AR 2 SS Plymouth) and 190 (AW 2 SS Dodge). A single Belvedere driven by Chrysler engineers Scott Harvey and Peter Hutcherson was entered into the 12-hour endurance event.

"The guy who co-drove that Hemi car with Scott Harvey at Daytona in 1965 was Peter L. V. Hutchinson," says Tom Hoover today. "He worked for me for a few years and was involved in the Weslake-head small-block program we did for Indianapolis with Granatelli. He had a lot to do with that and the Trans-Am cars the next year. What people might not know is that L. V. was the grandson of Walter P. Chrysler's financial man."

This car was built around Chrysler Engineering chassis 023, which was the prototype for the 1965 B-Body circle-track program and documented extensively through Engineering Document 4208.8. The car was equipped with a drag-package 426 Super Commando engine, extensive fiberglass parts including a bubbled hood, and full roll cage.

Larry Adams worked with Larry Rathgeb (plus notable engineering adjuncts, including members of the Ramchargers including Dan Knapp and Dan Mancini) to get this program off the ground. Interestingly, Ronney

Householder was not the proponent of this effort; that fell to Pete Dawson of product planning, an associate of Tom Hoover's and the factory point man on the Summers Brothers land-speed effort. Like the drivers, Dawson had a penchant for road racing, and his close association with English racing teams could have been part of the catalyst to make an attempt against the Ferraris, Corvettes, and a serious Ford Cobra effort fielded by Carroll Shelby that year.

Alas, it was not to be; the car ran for about two hours before Hutchinson brought it in with a misfire. The engine was being serviced, and somehow (perhaps through a spark plug tube opening) a cylinder ended up with oil poured into it. When refired, this, in turn, bent a connecting rod. The team put the wounded car back on the track, but the engine gave way, according to period reports, "in spectacular fashion" soon after. Because of this showing, plans to run additional GT events with this car in 1965 were curtailed, and the incident disappeared into history, except when seeing rare images of the big car cornering with all the sports cars.

Harvey, who successfully road raced A-Body models that year in addition to his Chrysler engineering work, also built a FIA-spec 1965 Hemi Coronet for David Pearson and navigator Fred Browne. This car, to be run in the Shell 4000 race across Canada from Montreal to Vancouver, used C-Body police disc brakes, oversize rear springs, 9x15 Dunlap tires (with identical Goodyear snow tires in the trunk), skid plates, and a 10.25 compression Hemi with extra oil capacity. The on-road/off-road rally, which was to last 100 hours between April 24 and 30, was a bust for Dodge, however, and Pearson's #114 is listed in the results as a DNF.

Indeed, according to the race report in Canadian enthusiast magazine *Track & Traffic* for June 1965, the team retired at the end of the first day (scheduled for 20 hours to Sudbury) after varied maladies, plus putting the car into a couple of ditches. Complaining of no brakes, no heater, and assorted other frustrations, the driver later

The late Cotton Owens remained a fixture in NASCAR for decades. He and the #6 Coronet that he re-created to honor the glory days are seen here at a Mopar event in St. Louis.

Jim Hurtubise recovered from burns suffered in an open-wheel race in 1964 to assist Norm Nelson in his charge toward the 1965 USAC championship. The duo ran Plymouths for several seasons; this photo is from 1967. (Copyright CR Racing Memories 0601072, Ray Mann Photograph)

called NASCAR's "Silver Fox" was quoted in the publication playfully saying, "Ah'm not gonna bust mah keaster on this thing no more!"

Pearson, however, may have been in this car or a similar example for a shorter but more treacherous course up Pike's Peak in Colorado on July 4, 1965, as part of the USAC stock car series. Nick Sanborn, a former Corvette pilot, won the timed acceleration race with a 1964 Hemi Plymouth. Parnelli Jones' Mercury was second, followed by Pearson driving a #6 entry out of Owens' operation, and USAC regular Herb Shannon in fourth in Clyde Robbins' #9 Dodge entry. Paul Goldsmith suffered the ignominy of a DNF, but survived intact when he overcorrected on a corner to send Ray Nichels' #25 Plymouth to the brink of disaster when he went off course.

But the USAC and ARCA efforts were not failures by any measure. As Ford had decided against formally participating in the series, Ray Nichels' "Go Fast Factory" cars dominated the USAC series, with Norm Nelson leading the way in points with a two-car effort he fielded together with driver Jim Hurtubise. A. J. Foyt also piloted a Nelson entry on occasion. Goldsmith was second in the Nichels Engineering Plymouth, followed by the Ford of Don White, who moved to Dodge for 1966. The ARCA title went to Jack Bowsher in a Ford for the third consecutive season, but Iggy Katona was pressing hard in his Plymouth all season long. Ernie Derr was the IMCA champ in a Dodge.

Back to NASCAR

The July 4 Colorado hill-climb event occurred on the heels of NASCAR's re-emergence, as far as Chrysler was concerned. Throughout 1965, attendance was way down with so many name drivers sidelined. The track promoters were angry, and finally Bill France and Harry Banks came to an agreement, adjusting the rules once again. The formal announcement stated that Chrysler would be allowed to run the Hemi engine. On larger tracks,

Older equipment was often recycled and used. Here is Billy Foster in his #22, a 1964 Dodge, which records show he raced only in late 1965. This may be at Wentzville, Missouri. Foster was USAC's 1965 Rookie of the Year. (Copyright CR Racing Memories 0602046, Ray Mann Photograph)

the engine would need to be in a 119-inch-minimum wheelbase car (the Fury or Polara). It could be used in the midsize 116-inch Belvedere and Coronet models on short tracks. Householder responded they would not run the big cars due to their non-aero styling, but he perhaps acquiesced when it was agreed the standard B-Body would be allowed on the bigger tracks for 1966 at the smaller 405-ci displacement.

As a result, the Hemi Furys were on hand at Daytona's Firecracker 400 the same day that Goldsmith's Pike Peak effort flirted with disaster. Buddy Baker in the #86 Plymouth actually posted a runner-up finish to A. J. Foyt, driving the Wood Brothers Ford. A more notable occurrence was the lifting of France's lifetime ban of Curtis Turner in late July. A timber investor/developer by trade, Turner was a truly flamboyant figure in stock car racing. Turner ran Hemi Furys at Spartanburg and Darlington and then landed a ride with Ford. The big Hemi Fury models are merely a footnote in racing history. It is unknown if one even led a lap that season.

By Bristol on July 25, however, several teams were back in action with 405-ci Hemi power in the midsize cars. Notably included was Richard Petty, who was also wrapping up his responsibilities with the rebuilt *43 Jr.* drag car. Petty won in Nashville the following Saturday night, ahead of Ned Jarrett's Ford and independent Dodge racer Buddy Arrington. Before the season was over, Petty also won at Asheville, North Carolina; Hickory, North Carolina; Manassas, Virginia; and Augusta, Georgia (which counted as the first points race of 1966, plus scored a large number of top-five finishes elsewhere). Also after Labor Day 1965, David Pearson's Cotton Owens Dodge won at Richmond, setting the stage for his flat-out 1966 effort.

Hemi Sports Racing Cars

There were also two noted Hemi-powered sports cars in the 1964–1965 seasons. For them, the place to compete was the United States Road Racing Championship begun by the SCCA in 1962 as a professional class for open-top sports cars and GT cars. This was an immediate predecessor of the Can-Am series and ran through 1968.

The first car with Hemi power that stood out was the custom-bodied *Hussein* Cooper-Monaco of Texas oil man John Mecom, which began life in 1964 with a NASCAR-bred Ford 427. It became *Hussein II* when a Ray Nichels Hemi engine went into the mid-mount engine bay late that season. Aggressively wheeled by A. J. Foyt, the car posted a runner-up to Roger Penske in the race at Nassau, Bahamas, that December. However, the engine weight was not conducive to good handling, and the car never won an event. As of this writing, it is in the Indianapolis Motor Speedway Hall of Fame museum.

At about the same time as Foyt's efforts in the Bahamas in the *Hussein*, a second open-top road race car was built by Bob McKee under the direction of Ronney Householder, reportedly being constructed for Richard Petty. When Petty's drag racing efforts proved lucrative, it was reported in *Car Craft* in February 1965 that the car would go to Bob Montana, a former fighter pilot who owned Town & Country Plymouth in Phoenix and had a penchant for racing. Town & Country was the dealership where the Sox & Martin team had repaired *Paper Tiger* during the 1965 AHRA Winter Nationals. The dealership name was also on the 558 Plymouth mule driven by Forrest Pitcock at the same event.

The McKey/Montana Hemi posted a class win in C/Modified and second place overall at Vacaville, California, in December 1965, but otherwise seems to have been plagued with fires, driveline issues, and other misfortunes on race day. It ran sporadically during the next few seasons, and after Montana and his family died in a private plane crash in 1971, his son-in-law inherited the car. It was found and painstakingly restored by John Rasmussen during a two-decade process to ensure its authenticity and is now in a private collection.

Richard Petty was back in the stock car wars by late summer 1965. The second drag Barracuda rolls into Bristol for an AHRA race in 1969. This car is being restored by Petty's Garage at the time of this writing. (Photo Courtesy Phillip Smith Archive, quartermilestones.com)

ARCA and Grand National racer Ramo Stott was a fixture in Hemi history during the 1960s and 1970s. No displacement is given on this 1965 Belvedere, just a big Pentastar and the words "Hemi Power" on the hood. (Copyright CR Racing Memories 0601309011, Ray Mann Photograph)

CHAPTER SIX

1966

Road and Track

The Hemi Dominates Racing and Comes to the Street

When Bob Rarey, Bill Weertman, Tom Hoover, and the others at Chrysler Engineering had first laid out the plans for a new 7-liter version of the Hemi engine in early 1963, there had not been any serious intention of making it into a street engine.

Indeed, an experimental gas-turbine design was Chrysler's most interesting foray into updated powerplants when the second-generation Hemi engine under development was an experimental gas turbine design. It eliminated many of the parts endemic to the overhead valve engine environment. Most of the cars imported from Ghia in Italy for use with that experimental program were eventually scrapped in a dispute with the government over import tariffs. Under Bob Rodger's tutelage, however, Chrysler had actually planned a newly designed Dodge B-Body fastback with the turbine in mind named the Charger. In fact, possible turbine engine installation is reportedly why the 1966 Charger had a full-length center console at its debut.

The turbine proved to be less efficient and less practical than hoped. Besides that, the automotive subculture itself was demanding street performance. Couple that trend with the desire for a new Stock Eliminator drag racing package, the need for a production Hemi engine to meet NASCAR's requirements, and the fact that the Race Hemi could be converted into a production engine with mostly minor changes, and the formula was in place to change history. Although more expensive to produce than a similar-displacement wedge design, efficiencies through mass production could make it viable cost-wise as a dealership option.

The Street Hemi: A Race Engine with Benefits

Many consider the Street Hemi to be the equivalent of a street H-bomb, but it really was in keeping with the times. Ford Motor Company had 427-ci engines in its full-size cars but stayed with its 390-ci package as the top street engine in the midsize Fairlane and Comet lines (except for some special race packages) until 1968. Meanwhile, Chevrolet and the other GM brands were starting to aggressively market new performance street cars up to 400 ci (which was a corporate displacement limit on midsize vehicles) and also had 427-ci or larger engines in their luxury models. The Pontiac GTO, Olds 4-4-2, and Chevelle SS packages were all formulated with this in mind, and these cars could be optioned quite profitably as well.

Post coupe Plymouths, such as this one owned by Canadian Ray Dupuis, were a primary reason the Hemi ended up in a street body for 1966: to create legal race cars in NHRA Stock Eliminator.

In 1964 and 1965, Chrysler had already offered the largest-displacement midsized street models in the world using the 426-S single 4-barrel wedge; the Hemi was the same displacement. In fact, the company had been considering a multiple-carburetor version of the 426S wedge, and it was already in process when the development of a Street Hemi began. After being banned in NASCAR as experimental in October 1964, the plan to convert the Race Hemi for highway/production car use began to germinate.

The biggest concern now was streetability rather than durability. Everything that had been learned up to that point had created a very strong architecture for power creation. Now the Hemi had to be built to allow the engine to run efficiently in various weather conditions, require less-intensive maintenance, and use high-octane pump gasoline. The package also needed to be reasonably affordable to the end user, although ordering a Hemi mandated other options in the driveline for durability.

By early 1965, plans were already being laid for a possible introduction with the 1966 model year. The street engine was eventually coded A102. Bob Rodger and Bob Cahill sent a letter to Product Planning on January 6, 1965, asking for changes to make the engine into a package for NHRA Stock Eliminator. This required a production model to be legal for competition and could resolve the political issues with NASCAR as well. Coupled with major redesigns to the B-Body styling for the new year, as well as the Charger's debut, the Hemi engine's wide dimensions needed to be taken into consideration as those cars' structural changes were finalized. However, this proved to be a non-issue beyond minor adaptions for installation.

426 Elephant Highway Evolution

Rodger and Cahill requested the following changes for the 426 Street Hemi: two 4-barrel carburetors, cast-iron exhaust manifolds, camshaft and manifolding for drag race efficiency while maintaining drivability in various weather scenarios, increased driveline reliability (automatic and 4-speed), forged pistons, and maintaining the short-block's durability. Furthermore, the cars were given limited warranty coverage (which was void if raced), no air conditioning was available, and they considered using a hydraulic camshaft. The latter did not occur on the Hemi until 1970, even though work was done on hydraulic cam feasibility during the creation of the 1966 version. This was likely dropped at the time due

Once released for street use, the Hemi was only detuned from its race configuration to make it drivable in challenging weather. Indeed, the parts durability of the A864/A990 versions remained part of the Street Hemi until the end of its production in 1971. The major adaptations for 1966 were the intake/carburetor layout, cam timing, and production-line exhaust manifolds. This car is a low-mileage original owned by Tony D'Agostino.

Soon recognized as the most legendary powerplant of the muscle car era, the Street Hemi stood alone among Detroit's offerings as a true race-engine option available for multiple years in multiple body styles. D'Agostino's 1966 Satellite, a race car in its early life, is a prime example.

In the early days of the muscle car era, engine types and horsepower ratings were often understated. This little chrome emblem located on the front quarter panels was one of the few cues used on Hemi-powered Chrysler products in 1966.

to RPM requirements, as the hydraulic tappets were only good to about 6,400 rpm.

The Hemi was promoted as a street engine, but it was never far from its racing roots and required more-aggressive maintenance for good tuning. NASCAR engine homologation and drag racing legality were its primary catalyst, and the large head ports were not responsive at low-RPM street levels. Many lax owners and magazine test drivers were subsequently frustrated by the engine's sluggish street manners below 4,000 rpm and its need for attention. Dealers learned early on that comparable wedge engines were optimal for all but the most insistent buyers, most added mileage a quarter-mile at a time.

By 1970, however, when racing rules were more liberal and the new E-Body sports models had arrived, changes became more attractive for simple streetability.

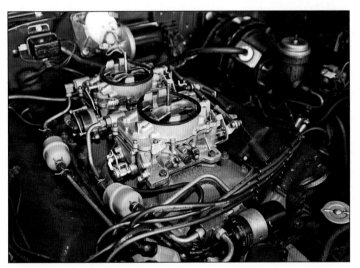

The inline intake did not have the ram effect of previous versions, but it was effective as a street unit. Two Carter AFBs were selected as carburetion. If you were brave enough to stand on it and get the secondaries to open fully, acceleration above 4,000 rpm was blinding. Mileage? Over 4,000 rpm, consumption was needle-moving.

This is an NOS Street Hemi air cleaner from 1966 (provided by Kramer Automotive). The circular chrome dome was the initial calling card for the engine, used until fresh-air layouts became popular toward the end of the decade.

"You have to realize that the 1970 changes were the 'civilizing' of the Street Hemi; it was really a major deal, a quantum leap forward," recalls engineer Tom Hoover. "For one thing, we had added the deeper 5-quart oil pan and windage tray by then. The previous versions had used acceleration baffles in the pan, but not a tray. The engine used the latest tappet technology and went to a hydraulic tappet version of the cam.

"More important was the wiping-type valvestem seals and that required the single-coil valvesprings. On the piston, the top ring land was changed, which quieted some of the tapping when the engine was cold. If you had good enough ears, you could hear the difference. These changes really were a major step in making the engine more acceptable to the customer."

But all that was in the future. On January 12, 1965, just six days after the initial Cahill and Rodger request for a street version of the engine, W. J. Bradley of the product planning department issued a product description of the Street Hemi package. Development was rapid for the fall 1965 introduction of the new models, but this was a pretty straightforward process for the people already involved with the race versions. They designed a twin, 4-barrel, dual-plane aluminum intake based on the runner structure of the existing NASCAR model.

Although this eliminated the ram-tuning effect of the earlier drag racing models, it made mass production and owner adjustability more feasible. This in turn hosted two Carter AFB (aluminum 4-barrel) carbs, 4139S front/4140S rear, and a large chromed, semi-silenced air cleaner underneath. A steel heat shield bolted to the bottom of the new intake manifold prevented oil in the lifter valley from heating the incoming fuel charge. A pair of short-runner cast exhaust manifolds was designed primarily to make installation in the production environment easier.

The heads were cast-iron and unchanged from the A864 versions except for a design change to the valve cover rail for simpler cover-lip stampings. The rocker gear and valve designs were basically identical to the race versions, retaining the dual-coil springs. Cam timing was shortened in terms of duration and overlap, but this was not a big factor in the racing environment, where aftermarket cams were legal. Although valvespring rates were not as steep as on race versions, the Street Hemi's high pressure still garnered notoriety for wearing out camshafts much more rapidly than other Chrysler engines. Regular valve rocker arm checks and adjustments were encouraged.

Still, most crucial to the street model was cold-weather driveability. To this end, the passenger-side exhaust manifold was equipped with a pair of steel heat-riser tubes

FLYING MILES: A LOOK AT LAND-SPEED RACING

Goldenrod is now in the Henry Ford Museum, restored. Here it is on display at the 1993 Chryslers at the Carlisle show, where it appeared thanks to the Summer Brothers and the persistence of (the late) Dick Towers.

Bill Summers reasoned that if he could mount four engines in a row to achieve less frontal area than previous efforts, he could top the record. Chrysler agreed to loan four built- and dyno-tested stock 426 Hemi engines for the effort. While the design and construction of *Goldenrod* continued, Sir Donald Campbell broke the Cobb record in late 1964 with a speed of 403.10.

Hot Rod covered the car's development extensively in the March 1965 issue, noting that, in addition to Chrysler, the Summers' effort was assisted by rudimentary wind-tunnel testing at Caltech. The final car stretched to 32 feet long, 48 inches wide, and 42 inches high, with the rear area narrower than the front portion. Custom-cut 16-inch rims and specially formatted Firestone tires went on the four hubs.

The engines were mounted in pairs, back to back. The output end of the crankshafts connected to a common drive rod that ran down one side of the length of the car. It eliminated issues arising from the four engines torqueing over in one direction. A pair of 5-speed transmissions and transfer cases took the output from either end of this drive rod. As the driver, Bob Summers straddled the rear axle in the rear.

On damp salt at more than 250 mph, *Goldenrod*'s first attempt was on Sunday, October 24, 1965. USAC did the timing. The record required a two-way (forward and return) run within one hour on a straight 10-mile course. The outbound run topped 400 mph in the flying mile, but a drive bearing was damaged on the return run, so it achieved "only" 365 mph on the way back.

The team returned to its Ontario, California, shop, fixed the damage, and returned to Utah for another try on November 12. This time, the car took Campbell's record with a two-way average of 409.277 mph, with a top speed of 412.202 mph on one run.

The following day, the four unblown Hemi engines reportedly pushed the car to a 425-mph time, but no

In drag racing, the goal is to have the lowest elapsed time between two points, counted in thousandths of seconds. In circle-track racing, you win by being the first to finish a number of course laps. For many enthusiasts, the purest form of auto performance is found in land-speed racing. The objective here is pure mile-per-hour execution.

Although this type of racing can be on paved surfaces, the most prolific efforts at land speed have occurred on hard-packed shoreline sea sand (which is no longer viable due to human populations where such conditions exist) and the dry salt beds of ancient lakes, where a fine layer of salt during certain conditions serves as the surface.

Serving as two examples of the 426 Race Hemi are the 1965 land-speed effort of the Summers Brothers and the FIA/ACCUS endurance records of Bobby Isaac set in 1971.

Goldenrod: The Summers Brothers' Chart Topper

By 1965, Bill and Bob Summers had been part of the racing scene at the Bonneville Salt Flats in Utah for over a decade. Starting in the late 1950s and using a first-generation Hemi engine, the team had topped the 200-mph mark there repeatedly and entered the parts business. In 1963, the duo decided to tackle the long-standing world record of Englishman John Cobb, who had run a 394.196-mph time in 1947. To that end they began to lay the groundwork for *Goldenrod*.

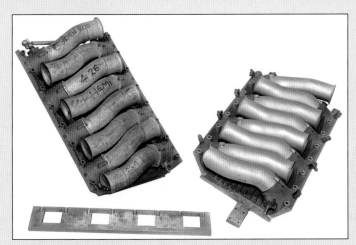

The original prototype intake (left) for Goldenrod was built by Mike Bucket and tested for sonic performance before the formal order went to Hilborn (right). The plate (bottom) was for Hemi intake prototyping. Jim Kramer is the caretaker of these parts.

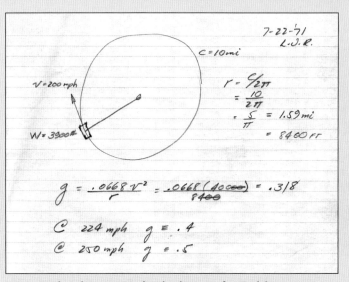

Larry Rathgeb's original calculations for Bobby Isaac's multi-mile speed records, dated July 1971, are in the Wellborn Musclecar Museum's collection.

return run was ever made. As of this writing, no other naturally aspirated piston-driven vehicle has beaten that time. Not bad for a couple of hot rodders.

Bobby Isaac and "Wing Car over Bonneville"

With the pressure off due to an abbreviated race schedule, Harry Hyde and Nord Krauskopf decided to refit one of the team's now-dormant #71 Charger Daytona stock cars for an attempt at the record books at Bonneville. In September 1971, Bobby Isaac had the opportunity to set records in a number of classes, including several endurance records using a 10-mile circumference course. Larry Rathgeb's original hand-written calculations estimating Isaac's g-force potential, fuel capacity, car construction, and drag coefficients are still in the Harry Hyde paper archive at the Wellborn Musclecar Museum in Alabama.

Although the team was allowed up to 480 ci, Hyde elected to use a standard-displacement 426 Hemi. He considered it his best qualifying engine, staying with the bathtub intake manifold and making some aerodynamic adjustments. USAC chief steward Joe Petrali scored the effort, and engineer George Wallace took two weeks of vacation to be there.

The project had a four-day schedule. Isaac went 218 mph on the second set of test runs on Sunday. On Monday, they began to hit the books. In just one try, on the straight-line flying mile, Isaac beat the 188-mph numbers Mickey Thompson had run for Ford three years prior: 216.945.

Next, he went after records in endurance racing, which were measured by timing a set number of laps or partial laps on a 10-mile closed-loop course. The hope had been to break them all the way to the 500-mile mark, but the condition of the sand in 1971 was so poor, the track was not a true circle but an oval. Still, Isaac wowed the handful of onlookers by dirt tracking the car at more than 200 mph, rooster tails of salt flying off it in the corners. Wallace wowed them by riding along at those speeds before the run started.

The new record for 100 miles was an average of 194.290 mph. Soon after that was achieved, according to a period report Deke Houlgate filed with *Stock Car Racing* magazine, the car became loose in poor salt, hit several marker poles, and smashed the windshield, ending the day's efforts.

After a day of repairs, the plan was to go after the 10-mile length standing-start records held by Thompson's Mustang (183.6) and an Unlimited Class (190.6-mph) record set by Abe Jenkins in the legendary *Mormon Meteor*. On the return run with a tailwind, Isaac exited the 10-mile length at 219 mph, but again the salt's condition snagged him.

This second 10-miles-long "ride in the marbles" put the wing car up on the embankment of the pond where Craig Breedlove had ditched his jet car back in 1964, and damaged the headers. To try to make good on the 60-minute turnaround, the car went down course the other way with the headers completely removed. The final

FLYING MILES CONTINUED

record was clocked in Unlimited, B/Class, and Stock Car at 182.172 mph.

The Dodge Charger Daytona was a unique car, designed like no other for the sake of speed. Harry Hyde credited the wing for its success, but according to Houlgate, Joe Petrali, who was himself a salt racer of some reknown, had the last word about dirt-track expert Bobby Isaac and the 28 records he had just set.

"I don't think you realize what this man has done," he told the small group on hand. "Europeans have tried it, Indianapolis drivers, Canadians, but nobody ever did this, not like this."

Both cars survived. *Goldenrod* is in the Henry Ford Museum in Dearborn, Michigan. The K&K Insurance Daytona is the centerpiece of the Wellborn Musclecar Museum in Alabama.

Other Chrysler wing cars have chased the barrier of speed over the years. This is the big-inch Indy Cylinder Head-powered 1971 Hemi Dodge Daytona of Gary and Pam Bieneke at a paved land-speed event in Maxton, North Carolina, in 2010; they later topped 200 mph with it at Bonneville.

that recirculated exhaust heat through a port built into the back of the intake. This passed through a small chamber under the rear carburetor during warm-up. In turn, a coiled bimetallic heat valve controlled the operation on the manifold, which closed the riser tubes once the engine reached its operating temperature. These cast-iron manifolds were effective on the street, but were often discarded in favor of tube-type headers for better performance, so this important characteristic for street use was lost in the process.

A final adaptation was to lower the static compression ratio. One benefit of the hemispherical engine design was the ability to easily change these ratios without major modification. A forged piston with minor valve reliefs

brought it down to 10.25:1 so it could run on Sunoco 260. A floating piston pin was now used thanks to a bushing in the connecting rod's small end. Other than that, the bottom end was basically unchanged from the Race Hemi.

This Street Hemi exhaust tube cutaway resides in the Garlits Museum Engine Room. The recirculating riser tubes mounted behind the intake from the passenger-side manifold greatly helped if you were driving the car in colder climates. They used exhaust heat to warm the manifold quicker and closed when the engine achieved operating temperature.

One simple way to see the difference between the early Race (right) and Street Hemi (left) heads is to compare the valve covers. The early K-style heads have a dimple in the casting and cover. Street Hemi heads have a simple 45-degree angle on that corner. Both examples were provided by Kramer Automotive.

The chamber underneath the rear carb was used to heat the manifold for cold-weather driving. Swapping to headers or blocking off the tubes increased performance on the track but made the car more challenging to warm up if you bought it for dual-purpose usage. This cutaway example resides in the Garlits Museum Engine Room.

A forged Tufftride-treated crankshaft, the rods from the A990 drag engine, and the four-bolt mains were all in place. A baffled oil pan with street-clearance depth was bolted underneath it all; the windage tray was added in 1968.

The rest of the driveline was sorted out for durability in 1966. When optioned with the heavy-duty Torque-flite automatic transmissions using a higher-stall torque converter, cars received the 8¾ differential with a standard 3.23 gear. A Sure-Grip dual-axle traction was recommended but optional. Manual-equipped models received a 3.54 gear as standard, using the Dana 60 differential from the truck line; all Hemi Danas were Sure-Grips. Steeper gears were available as well. For Hemi cars in 1966, a 14 x 5.5–inch steel wheel was standard, with Goodyear Blue Streak tires.

Although originally considered for a C-Body adaptation under code A103, the Street Hemi arrived in 1966 available only in the B-Body lineup. There is evidence that a 440-ci Hemi for a stillborn Chrysler 300 project was considered during the development phase of the engine in 1963 and 1964. This would have been built solely in luxury trim for the 1966 introduction of the 300M. Moreover, it would not have required the durability of the race engine in that environment.

However, the 300 letter series was discontinued after the L series models of 1965. Because of the warranty and spe-cial tuning needs endemic to the Street Hemi, this option may not have done the corporation's reputation any good with this particular market share. Instead, a 440-ci wedge for full-size models was introduced in its place for 1966.

Building engines for the Street Hemi program in volume still meant that production was done at the small Chrysler Marine & Industrial plant in Marysville, Michigan. Bob Rodger alluded to a possible production line at the Trenton Engine plant in Trenton, Michigan, but volume apparently never justified the change. The 426 Hemi could not be simply thrown together. Even though the engines were not blueprinted in the truest sense of the word, care in assembly was still very important.

In a period story by Roger Huntington in *Super Stock & Drag Illustrated* magazine, Bob Rodger noted that the market share for more-expensive muscle cars that had developed around the new-for-1965 midsize GM lineup was a major factor in the decision making of the Street Hemi. Pricewise, the Hemi option added approximately $900 to the base price, but that cost also included some of the heavy-duty upgrades that would have normally been added optionally to other brands.

Chrysler's badging for the Hemi was understated: Simple, small, chrome 426 Hemi emblems were added to the front fenders behind the wheel opening. The center hood marker on the Belvederes read 426 vertically, and the early group of street Plymouths received small, discreetly located HP2 tags. This callout has been a matter of dispute among Chrysler aficionados, but according to Willem Weertman, this referred to Hemi-Powered (Squared), based on the dual 4-barrels on the street engine. It was replaced with the chrome 426 Hemi logos at midyear.

One unique thing about 1966 Hemi production was that the engine was available in a variety of B-Body styles. Rumors of a factory Street Hemi station wagon

In 1966, the Street Hemi was available across the B-Body lineup; it became a muscle body–only option starting in 1967. As a result, a handful of four-door examples were created that year. This red Coronet Deluxe, owned by the Rohde family, was shown at the 2014 Muscle Car & Corvette Nationals.

have arisen but have never been authenticated. Ramcharger Mike Buckel built one for himself but not off the assembly line, and it was a notorious Top Eliminator winner on Woodward Avenue for two years running. A small number of four-door examples were built for police work, including one for the U.S. Treasury that is now in the Garlits Museum of Drag Racing in Ocala, Florida. With two-door post coupe models, drag racing was about to receive a serious dose of the Street Hemi, but first it was back at Daytona for a return to Grand National racing, an environment where the Hemi always proved its marketing value.

Goin' Round in Circles

As mentioned previously, Chrysler had been visibly absent from NASCAR for the first half of 1965, returning at midseason in the C-Body full-size designs for superspeedway use and in the B-Body in short-track action. The Street Hemi was now part of the midsize B-Body factory lineup and available to anybody. This meant that Bill France could do little to prevent these cars from running in his sanctioning body, especially after seeing the engines being constructed by the hundreds in December 1965.

Truth be told, 1966 went down as something of a repeat of 1965 for NASCAR. Ford announced on April 16 that it would boycott the series when France did not give the SOHC engine the same weight breaks he had created in the middle of the 1965 season to help get the Chryslers back. For parity, NASCAR had mandated a 405-ci limit on cars with a minimum wheelbase of 115 inches (Category 2), and 430 ci on full-size models with a minimum 119-inch wheelbase (Category 1), but had added a pound-per-inch restriction on overhead-cam engines as well.

Testing by Ford in December 1965 at Daytona with an SOHC Galaxie had shown the engine could not compete with the smaller Chrysler models, even at the smaller 404-ci displacement that was developed by Chrysler as A117. Although author William LaDow uncovered that Ford had formally announced that it fully intended to race this engine during 1966 at a late 1965 corporate function in Detroit, the SOHC Ford engine never made a competition lap on the Grand National circuit.

France did everything he could to keep other competitors involved against the Chryslers, which began dominating again in 1966 with the return of the Hemi. As mentioned, this already included reinstating "banned-for-life" Curtis Turner, who ended up racing for Ford in 1966 after his brief foray with Plymouth. But Turner's real comeback was driving a trick Chevelle with Smokey Yunick in 1967 (covertly assisted by Chevrolet's research-and-development arm). Before then, though, Yunick's young driver Mario Andretti wrecked Smokey's special one-off 1966 Chevelle during the Daytona 500 in 1966.

There were still a handful of other GM independents racing. Under the pound-per-inch rules, Bobby Allison even had some short-track success with a small-block Chevelle due to its favorable weight and strong high-RPM power band, winning three events that season.

Still, the most visible example in the 1966 rules controversies occurred at Atlanta in August 1966 at the Dixie 400. The highly visible aerodynamic changes to both Yunick's Chevelle and the Holly Farms Ford Galaxie of Freddy Lorenzen and Junior Johnson were allowed while France tossed out points leader David Pearson and Cotton Owens' #6 Charger on a somewhat-bogus vehicle height technicality. The weekend after this event, Ford returned to the series. An accommodation was made to let the unibody Fairlanes race with a special Holman-Moody–designed Galaxie half-chassis front clip, and Fords won four of the last five events of 1966 season with this combination. Nevertheless, the Chrysler Hemi engine's first full season after the dark days of 1965 was again a story of dominating circle-track racing.

Hemi Heroes on the High Banks

The 1966 NASCAR season began with a number of the Chrysler drivers returning in their 1965 models, which were considerably smoother than the sharp-edged Elwood Engel–designed 1966 B-Body sheet metal. Of the 49 Grand National races held that season, 15 were on dirt. Of the 34 others, 2 were at road courses (Riverside, California, and Bridgehampton, New York) and 12 were on tracks that were considered superspeedways. Richard Petty was in front at the checkers for the first 1966 season Grand National race (held in November 1965) in Augusta, Georgia, in his 1965 Belvedere. After Ford's Dan Gurney won Riverside for the third straight time in early 1967, the Chryslers really turned on for the big event at Daytona.

Paul Goldsmith chose to run a 1965 model Belvedere at early-season races in 1966. The #99 was the winner of the first qualifying race for the Daytona 500 and also won at Rockingham that season. (Copyright CR Racing Memories 1204005, Ray Mann Photograph)

James Hylton waged a successful run at NASCAR's Rookie of the Year crown in 1966, finishing second in points to Pearson despite not winning a single event. (Copyright CR Racing Memories 0601044, Ray Mann Photograph)

In the first 100-mile qualifier at the Florida speedway, Paul Goldsmith, in a 1965 Plymouth, finished first; followed by Petty in his new 1966 Plymouth; and Don White in a 1965 Dodge. Goldsmith and White were both out of Ray Nichols' Indiana shop, as was Sam McQuagg, who put the brand-new 1966 Charger design into the sixth spot. In the second 100-mile qualifier that afternoon, former Mercury driver Earl Balmer won to place Nord Krauskopf's #71 K&K Insurance 1965 Dodge next to Goldsmith on the front row for the 500.

On race day, however, it was as if the Pettys had never left. Richard led 108 laps before rain shortened the 200-lap event to only 198. He was a full lap ahead of second-place Cale Yarborough in Banjo Matthews' Ford when the race was called. Petty won seven other events in 1966, but the big story for NASCAR was Dodge and David Pearson.

Pearson finished third at Daytona in Cotton Owens' Spartanburg, South Carolina–based 1966 Charger, but spent most of 1966 running Owens' well-tested 1964 Dodge in short-track action. He won four straight events in April and some others, and then took a 1965 Coronet to victory on the Bridgehampton road course. Despite the problems of not racing at Atlanta due to the aforementioned legality issues (where Fred Lorenzen crashed Junior Johnson's "more-legal" Ford early on, Yunick's

Chevelle broke, and Petty emerged victorious yet again), Pearson never lost the points lead following his runner-up finish to Gurney at Riverside. He won 15 events total that season and finished a big 1,950 points ahead of young James Hylton.

Hylton, racing for independent owner Bud Hartje, had not won any races, but had finished in the top 10 at 32 of the 41 events he attended in his Dodge to get his points total. Petty was third, having raced at 39 of the 49 events that year, with 22 top-10 finishes.

Chrysler products driven by McQuagg, Goldsmith, Jim Hurtubise, Marvin Panch, Jim Paschal, Paul Lewis, and LeeRoy Yarbrough also made NASCAR Grand National winners' circle appearances in 1966. Although this was indeed dominance, there was little challenge after Ford announced its withdrawal, and the fans stayed home too. Other than Gurney's win at Riverside and Dick Hutcherson's crash-plagued victory at Bristol, Fords had been shut out during the first 10 events of 1966 and no relief was in sight.

Until Ford's boycott led to the new legality of tube-chassis suspension changes in NASCAR stockers that August, the Hemi was scarcely challenged; only the drivers' names and body designs changed. Most interesting may have been McQuagg's win at the Firecracker 400 in Nichels' #98 Charger. This was the first appearance of

LeeRoy Yarbrough (kneeling left) with car owner Jon Thorne (standing), and crew chief Jimmy Thomas (kneeling right), on the tarmac at Daytona in 1966 with the #12 Charger. They raced in 10 Grand National events, won the fall race at Charlotte, and were the 1967 Daytona 500 Qualfier #1 in this car. (Copyright CR Racing Memories 0601044, Ray Mann Photograph)

Sam McQuagg claimed victory at the Firecracker 400 in part because of a rear deck spoiler authorized as a Mopar factory part immediately prior to the race. Ken Garrett owns this 1966 Hemi Charger.

the little deck spoiler that greatly helped downforce and was a harbinger of future aerodynamic improvements.

Indeed, airflow over the body structure wrote the next major chapter in NASCAR's increased performances. Although France did what he could to appease Ford, eventually with success, the Hemi never came to NASCAR to do anything but win. When the SOHC did not become a

The Holley 3-barrel was not NASCAR legal after 1964. However, the cut-down plenum entrance on this bathtub manifold behind it suggests it was used in other sanctioning bodies. Note the Holley shown here (provided by Kramer Automotive) does not have the proper LeMans float bowls for a bathtub application.

The Garrett Charger came from the dealership with the small but effective NASCAR-legal spoiler wing installed on it.

production reality after all, the engine Ford used in 1967 was still the wedge. It was greatly improved with the next batch of great ideas, which included two carburetors.

In defense of Ford on the SOHC street availability issue, the engine's exotic design, dimensional characteristics, and tuning needs made it a much more challenging production-line installation compared to the Hemi or the new big-block Chevrolet engines. The cost of putting it into a street production vehicle, even in limited quantities, certainly played into the decision not to race with it. Ford's next true racing engine was the more conventional Boss 429, which was a semi-hemispherical design.

The Race Hemi was not simply for the Grand National circuit, though. In other circle-track efforts, Norm Nelson grabbed success in the USAC circuit in his 1966 Belvedere, winning 7 events and never finishing outside the top 10. The Coronet found takers too. Six-time IMCA champion Ernie Derr of Keokuk, Iowa, took home the IMCA crown in a Dodge, while Iggy Katona took home the ARCA season title driving both a Plymouth and a Dodge. Without question, the engine ruled circle-track racing during that inaugural year of street production.

Hemis in NHRA Stock Eliminator

As mentioned, the initial push for a Street Hemi had been not to simply satiate the NASCAR issue, but to move the engine into Stock Eliminator. The 1966 season was one of the most important for this category in the NHRA's history, as manufacturers offered more high-performance cars for Stock that season than ever before, or since. Chevrolet produced its new Chevelle SS 396 in volume, but a more serious GM big-block effort came from Oldsmobile, which quietly offered an effective new tri-power/lightweight 4-4-2 model drag package (code W30/L69) despite the corporate no racing edict.

Pontiac did not have a Stock package per se, but through Knafel Pontiac in Akron, Ohio, it secured the services of Arlen Vanke. With Knafel's backing, Vanke and his associate Bill Abraham of Firestone put three cars into class wins at NHRA's Springnationals at Bristol in 1966. One was a 1963 steel-nose Plymouth! After the GTO won C/S and then the overall Junior Stock crown, "Akron Arlen" received a call from Dick Maxwell and agreed to come back to Chrysler under contract. Vanke played a role in the factory drag testing programs for several years. He was close to Detroit and available to drive consistently. He also did special development projects.

Meanwhile, Chevrolet resecured the services of William Tyler Jenkins, also known as "Grumpy," winner of the 1965 Winternationals Top Stock crown in the *Black Arrow* Plymouth. Despite Chevrolet's official stance of being out of racing, efforts such as those of Yunick, as well as Mark Donohue and Jim Hall in the new Can-Am series, proved otherwise.

Jenkins did not receive a factory support deal from Chrysler for the rest of 1965, so he switched to Chevy. He spoke to Vince Piggins, head of the Chevrolet Product Promotions department, about a special project car. It was a Chevy II featuring the recently released L79 327/350-hp Corvette small-block; it was a very well balanced package for drag racing. Although Jenkins was not sponsored with any actual money, Piggins pushed through the production of a special Corvette-powered Chevy II under RPO L79, and this combination was factored by NHRA into A/Stock, which happened to be where the new Street Hemi was as well.

At the time, the rules in Stock required a class breakdown on a shipping-weight-to-advertised-horsepower number. According to research by auto historian Rick Voegelin, Jenkins gave up 99 ci to the new Hemi, but he also had a 742-pound weight break compared to the Hemi Belvedere's minimum shipping weight (3,175 for the base V-8, plus 475 for the Hemi equaled 3,650 pounds). The result was that the Chevy II (at 350 advertised hp) and the 426 Hemi (at 425 advertised hp) were evenly matched and, as both were 4-speeds (there was no automatic option for the L79 from Chevrolet), raced heads-up when they were against each other.

During NHRA events, following class eliminations, there was a breakout into two elimination categories: Top Stock (which consisted of manual and automatic Super Stock and A/Stock cars running off their respective record indexes) and Junior Stock (which contained everything for B/S down, and raced off a record-handicap basis). Stock rules required a 7-inch tire maximum; no changes to heads, carb, or compression ratio; and an intact interior with complete exhaust systems. In Top Stock, an intake manifold swap was permitted as long as it replicated the OEM example and the carb remained in the OEM location. A replacement flat-tappet cam was also permitted.

In Stock Eliminator, paperwork filed with the AMA gave the NHRA the numbers needed for legality. Engineers with all companies were able to create mathematical combinations that could favorably be factored for NHRA class racing. For instance, the 426 Chrysler Hemi, 427 8-BBL R-code wedge Ford, and high-compression L88 Chevrolet Corvette engines all came in at an advertised 425 hp at a given RPM. Needles on factory dynamometers told the story that those numbers were certainly true at that RPM. Of course, the needle was still moving upward as the RPM increased, but for 1966, that advertised amount was the number the NHRA used for its factoring ratios.

The previous year's numerous Hemi Super Stock cars were still legal. But the aluminum-nosed Hemi and Max Wedge models of previous seasons remained without a place to race unless converted to A/Modified Production, as all-steel bodies were still required in Stock. Some

Don Grotheer won the A/S class at Pomona in a Hemi Belvedere. From Oklahoma City, Grotheer became one of the biggest players in the following years for the Chrysler camp, and he was also one of the better 4-speed pilots of the era. He bested Bill Jenkins for the A/S class title at the 1966 NHRA Winternationals. (Photo Courtesy Ray Mann Archive, quartermilestones.com)

were simply parked while many others were modified for match racing. As a result, the 1965 cars were still dominant in the two Super Stock classes, S/S and S/SA. They made history once again when the 1966 NHRA season opened at the Winternationals in Pomona, California. Also at this event, the NHRA had its first chance to tout female drivers.

Shirley Shahan: Beating the Boys

California housewife Shirley Shahan had a 1965 A01/A990 Plymouth named *Drag-On Lady*. (Her husband, H. L., had spent much of 1965 working with Butch Leal after his stint with young Hank Taylor.) The week before Pomona, Shahan had shown her skill when she posted a runner-up finish at the AHRA Winter Nationals race in Irwindale, California, to Darrell Droke's factory-backed SOHC 1965 Fairlane in the Mr. Stock Eliminator race. The Tulare, California–based couple raced this same Plymouth, modified with fuel injectors on nitro, during heads-up match races and converted it back to Stock for the NHRA Winternationals.

Shirley's Plymouth was classed in S/SA, and her sole competitor in class at Pomona was none other than 1965 Stock World Champion Joe Smith in the Fenner Tubbs' 1965 Plymouth out of Texas. Smith won class over Shahan in a close 11.32 to 11.33 battle. In S/S class, Butch Leal's 1965 A990 *California Flash* stick car won on a single, while Don Grotheer's A/S 1966 Street Hemi Plymouth beat Jenkins' L79 Chevy II deuce for that class title. A pair of steel-nosed Max Wedge Plymouths ran off for the A/SA title, with Richard Charbonneau emerging as the champ. A pair of Street Hemis was in the class as well, including Roger Lindamood of *Color Me Gone* fame in a Dodge Coronet sedan.

The final field on Sunday at Pomona in Top Stock featured 24 entries. Shahan parlayed excellent driving on the narrow tires with times well within the 11.15 breakout (class record) index for S/SA. In the final, she was up against Ken Heinemann in the new 1966 *Brand X Eliminator* Plymouth Hemi Belvedere. Heinemann left first on the 11.84 A/SA index, but Shirley caught and passed him at the top end, running an 11.26 to the Brand X's 12.01.

No New Super Stocks for 1966

Chrysler had built Super Stock packages every year since 1962, and a Dodge version (and likely Plymouth as well) had been planned for 1966. Announced in a letter to the NHRA dated January 20, 1966, it would have used aluminum heads with larger valves, a scooped hood, and a cross-ram intake among other things. However, it was canceled on March 24 when Chrysler found that the heads would not be ready for production before June, too late for the season. Unfortunately, the minimum shipping weight for the lightest Coronet was 3,215, 40 pounds more than the Belvedere. The Charger, at a massive base weight of 3,499-pounds, was even heavier, so no Hemi Dodge was competitive in class racing that year.

"I had bought a new Coronet and took it up on North Woodward right after I had driven it around a little," Tom Hoover recalls. "I got into a race with a Chevelle, and I said to myself, 'Damn. This guy is staying right with me; this can't be right.' So when I got home, I began trying to figure out what had happened.

"Finally, I wondered if the guy who installed the cam up at M&I [Chrysler Marine & Industrial] had a tooth retarded on the gear. Maybe the cam was installed at 94 degrees instead of 104. Well, it was! I moved the cam to where it was supposed to be, and the car went 103 mph and change on its first pass when I finally got it out to the dragstrip.

"Still, I really had to work hard to get my Coronet down to 3,400 pounds. It was a lot of work, but I finally did it. In 1968, apparently the body people became aware of how much metal they were using and got cars back down closer to where they had been in 1964."

Shirley Shahan, seen here at Indy in 1965, won the 1966 Winternationals Ms. Stock Eliminator title in this car after beating Ken Heinemann's Brand X Eliminator *1966 Belvedere in the final round. Classed in S/SA, it proved the 1965 packages were still potent in NHRA competition, but husband H. L. Shahan also converted her car to run on injected nitromethane occasionally. (Photo Courtesy Ray Mann Archive, quartermilestones.com)*

Ramchargers member and the man credited with many of the Hemi engine's advancements, engineer Tom Hoover poses with the 1966 Coronet that he bought new. This car is presently in a private collection. (Photo by David Hakim, Courtesy HP2 Communications)

The only Street Hemi Charger of note to actually compete in 1966 went to Al Eckstrand, who had relocated to England that year. Through Dodge Division Vice President Byron Nichols, he was given a 1966 Hemi Charger pilot car to use in exhibition racing around Europe. At that point, Eckstrand began formulating plans for performance car driver training with American service personnel stationed overseas, a program that later took him to Vietnam and beyond. The Charger, which today is in the Walter P. Chrysler Museum's holdings, was the start of that project and the only Hemi car ever involved in it.

Al Eckstrand (right) with the pilot Hemi Charger that he used in driver demonstrations in Europe following his move there. It was given to him by Byron Nichols. A pilot car was a carefully built initial example to test production techniques and parts fitment before the assembly line fired up. Al later restored it and returned it to America. Then he traded this car to the Chrysler Museum in Auburn Hills for one of the first Vipers built. He is seen here with the museum's Brandt Rosenbusch (left) on the day the car was acquired for the collection.

On the other hand, Street Hemi Plymouths in Stock were visible and working. In addition to the racers already running these cars, the effort received a big boost that spring thanks to a former associate of Bill Jenkins who built headers in York, Pennsylvania.

The A/Stock Wars: Heavyweight versus Bantam Weight

Jere Stahl was not unknown in drag racing, as his Jenkins Competition–powered Junior Stock Chevrolets had been notorious record-setters in the lower classes. A master fabricator, Stahl was asked to build some headers for a new 1966 Hemi Plymouth, which had been loaned to *Super Stock & Drag Illustrated* magazine for a road test. After making a couple of passes in it at York U.S. 30 Dragway for the magazine story when Ronnie Sox was unavailable, Stahl realized that this combination, street or not, had some great possibilities. Shortly after, he ordered the lightest Belvedere I possible from his local dealership and turned to engine builder Bill Stiles for a tune-up. Stiles, also of York, was available because Dave Strickler had chosen to build a match race Corvette Funny Car for 1966.

The car made its formal debut at the NHRA Springnationals in Bristol that June, where Stahl came up against Jenkins in the class finals for A/S. An 11.96 in the mountains was enough for the win, although Jenkins fouled at the start before running 12.25. Beyond the altitude factors at Thunder Valley, all 4-speed entries had to gingerly find traction on 7-inch-wide tires regardless of track location. Stahl's header business came in handy in an unusual way.

That summer, he had the chance to ride back to Detroit with members of the Ramchargers team following a NASCAR-sanctioned drag race at Niagara, New York. They wanted to know about headers, and he wanted to know about suspensions. He left the Motor City with a copy of a confidential Chrysler Engineering drag suspension manual written by Jim Thornton.

Strickler had given Stahl one important secret to driving stick cars: Strike the narrow tires at the launch with good solid RPM. He now also used the new information to blueprint the Belvedere. Through the Chrysler product planning department, he obtained a set of special Super Stock springs created for the defunct 1966 SS program. Later in the year, also through Chrysler, Stahl managed to obtain a pair of road race NASCAR transmissions built by BRM, the Formula 1 racing team in England. One of these close-ratio designs included a very high 2.14 first gear; conversely, the standard A833 first gear was 2.66. Coupled with low tire pressures, using the higher

Intended to be mildly detuned for street use in 1966, the newest version of the 426 Hemi engine was the top player in Stock Eliminator, even in the heavy B-Body models. This 1966 cutaway example is a former Dodge auto show display; it is now in the Wellborn Musclecar Museum.

Jere Stahl's 1966 Belvedere was the first Street Hemi to take a national event title when he won over Mike Schmidtt at Bristol. Here at Indy, the car is sporting the spoiler design to keep air out from under the car. (Photo Courtesy Ray Mann Archive, quartermilestones.com)

transmission ratios, Stahl's Hemi almost bogged off the line and then picked up the pace without tire spin.

This gearing and tire setup proved to be effective in competition. At Sunday's Top Stock finals in Bristol, Jenkins' Chevy II fell to Joe Smith in the second round, but Stahl defeated Smith in the semifinals. In the money round, Stahl faced 1965 World Champion Mike Schmidtt's big AA/SA 427 Galaxie and won, taking home the first big NHRA win for the Street Hemi package.

At Sanford, Maine, the following weekend, Stahl and Stiles reset the national record in A/S to 11.76. The car ran as fast as 11.49 at the event, but everyone wanted the record to stay soft because it was the index for any class handicap. In July, Jenkins took it down to 11.64, which ended up being the index at Indy about a month later.

Top Stock at Indy and Tulsa 1966

Stahl and the other Hemi racers did not have the same fan appeal that Jenkins received by being "the little mouse that could" against the big bad Mopar factory wolf. As in NASCAR, drag racing's major sanctioning body was already unhappy with the way Chrysler could seemingly dominate at will. This was due not only to excellent engineering, but also to the sheer number of competitors. Literally hundreds of Chrysler Max Wedge and Hemi automatic models ruled the upper echelons

of NHRA stock car racing (S/SA, A/SA, B/SA, and C/SA), while stick versions held their own in S/S and A/S.

Other than the special 1966 4-4-2s, which ended up totaling only 54 units, General Motors had little visible involvement beyond the L79 Chevy II until the performance COPO era began in 1968. Although Ford built 57 427-ci Fairlanes late in 1966, the company remained focused on fairly exclusive experimental models going to specific racers after its 1964 Thunderbolt Fairlane release. Moreover, the all-steel-body rule enacted for 1965 had eliminated the Fairlanes in Super Stock, so Ford was focused mainly on fuel-burning and wheelbase-changed XS racing for 1966, with a handful of special cars running in the fading FX classes.

At Indy, the crowd cheered Jenkins on each run. He had even bolted a large Chevrolet emblem under the front bumper. It was not meant to be an advertisement but rather a wind foil to keep air from under the car. Stahl also added a similar flat plate, labeled Plymouth, for the same reason, but the NHRA eventually asked them all to be removed so the cars retained the stock appearance. The A/S class title went to Vanke's new 1966 Belvedere, but on Monday the 32-car Top Stock final field again came down to Stahl and Jenkins. It would have been a close race at 11.73 to 11.76, but Jenkins again left before the tree was activated and fouled it away.

That left just the NHRA World Finals in Tulsa. Coming back from Indy, Jenkins' truck driver totaled the rig and race car. Jenkins, assisted by Roger Penske, quickly secured another Chevy II, swapping in the driveline from his wrecked car. Stahl never missed a beat and showed up at Southwest Dragway in Oklahoma with his now-proven combination and the 2.14 first-gear crash box.

Once again, they marched through eliminations, and it was Stahl and Jenkins in the Top Stock final one last time in 1966. Although close at 11.65 to 11.73, the Hemi prevailed and the Grump's Chevy II was completely shut out in NHRA final rounds in 1966. Jere Stahl had garnered the Hemi its second NHRA World Finals title in a row.

With so many cars not legal for Top Stock, and so many changes to what Detroit was producing, the NHRA had already announced that it would introduce an entirely new category of classes under the name of Super Stock for 1967. These entries were allowed more serious changes than Stock, and it was here that the Hemi wrote the rest of its door-car history of the 1960s.

Other Race Hemi Accomplishments

In AHRA, with its myriad Formula classes, focus on the Stock divisions was not as strong as in the NHRA. Ford was deeply involved in this organization that season, and the company's Mustangs took a lion's share of the victories in the upper classes. NASCAR's Drag Racing Grand Stock Series had a number of classes for stock cars, but was best noted for match race–style Ultra Stocks, which ran on several weight indexes. When the smoke cleared, the 1965 Dodge of Melvin Yow, in gas-burning, match race trim, won the Grand Stock crown in the NASCAR group.

Among the things Ford focused on in 1966 was increased participation in Top Fuel with new supercharged SOHC engines. In the end, Pete Robinson emerged from the "winner take all" finale at the NHRA World Finals at Tulsa as the NHRA season champion in his Ford rail. Nevertheless, Chrysler Hemi-powered fuel and gas dragsters were more than competitive in all sanctioning bodies. This was thanks to the work of the Ramchargers, Don Garlits, and other dragster campaigners with the late-model Hemi (see associated sidebar of Top Fuel), and a vast majority of competitors using the refined 392-ci design. In Top Fuel, the Roland Leong/Keith Black *Hawaiian* team again won both the Winternationals and Indy Nationals for the second straight year, this time with Mike Snively driving. Jimmy Nix took home a Top Fuel crown at Bristol. All were won using 392-ci power.

Moving into fuel-burning ultra-stock racing, Chrysler chose to focus its factory sponsorship on just a couple

Don Prudhomme was on his own in 1966. After losing the Drag Racing *magazine number-one spot to Garlits' 426 rail at Half Moon Bay early in the season, he was at Indy in this gorgeous streamlined body with 392 Hemi power. Mike Snively now drove for Roland Leong/Keith Black in* Hawaiian, *which Prudhomme vacated at the end of 1965, and Snively ended up in the Indy winner's circle. (Photo Courtesy Ray Mann Archive, quartermilestones.com)*

Even though a Ford won the Top Fuel crown in 1966, Hemi-powered competitors continued to dominate at most events. The 392-ci Hemi, refined for horsepower in the supercharged environment, remained in a majority of entries. Delaware's Joe Jacono, seen here at Tulsa for the NHRA World Finals, won a NASCAR Top Fuel title in a 392-ci Hemi. (Photo Courtesy Ray Mann Archive, quartermilestones.com)

Sox & Martin's Baccaruda was a one-off creation, but Sox himself admitted 1966 was a hard year to keep up with the Fords. The car ran with a fuel-burning injected engine during 1966, and Sox went to final rounds in class at both Pomona and Indy with it. It is seen here at Cecil County in 1966. (Photo Courtesy Charles Milikin, Jr.)

After the team moved to Super Stock, the old Baccaruda raced at the NASCAR drag races in Richmond, Virginia, in 1967, after being sold to the Buckeye & Vernon team. It was reportedly disassembled for parts for that team's new 1968 Barracuda. (Photo Courtesy Kramer Automotive Film/Print Library)

A few brave souls took the next step forward after altering the wheelbase by adding a supercharger. Hank Hankins and The Trader Plymouth are in the pits at Richmond Dragway in 1966; later images exist of this car after it was wrecked in an on-track incident. (Bob Plummer Photo, Courtesy Kramer Automotive Film/Print Library)

Shirl Greer of Kingsport, Tennessee, built his S/SA Tension Dodge into an early ultra-stock for 1966 using fuel injectors. One unique change Greer made, similar to that on the Garlits/Cook Dart, was centering the steering position with a tight cage around the driver. Greer documented a round-win record of 90 percent that year. Here he is racing Malcolm Durham's Strip Blazer Corvair at Aquasco, Maryland, in the summer of 1966. (Photo Courtesy Kramer Automotive Film/Print Library)

of entries for the new season. The two players receiving full deals were the most visible drivers from 1965: Dick Landy for Dodge and Sox & Martin for Plymouth. Both teams went to the A-Body platform; Sox & Martin with a Barracuda named *Baccaruda* and Landy with a well-constructed Dodge Dart. Both cars started 1966 where 1965 had ended: injected on nitromethane.

The cars and their Ford counterparts ran at Pomona that year at the 5.00-pound-per-inch C/Fuel Drag-

ster division (which meant a scant 2,130 pounds for a 426-ci engine) of Competition Eliminator. Sox posted a runner-up to Gas Rhonda's Mustang in the class final. However, the NHRA's biggest change for cars of this ilk occurred on April 1, 1966, when it announced an entirely new group of classes to be run under the title of XS, for Experimental Stock.

A/XS cars, injected at 2,000 pounds and running any fuel, were placed into Competition Eliminator while

B/XS-E/XS (weighing between 2,600 and 3,400 pounds) were for gasoline-powered entries in the Street Eliminator division. Bodies needed to be 1964 or later, a single engine only, and no superchargers. Later in the season, the NHRA added the formerly hypothetical S/XS class for supercharged and fiberglass tube-chassis cars.

Funny Car popularity continued unabated in 1966, as many racers found easy bookings and match race money available. New entries featured a variety of innovations; they sprang up almost organically nationwide, some quite rough-hewn. By establishing some ground rules, the NHRA attempted to control the situation with XS, but this arena was ground zero because necessity is, after all, the mother of invention.

So much was happening around the country but it's really beyond the scope of this book. Following are a few of the emerging scenarios.

Ultra-Stockers and the XS Factor

At the top remained the supercharged fuel burners. These included 392 and 426 Hemi cars such as the *Mr. Norms* entry; a new 1966 Charger arrived for the team at midseason. Several glass-steel hybrids such as Bob Sullivan's 392-powered *Pandemonium* and Larry Reyes' *Kingfish*, both Barracudas, also were running by 1966. Promoters quickly saw the value of racing the supercharged cars against one another, and events such as Capitol Raceway's King of Kings Invitational brought the more notorious blown entries together.

Added to this group of what the NHRA later termed S/XS were the new SOHC-injected Comets that Mercury had created. Now considered the first of the liftoff-body Funny Cars, they were trendsetters. Don Garlits and Emory Cook also returned using this same basic format with Garlits' *Dart II*, but were ruled ineligible for S/XS by NHRA.

The next step down was A/XS, which is where Sox and Landy first ended up after the C/FD change, racing against the lengthened Ford Mustangs that had been built by Holman-Moody for the new season. The vehicles used in the XS classes were evolutionary combinations of lengthened and altered wheelbases, minor engine relocations, and hybrid-part bodies. Most still had functional driver's doors, fuel injection, and transmissions that year. With a 2,000-pound minimum weight limit, the so-called Funny Cars were becoming much more functional, but issues with aerodynamics and safety were becoming more serious.

Toward the end of 1966, the decision to supercharge the Landy machine showed just how serious, as Landy was burned slightly when he had a transmission explosion and small fire during a test session with Chrysler corporate personnel from Detroit on hand. The cars, still wheelbase altered, were looking less and less like production cars, and Chrysler decided to refocus for 1967 on the newly announced Super Stock classes instead. Sox once recalled to me that *Baccaruda* was one of his all-time favorite cars, because "all you had to do was turn up the wick, and off it would go."

Turning up the wick was more than simply the mechanical tune-up that year. In addition to heavy nitro loads, the use of hydrazine, a fuel additive, was

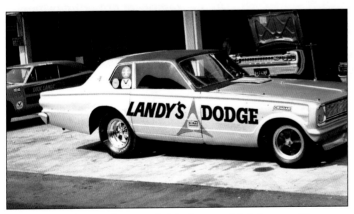

In 1966 Dick Landy raced this Dart, which began the year injected and ended it with a supercharged combination. A fire in late-season testing was a catalyst to the factory forsaking the ultra-stock/funny ranks to go to Super Stock in 1967. It is seen here on the day it was sold by the team in late 1967. Gene Kidder, the new owner, destroyed it in a Florida crash in 1969. (Photo Courtesy Landy Family Archive)

Piloted by Mike Buckel, the Ramchargers Dart pulls the wheels off the ground on the cover of the Cars magazine Super Stock Internationals event program from Cecil County Drag-O-Way in 1966. That young lady was obviously hearing the sound of Mr. Hoover's Hemi and was not appropriately dressed for the starting-line environment. The use of hydrazine by the team certainly solidified its reputation as the mad scientists of drag racing. (Photo Courtesy Mike Goyda, goyda.com)

growing in popularity. Chemically coded N_2H_4, it was a highly toxic chemical used in rocket propulsion that had to be kept on ice to remain stable; even its vapor could be fatal. It could be added in small quantities to nitromethane to create more power, but had to be introduced to the fuel cell immediately prior to the race and required the fuel system to be cleaned out as quickly as possible following the pass. If not, the compound turned into a highly explosive jellylike substance.

The use of hydrazine pushed the injected Chrysler cars down into the 8.50 or better range (and Mercury's Comets went even faster). Soon after, the supercharger became standard equipment for Funny Car racing, and the experiments with test tubes and rubber gloves ended. One of the sport's major suppliers of nitromethane, Commercial Solvents, threatened to quit selling nitro for drag racing if the use of hydrazine as a racing fuel was not curtailed.

The Ramchargers' Dart was similar to Landy's car in appearance. It was built at the team's remote garage in Ferndale around a commercial chassis using a fiberglass body.

"We sometimes referred to the 1966 Dart as the birdcage car, like a Maserati," remembers Tom Hoover. "The roll cage was tied to the whole structure of that car. The chassis came from Woody Gilmore, and Al Bergler in Detroit had done the aluminum tinwork inside it.

"There was a real problem with it, though, that we did not discover until midseason. Under the strain of racing, we had bent the stock rear housing so that the back tires were toed-in by 3/8 inch. If you want to make a car squirrelly, do that; it will change your life. Once we built

a structure to prevent that, the 1966 car was a completely different animal to drive. It worked well."

The car was soon into the 8-second zone, and the team tested and raced with a hydrazine combination that year. Mike Buckel was usually the driver now, and while the team found the subsequent power increases were solid, many times it was at the expense of engine internals, particularly piston tops and ring lands. At the team garage in Ferndale, team members could not replicate the destruction even by slamming a vise-held piston with a sledgehammer. Speed costs money. How fast do you want to go?

B/XS and Beyond

The NHRA 2,400-pound B/XS and lower classes were primarily for homebuilt and independent machines, though some of the Fords and Ronnie Sox moved from the fuel combination used in match racing to gasoline to be able to stay in Street Eliminator on race day. Indeed, while independent racers had to run on gasoline at NHRA shows, many of them regularly raced on fuel elsewhere.

For instance, Shirl Greer of Tennessee took out all comers in the 2,400-pound Fuel class on Saturday at the 1966 Super Stock Nationals, held on Long Island's New York National Speedway that year. Greer had converted his 1965 A01 Dodge named *Tension* to a straight front axle/centered driver design by this time and was running low-9-second times. He beat often-quicker competitors (including Sox and Ford ace Bill Lawton) that night through good wheelstand control and simple consistency.

Finally, some of the drivers from the 1965 altered-wheelbase program still had sponsorship deals for parts.

As an example of opportunity meeting need, the Jon Thorne Racing Enterprises Jayhawker used a wheelbase-changed 1963 body and a 1964 Plymouth aluminum nose to get in on the action. Thorne was a well-heeled heir to a business fortune and had cars in competition in both drag racing and the Grand National circuit.

The introduction of match racing and NHRA's XS classes resulted in many interesting combinations during the 1966 season. This is the shortened Jake's Speed Equipment Plymouth out of Louisiana, campaigned by Paul Candies and Leonard Hughes, who became a big part of 1970s Funny Car and Top Fuel racing. It has been restored by Jet Townsend.

Gene Snow, on his way to winning the 1966 NHRA Nationals in Competition Eliminator in his C/FD-classed Dodge Dart, was able to run close to his own 9.33 national record as he drove through Monday's handicap eliminator. (Photo Courtesy Ray Mann Archive, quartermilestones.com)

A few of them built new cars using a set of scaled A-Body build-up plans the factory had created; several others stayed with their 1965 models. To keep up with the changes, however, these cars were now fairly radical. Bobby Harrop escaped unharmed but destroyed his *Flying Carpet* Dodge at Cecil County's season opener in 1966 after setting the engine position back. The roof was taken off *Melrose Missile* by Cecil Yother to make it into a roadster.

Indy 1966

With the Ramchargers' dragster in as low qualifier, Emory Cook piloting Garlits' new *Dart*, and Stahl and his cohorts in Stock, the 426 contingent looked strong when Labor Day arrived. In A/XS, Sox and *Baccaruda* lost in the class to Bill Lawton's Ford Mustang. The most visible Hemi cars in NHRA B/XS gas action at the Nationals in Indy were the 1965 Plymouths of Lee Smith and Vernon Rowley (in the ex-1965 Sox & Martin *Paper Tiger*); Rowley won the class with a 10.11. The ex-*Lawman* 1964 Plymouth was still in the able hands of Joe Aed and Carl Housley, who won B/Altered honors. On Monday, however, an unsponsored Dart named *Rambunctious*, which had been classed into C/Fuel Dragster, put the first Hemi Funny Car into the winners' circle at the Nationals.

Oilman Gene Snow had become established out of the Fort Worth, Texas, match race scene, and had built a nitro-burning 1965 Dodge Dart. For 1966, the car was updated with a modified wheelbase, more fiberglass, and an injected Hemi. Wanting to stay with his fuel of choice, nitromethane, Snow elected to be classified with dragsters instead of detuning for XS. He won the class to take a spot in the Competition Eliminator field and then ran off his own C/FD class record to score round wins. He went flat-out to 9.04 in the final to win on Monday over a B/Gas dragster.

Snow was also back on the map at Tulsa, where the NHRA again adjusted the rules for Funny Cars, finally choosing to create a handicap Funny Car eliminator for all cars that were in the S/XS and A/XS fields. Snow won the A/XS class title over Hubert Platt's factory-assisted Mustang and then went to the final round of the NHRA's first Funny Car Eliminator before he foul-started against Ed Schartman's SOHC Comet.

In the end, 1966 was a year of transition and the staging ground for the rest of the decade. The Street Hemi had arrived, the cars were back on the circle tracks, and drag racing was growing in popularity and performance. Boredom would not be a problem.

In 1966, transitions occurred rapidly and opportunities opened up. For instance, racers in Super Stock found it was possible to convert legal cars to "more legal" versions thanks to reversible wheelbase mounting points and add-on parts. This is Ken Montgomery and his 555 Plymouth, running in U/S (Ultra Stock) trim at a NASCAR drag race at Richmond, Virginia. (Bob Plummer Photo, Courtesy Kramer Automotive Film/Print Library)

CHAPTER SEVEN

1967
Conquering the Competition

Hemi Drivers Rack Up Wins and Championships

The custom color that the Petty team had mixed up by accident in the early 1960s became Petty Blue during the 1967 NASCAR season. The same Hemi technology that had first proven itself during the 1964 Daytona 500 had now been refined to the extent that it was making circle-track history.

Richard Petty, at 30, was in the process of winning his second Grand National title for Plymouth that year. He was also rewriting the record books for NASCAR's premier series in ways that still have not been challenged.

By the middle of the season, May 13, when he won the Rebel 400 at Darlington, Petty had taken home a record 55 career victories, surpassing the 54-win record formerly held by his father, Lee. He toppled Tim Flock's 18-win single-season victory record from back in the Keikheafer Chrysler 300 era when he took home his nineteenth title of the year on August 12 at Bowman-Gray Stadium in Winston-Salem, North Carolina. This record occurred in the middle of a run of 10 consecutive race victories on the Grand National circuit, another record that has never been equaled. Indeed, the 27 wins from 1967 alone equal more than 10 percent of the 200 race crowns bestowed on the man who became recognized as King Richard in 1967.

Chrysler's Hemi engine in NASCAR was now technically four seasons old, but other than very minor changes for durability, it had not received any significant development since Petty had scorched Daytona with it at its introduction. Development of the potential A148 race engine (see the sidebar on page 167, "Tom Hoover on the Hemi Engines That Were Not") never went beyond initial dyno testing; the sanctioning body's limits on displacement had focused attention on higher-RPM durability.

After two years of manufacturer boycotts, however, it was hoped that things for NASCAR would finally settle down a little as both Ford and Chrysler found ways to race head to head. The fact that Petty dominated that year was not so much due to the Hemi engine as a superior powerplant, but more about his natural talent as a driver. In retrospect, the rules had been rewritten in 1967 to allow Ford to make some headway.

The engine that roared. This Chrysler publicity image of an A864 circle-track Race Hemi (and its externally identical A117 404-ci cousin) helped Richard Petty rewrite the Grand National record books. Note the bathtub intake and shorty headers. This example does not have additional crankcase ventilation, or increased oiling capacity. (Photo Courtesy Chrysler Group LLC)

Seen here at the Mopars at the Rock show that Steve Earwood promotes annually at Rockingham Dragway is one of the two #43 Plymouth Belvederes that Richard Petty raced during the 1967 season. The records Petty set that year will likely never be broken. In those 27 victories, he won 10 of them consecutively.

Tiny Lund at the 1967 Daytona 500, where he finished fourth, due to running out of gas. Lund had run a Dodge D500-1 for the Petty family at Florida's old Titusville-Cocoa Speedway in late 1956. He was among several drivers who wheeled Petty Plymouths in the 1966 and 1967 seasons. (Copyright CR Racing Memories 0603, Ray Mann Photograph)

As previously stated, NASCAR had developed a formula for using power-to-weight ratios for competition that started in the middle of 1965. In early 1966, Ford's racing bosses Leo Beebe and Jacques Passino tried earnestly to convince NASCAR that the SOHC engine would soon be available as a production engine, announcing in December 1965 their intention to run the engine during the 1966 season. Although persuaded to legalize it, Bill France had added extra pounds to the overhead-cam design (10.96 for overhead-cam designs versus 9.36 for in-block camshafts). Moreover, the SOHC would be legal after the engine was available for purchase in a production vehicle, which representatives from ACCUS tried to do through dealership channels unsuccessfully.

In April 1966, at the behest of Henry Ford II, the company pulled out of NASCAR in protest. However, seeing an effect on sales and product promotion, Ford and Mercury returned late in the 1966 season with a promise of parity from France. He allowed them to run a specially designed Holman-Moody Galaxie tube-frame front structure on the unibody Fairlane and Cyclone models. This was the first such chassis restructuring legalized in NASCAR car building.

Other big changes helped the Blue Oval guys in 1967, at least on the big tracks. One was the allowance of special circle-track tunnel port parts, which NASCAR ruled were simply replacements and did not require a production-engine variant.

The second was the legalization of dual 4-barrel carbs on wedge and semi-hemi engine designs. This change greatly increased power for both the Ford 427-ci wedge and the Chevy 427-ci rat motor. It allowed Curtis Turner, in Smokey Yunick's Chevelle, to record the first 180-mph qualifying lap at Daytona that year. The dual-carb setup also gave much better mileage due to superior fuel distribution characteristics, a factor in long green-flag races.

Finally, the modified smaller Fairlanes and Comets replaced the big Galaxies and Marauders of yore in 1967. With that body design legalized for the series (possibly by a small production run for drag racing with 427-ci side-oiler engines), simply add in Ford drivers such as Dick Hutcherson, Ned Jarrett, and 1967 Daytona 500 winner Mario Andretti, and suddenly it looked like time to go elephant huntin'. The problem for Ford was that no one told Richard Petty. He recorded 40 top-10 finishes en route to dominating the 1967 season.

One thing to remember is that, on the short tracks, mere horsepower was not the only issue. You had to be smart enough to stay out of trouble on a half-mile full of race cars, and Petty was among the best at staying out of harm's way. Of course, being the race leader didn't hurt.

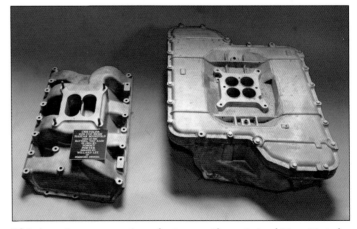

This is a size comparison between the original Hemi intake (left) and the bathtub (right), giving ample evidence of the plenum area used to ram tune the runners. These examples reside in the Garlits Museum Engine Room.

In 1967, 49 Grand National events were held, with 14 of them on dirt, 34 on pavement, and Riverside as the sole road course. Thirteen of the paved races were on superspeedway facilities, including Daytona's Twin 100 qualifiers. Ford had success all four times at Daytona in 1967 with Andretti in February and Cale Yarborough in July taking the race crowns, plus both spring qualifying races. Ford also won both races at Atlanta and the late-season speedway run at Rockingham, but the Hemi cars still proved to be potent everywhere except that season opener.

For Plymouth, Petty took home superspeedway titles at both events at Darlington, plus the first Rockingham event. Jim Paschal won the World 600 in Charlotte in May. Buck Baker also won at that track with a Dodge in October to snap Petty's record 10-race winning streak. But where Petty proved his prowess was in places such as Martinsville and Richmond, Virginia; Hickory, North Carolina; and Columbia, South Carolina. They were all places where he won both events that season.

Some detractors in the modern era have stated that Petty won because these were so-called small events. In reality, all of them featured many top name drivers and not a single one of them laid down to allow that blue tail panel to move up ahead of them. Dirt or pavement, superspeedway or short track, Richard Petty was indeed king.

Circle-Track Parts and Changes

After the 1965 boycott the circle-track Hemi benefited from better manifolding. Using the analysis done on the factory cross-ram intake for drag racing, Chrysler engineers cast and built an intake manifold that brought the ram-tuning effect to the NASCAR program. Known as the

bathtub or "tub" manifold, it featured eight horizontally crossed square tubes inside a large internal plenum. The plenum was topped with a lid that had a deep depression for the single carburetor, sunk down to clear the cowl air induction unit. It was used exclusively in circle-track applications that required a single 4-barrel carb.

"There was a step between the first A864 intakes that were used at Daytona in 1964 and the bathtub intake," remembers Tom Hoover. "Forbes Bunting created a true high-rise intake for the Hemi, probably late in the 1964 season. It was a dual-plane. I'm thinking it was magnesium, but this one had a carb pad that was about 1.5

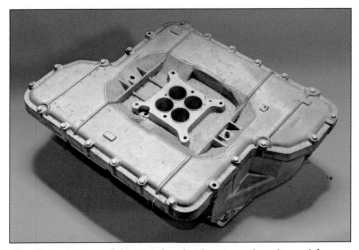

The factory was able to take the lessons developed from the drag racing program and apply them to the circle-track engine. The sunken tub inset allowed the carb to remain low enough so that the cowl induction air cleaner was not impacted, although it resulted in the runners being closer to the lifter valley. This example resides in the Garlits Museum Engine Room.

The standard Hemi NASCAR intake looked like this during the early days, similar in design to the Street Hemi version machined for two Carter carbs. This one (which resides in the Garlits Museum Engine Room) was reportedly on a car during the 1964 500. The center divider relief facilitated the use of the Holley 3-barrel carb, which did not last long in Grand National racing.

The design necessitated the use of Holley carburetors with LeMans-type center-mounted floats and end feeds. The secondary benefit of this carb design and its special float system was greater fuel control under cornering. This example was provided by Kramer Automotive.

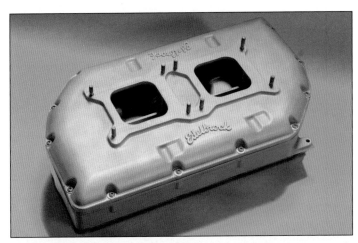

Released in the late 1960s, Edelbrock's Rat Roaster is said to have been the final result of the work initiated on the bathtub NASCAR intakes. It was available in several styles. This one, which resides at the Garlits Museum Engine Room, is set up for twin inline carbs for Super Stock racing.

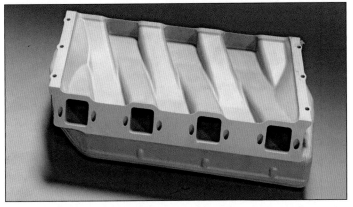

The underside of a Rat Roaster shows how the cylinders' locations cross over, with enough length to create the ram effect in each runner as the open plenum area under the carburetors is filled with the air-fuel mixture. This example resides at the Garlits Museum Engine Room.

The interior of the Rat Roaster intake on the left features a vertical center divider for evening out fuel distribution between the banks of cylinders. The one at right is as-cast from Edelbrock with no changes. These examples were provided by Kramer Automotive.

inches taller than the first version. This was not simply a raised carb-mounting point, but a careful rework, as if you had stretched the intake like rubber. It made all the runners longer. It worked, but you had to do whatever you could for hood clearance.

"Wish I had one of those things now; they were really neat," he adds with a laugh. "With three Holley 2-barrels, it would have been a great Six Pack design for the Hemi; a real winner."

Like the cross ram, the tub used the sonic effect, which both created natural supercharging via sonic waves in the intake runner and balanced the cylinders better than a standard straight runner-style or dual-plane intake could. Initially available in 1966, the tub was in wide use during 1967 on Petty's Plymouth and the other Chrysler factory entries. The intake design certainly helped make up for the lack of carburetion on the Hemi compared to other engines, and it possibly played a role in the horsepower-on-demand situation that hard-cornering short-track racing and its attendant effect on carburetion entailed.

Later on, these same elements were offered to drag racing fans who required inline Street Hemi carbs using Edelbrock's aftermarket Rat Roaster. This aluminum unit was made with interchangeable tops for level-mounted single or multiple carburetion in drag racing applications, and it did not have the carb-mounting depression that the NASCAR intake used.

Subsequent dyno testing with various styles of carburetors coupled with detailed information released through Chrysler Engineering resulted in individual racers adding internal fuel dams to the base area, which helped direct air-fuel movement to or from specific cylinders. It was not recommended for the street due to the possibility of fuel puddling in the floor area, which could have explosive consequences if the engine backfired the next time it was started.

"Rat Roaster had no accommodation for either exhaust or water heat," says Hoover, "so when it was cold, it was pretty 'sneezy.' The cross-ram was that way too. I remember Dick Maxwell and his wife tried to drive around Detroit in their 11.0 Max Wedge one winter with the cross-ram on it. It backfired and broke the nose off a new starter. Scary; none of them were really made to run if it was below freezing."

Ironically, another area that appears to have created a positive improvement was reducing displacement. As we have seen, France made a number of attempts to limit power by requiring specific engines to run at smaller sizes. For instance, most Mopar NASCAR entries were Category 2 cars requiring a minimum wheelbase of at least 115 inches and limited to 405 ci. Weight was based at

BANZAI SUMMER

One of the most dramatic episodes in the history of the Race Hemi in drag racing occurred during a few months in 1967, primarily because of the new package car's weight and lack of compression. To get a solid response from any race car, the goal is to get it to launch high up in the RPM band. Although this was easy with a clutch (simply wind the engine up and let it go), the Torqueflite and torque converter presented a problem. Factory-backed driver Jack Werst found a solution in a unique driving technique and a heavy-duty transmission rebuilt by a fellow Pennsylvanian who went on to garner fame as the tuner of several noted nitromethane entries.

Brian Kohlmann in the ex–Jake's Speed Equipment car suffered a massive transmission explosion during an exhibition run at Frank Spittle Super Stock Nationals Reunion in 1995. Torqueflite failure and high-RPM levels could result in massive destruction.

"We had some special transmissions made that year by a guy named Tim Richards, in Scranton, Pennsylvania, who later tuned Joe Amato's fuel dragster. We began doing what came to be known as 'banzai' starts with those transmissions," recalled Werst in an interview with me in 2003. As the antics continued, Werst was even called "Banzai" by some track announcers that summer. "The trick was to wind that Hemi up to 8,000 rpm in neutral and then drop it into first gear. KA-baam! The car dropped a half second under the index by doing that. It also caused some very bad transmission explosions in the car."

Of course, when the transmission exploded, pieces and fluid flew everywhere.

"I got a lot of ink doing those starts, but now I see it as being pretty foolish. I mean, I blew windshields out of the car, dashboards out of it. I'd try anything to get that thing to run."

Nevertheless, Werst set up his *Mr. 5 & 50* Plymouth to run similar to a stick car at Indy. With a Dana 60 rear and bigger springs, he figured he could easily win the SS/BA class title. He was not the only one. A period magazine writer stated that somebody from Chrysler had told him that a whole truckload of transmissions was on hand to get past the carnage.

The NHRA (and especially the likely recipient of hot oil and parts from such problems, chief starter Buster Couch) understandably was not inclined to permit it. As Jack and his Plymouth came around the corner to the starting line for his first run, he saw that they had posted a small round sign by the Christmas tree that stated "NO NEUTRAL STARTS."

Werst and his crew swapped the parts back for the automatic, but a red light ended his chances. A third Pennsylvanian, Tom Myl, won the SS/BA class, but the first Indy Super Stock title went to Jack's former engine builder, Bill "Grumpy" Jenkins and his Camaro.

9.36 pounds per cubic inch on all but the overhead-cam design. The code A117 Hemi displaced 404 ci, attained by reducing the crank stroke from 3.75 to 3.558 and using a slightly longer rod (7.714 versus 6.86).

"The real benefit to destroking an engine is not simply the moving reciprocating weight, or what is known as rotating inertia, but friction reduction. You are not moving the piston as far," Tom Hoover says. "One thing people talk about today is piston speed. This is the mean amount of travel the piston makes in a given amount

of time at a given RPM level. When you can reduce the stroke, piston speed can be safely increased, but friction is probably the most important factor. Reducing friction means reduced heat, which ups the thermal efficiencies. However, if the destroking exposes more surface area in the combustion chamber, you lose some of that.

"A good example would be to compare the 225 and 170 slant-6s. They made about the same amount of power. The longer stroke and larger displacement may have meant more torque, but it did not mean the engine

Iggy Katona of Toledo, Ohio, ran a Dodge Charger to take home his seventh title on the ARCA circuit. The Hemi helped many noted drivers in these smaller sanctions establish major achievements. (Copyright CR Racing Memories 0702004, Ray Mann Photograph)

was more powerful. Some of that was the frictional loss of the larger displacement, but what you want is the least amount of stroke and the highest possible RPM. That is what makes today's 500-inch 11,000-rpm Pro Stock engines so amazing. The biggest challenge then becomes making the valve gear work with the potential RPM levels.

"I don't recall that we did a whole lot of testing work on the 404 ci; we looked at a couple of camshafts for it. We did some testing in 1964 on a 396-ci engine that the rules had suggested, but was never really a big deal and didn't go anywhere. However, it was later a big wallop to go from 7 liters [the 426] down to 6 liters [366 ci] without making major changes to the block dimensions."

The displacement limits that NASCAR tried to mandate in the pre-restrictor plate era never proved to be a realistic solution to stem speeds and safety concerns, and endurance parts developed for greater RPM levels made the cars faster still. The major safety issue on the larger, faster tracks was not horsepower but wheels and tires. Goodyear and Firestone both worked diligently to develop versions of tires for specific track surfaces and conditions. However, even those tires sometimes came apart violently, and overaggressive cornering tore the rim lug-mounting points to shreds, resulting in wheel loss or worse. In fact, several drivers lost their lives while performing tire testing during the 1960s as the evolution continued.

Dominance Everywhere

When the smoke had cleared on the 1967 Grand National season, Plymouth had 31 event wins (Petty with 27, Jim Paschal the other 4). Dodge had 5: one each by Buddy Baker, Bobby Allison, LeeRoy Yarbrough, and 2 by David Pearson (before he left Cotton Owens' team at midyear to drive a Ford for Holman-Moody).

Although aerodynamics already played a part in the NASCAR equation, Ford spent 1967 scientifically devel-

oping a more streamlined fastback shape for its midsize cars. Ford fully intended to make 1968 a banner year.

Petty had won the NASCAR series, attending all events and racing in 48 of 49 of them (he could only run one of the Daytona qualifiers), but Hemi-powered Dodges and Plymouths were even more dominant in the ARCA circuit in 1967. Of the 32 events held that year, Dodge won an amazing 21 titles and Plymouth won 5. Iggy Katona, an elder statesman of engine racing at 51, took home his second consecutive crown in the series, the seventh and final championship in a career that had begun in the early 1950s.

Ernie Derr, another racing veteran, took his third IMCA title and eventually won a record seven consecutive crowns through 1971. Ford was also frustrated in the USAC Stock series in 1967 despite having Andretti, Foyt, and others onboard. Don White, running a Charger out of Ray Nichels' "Go Fast Factory," held off Ford standout Parnelli Jones to take home the third of Chrysler's 1967 Hemi circle-track championships. In the 22-race Midwestern series, White won nine events, including five of seven held at Soldier Field in Chicago, and he finished in the top three at many others.

Although Petty's victorious capturing of another championship was well documented, few recall that Dodge also won three circle-track National Championships in 1967. In USAC it was Don White. A lengthy story in the July 2, 1978, issue of The Milwaukee Journal *labeled him "The Richard Petty of the North" for his racing accomplishments. (Copyright CR Racing Memories 0603030, Ray Mann Photograph)*

Upscale Street

The biggest change from the production standpoint in 1967 was that the company chose to install the Street Hemi in only the most upscale B-Body models during its sophomore year. Two were new models, the Dodge R/T and the Plymouth GTX, based on the Coronet and Belvedere, respectively. Together with the Charger, these designs were the only street cars you could order with a Hemi through a dealer for 1967. Although more profitable per unit, the change actually hurt sales by cutting many buyers out of the picture financially.

All three models came with upscale sport equipment, including bucket seats, center console, special trim, and a new performance version of the 440 wedge as standard. When upgraded to the Hemi engine and associated mandatory transmission options, the sticker price was well above $4,000. Most were hardtops (there was no coupe option), with a handful of convertibles created. Unfortunately, showrooms had nothing close in weight to the basic Belvedere I sedan that Jere Stahl had driven to win the 1966 NHRA Stock Eliminator championship.

Another big change occurred for 1967: NHRA Stock and Super Stock had been separated into two divisions for the new season and had formulated rules for the new Super Stock class. The primary changes were the allowance of any tire that could fit into the stock rear wheelhouse, any intake as long as the OEM carb remained in the stock location, and any camshaft (including rollerized versions). A roller cam uses special tappets equipped with a cylinder that rolls against the cam lobe. It allows for much faster valvetrain response and more radical lift designs. Common in production cars today, it was a radical change from stock in the 1960s.

"The real benefit of a roller camshaft is the reduction of friction, as the horsepower required to move the valve gear is substantially decreased," says Hoover. "If it took 15 to 20

hp to run the valvetrain at a given RPM, the roller design used approximately half of that; it was a real change.

"The other thing was that you could use a higher ramp acceleration rate. The front face of the cam's lift surface, the opening side, could be designed steeper without scuffing the cam. It woke the engine up."

With gasoline as the only fuel, the new rules allowed cars to upgrade performance on the NHRA circuit much as they had done in match race trim. For 1967, there were 10 S/S classes, 5 for stick cars and 5 for automatics:

Class	Time (seconds)
SS/A-SS/AA	0.00 to 6.99
SS/B-SS/BA	7.00 to 7.69
SS/C-SS/CA	7.70 to 8.69
SS/D-SS/DA	8.70 to 9.49
SS/E-SS/EA	9.50 and up

After eliminations for each class, the final eliminator field was handicapped by the national record, with drivers receiving a .10 break-out margin if they went quicker than the index; overall, this was a source of ongoing frustration for everyone during the following seasons. More important, for the first time, due to the changes being permitted, the NHRA estimated the advertised horsepower-to-shipping weight instead of simply accepting the AMA paperwork as it had done previously in Stock. This one change became quite politicized between the manufacturers and the NHRA, especially when coupled with meeting the stated minimum requirements for production legality, which remained as 50 documented units to qualify for Super Stock homologation.

Super Stock was a very big deal in 1967, big enough that shifter magnate George Hurst put up a whopping $10,000 for the winner at the season-ending World Finals race, the largest single-race purse the sport had ever seen. It was his and the NHRA's ardent desire to see that money go to some campaigner in a brand-new muscle car. As you shall see, that did not happen, even though Chrysler created a run of new Super Stock package cars for 1967.

The RO23/WO23 Cars

Chrysler announced that there would be a 1967 Hemi package car created for the new class. In keeping with marketing the new R/T and GTX cars, the hardtop body was selected, which put the curb weight with Hemi motivation at just under 3,700 pounds. Indeed, once the heavy truck battery and big wheels were installed, shipping weight was listed as identical to the 1967 GTX and R/T Street Hemi minimum. Rather than revert to the magnesium cross-ram/

Super Stock and Stock were separated into two classes in 1967. Here is one of the package cars that was built by Chrysler to compete that first year, the Liberty "Belle" Dodge out of Wisconsin. These cars were not much different from regular street models. (Photo Courtesy Kramer Automotive Film/Print Library)

aluminum head A990 engine of 1965, the powerplant in these cars was much closer to the Street Hemi, and not a variant of what had been suggested and canceled in 1966. The result was a heavy car that was somewhat low on power, but there was a logical explanation for it.

According to author Jim Schild in his book *Maximum Performance*, these cars had been scheduled for A/Stock when the construction process was initially finalized on December 12, 1966, in product planning documents PC-72 and C-106. As noted, to meet eligibility for the new Super Stock class, a minimum of 50 units was required, so at least that many had to be built. To become legal for the new Stock class, the NHRA now required 500 units, although many of the era's top power packages never met that number.

Coded on the door-mounted VIN tags as RO23 for Plymouth and WO23 for Dodge, the cars made a late-spring debut and were not legal for S/S until mid-May because of a 30-day waiting period that the NHRA required to verify overall availability.

The 1967 RO/WO cars were mild compared to previous packages. Again, even though the NHRA allowed the use of fiberglass parts in Super Stock, partly in deference to Ford's special 427 Fairlanes of 1966, the 1967 Chrysler bodies were all steel, with only one major exterior change: a low-profile steel hood scoop similar to that used in 1965.

In a letter written on March 1, 1967, Domestic Product Planning Engineer Dick Maxwell explained to NHRA President Wally Parks that, as sales bank units, all of the cars were painted in code WW1 white with a standard black vinyl front bench seat. The sound deadener, seam sealer, and insulation were left off. There were no options. Deletions from the standard Hemi list were heater and radio (those areas in the dash had block-off plates installed), and the front sway bar. They all had drum brakes fore and aft, 7.75 x 15 blackwall tires mounted on standard white body-color 15 x 6 rims, and they were shipped without hub caps in the trunk. However, that trunk did hold a big truck battery mounted in a tray behind the

right rear tire as the 1965 version had, and the car had a special aluminum plate that was used to seal the inline Carter AFB carburetors to the hood scoop.

The engine was very close to the Street Hemi. In fact, the only significant change to this version of the A102 engine was to the stock dual-plane intake manifold. After

The engine in the restored Landy Dodge. The WO23-coded race cars were referred to by Dick Maxwell as SS/B Street Hemis and were quite similar to what could be purchased that year. Note the aluminum hood plate fitted to the OEM Hemi air-cleaner baseplate.

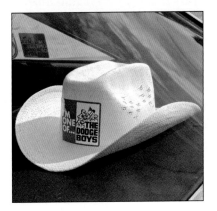

In addition to the Supercar Clinic give-away programs, Dodge also featured its noted Good Guys in White Hats promotions during this period. They gave away a bunch of these faux Stetsons through the dealerships.

The 1967 Dick Landy Coronet was converted using a standard R/T body and a special-order 1967 base Coronet hardtop that had been shipped with a Hemi engine installed. Members of the Landy family (wife Gean, son Richard Jr., daughter-in-law Peggy, and granddaughter Jasmine) pose with the car, which was restored by Erik Lindberg, and debuted at Mopars in the Park in 2009. It is now in the collection of Greg and Kathy Mosley.

You can see the differences between the factory Street Hemi intake (left) and the ones modified by Arlen Vanke (right) and used on RO/WO package cars. (These examples were provided by Kramer Automotive.) Removal of the center plenum wall greatly aided fuel distribution under hard acceleration. Opening the dual front ports beneath the forward carb allowed for faster throttle response, as the AFB carbs used vacuum to open the secondaries.

The back of the Vanke intake also has modifications, including the millwork between the two runner planes and the low divider wall added on the runner floor to alter the flow characteristics on the short center runners. This example was provided by Kramer Automotive.

development by the factory, Arlen Vanke was given the job of modifying the intakes for these cars by opening up the cast-in bores for the front carb, removing the center plenum divider, and welding a small dam to the floor for better fuel distribution on the shorter runners.

The carburetors were the factory Street Hemi Carters (4139S front and 4140S rear) that had been maximized via internal parts changes for this race-type environment; they retained the factory 10.25 compression piston. The cars used the standard full exhaust system with cast-iron manifolds as well.

Transmissions were either the A727 Torqueflite with heavy-duty internals, the reverse-pattern valve body, and a 2,700-rpm stall converter, or an A833 4-speed with internal slick-shift changes for easier shifting (but noisier than the standard unit). An R/C Industries scatter shield and heavy-duty clutch parts were in front of the 4-speed boxes, which used a Hurst short-throw shifter mounted to a location offset from the normal stock positioning. All automatics had the column shifter.

Differentials were either the 4.86 8¾ with the automatic or a 4.88-geared Dana 60 with the 4-speed. Approximately just under a third of each brand were built as 4-speed cars, with the remainder being automatics.

Based on normal production information, all 110 (55 Dodges and 55 Plymouths) cars came off the production line in one large sales bank group on Sunday, February 12, 1967, soon after the NHRA and AHRA season-opening events. Maxwell's March 1 letter to Parks specifically notes, "We started building our special SS/B Street Hemis last week." If the car were indeed assembly line built in early February, this statement apparently refers to some off-line finalization.

Tom Hoover states that none of the special manifolds were installed on the assembly line, so that was likely the cause, although Maxwell further noted in this letter that the production Street Hemi Carter carbs were being rebuilt at the engine plant for this program, presumably before the engines' final assembly.

Interestingly, also in this letter, Maxwell refers to a prior letter from Parks. He states, "In accordance to your

In a late-1966 magazine interview, World Champion Jere Stahl remarked that he did not think 1967 would be as easy as 1966. With his booming header business and the challenges of making his Plymouth competitive for Super Stock in the new season, that proved to be true. The car was later restored and became part of the Bill and Suzanne Turner collection.

letter of November 23, 1966, we have not changed the compression ratio or carburetor size." This statement sheds great light on why the cars were built the way they were. It is quite possible that a conversation had been ongoing between Chrysler and the NHRA to prevent the newer cars from superseding the abundant 1965 models, which were classed into SS/A for the 1967 season. Maxwell stated that the factory would offer a conversion package over the counter to anyone who desired to convert a Street Hemi hardtop to SS/B-BA specs.

Finally, the letter also breaks down the parts listed above. It also noted that the cars would get Mopar's vis-

cous fan drive and transistorized Prestolite ignition parts that had a recurved dual-point distributor. Incidentally, in this letter Maxwell consistently refers to these new cars as SS/B Street Hemis, not Race Hemis.

Maxwell then sent NHRA's Bill Dismuke a follow-up letter dated April 14, 1967, stating that the true total of more than 50 cars per brand had been completed by April 13. Again, this delay seems to have been because the later modification was made after construction. Perhaps as a result, these were the final package cars built by the assembly-line method, except for the 1970 Plymouth Superbirds in late 1969.

Starting in 1968, race vehicle construction for the drag program was done by funneling groups of semi-finished production cars to a division of Hurst Industries.

Changes in Race-Based Promotions and Fuel Cars

Chrysler formally chose to leave fuel stocker racing for 1967. The Ramchargers and Golden Commandos teams did campaign new Funny Cars in 1967, but these were independent of direct factory financing. Funny Car racing was in major transition in 1967. The NASCAR Grand Stock series outlawed all fuels but Pure Oil gasoline at its events in anything but dragsters that year. In addition, calls came from various editorial quarters and all the sanctioning bodies to ban nitromethane in stock-bodied representations. As history shows, that was not to be, but several dramatic incidents in 1967 did little to engender the Funny Car cause to the powers-that-be. These included an incident at Richmond, Virginia, where Mike Buckel put the Rams' new 1967 Dart up on the rear bumper as well as the death of popular driver Del Heinelt in a Ford Mustang at the NHRA Nationals.

Jere Stahl (left) and Bill Stiles (right) sign a pair of the popular 1/18-scale replicas of the 1967 Plymouth at the York Reunion in Pennsylvania. Both men were drivers in the Pro Stock era.

Jere Stahl and Bill Jenkins leave the starting line during a press event early in the weekend of the 1967 NHRA World Finals. Stahl had already announced he would be stepping away from driving to concentrate on his growing business. Unbeknownst to Bill Jenkins, an NHRA season championship would elude him until 1972, thanks in no small part to Chrysler's continuing development of the Hemi. (Photo Courtesy Ray Mann Archive, quarter-milestones.com)

At the 1967 Super Stock Nationals at Cecil County Drag-O-Way is Dave Strickler's old altered Dodge, modified from its 1965 origins by owner Chuck McJury for match racing on the NASCAR and gas circuits. McJury's Fury was later found and subsequently brought back to its 1965 appearance. It is presently part of Nick Smith's collection. (Photo Courtesy Kramer Automotive Film/Print Library)

Despite the lack of factory involvement by either Chrysler or General Motors, the outrageous antics of Funny Car racing made the turnstiles spin ever faster nationwide. Numerous independent drivers and teams arrived on the scene sporting all manner of engine and

By 1967, the face of drag racing was changing, but some first-generation cars were still running. Plain Busted was an independently campaigned entry from New York that had once been Bill "Maverick" Golden's 1963 Max Wedge Dodge. Many of these cars were raced until they were literally used up. (Photo Courtesy Kramer Automotive Film/Print Library)

In Funny Car racing, the fastback Charger body was selected by several Dodge teams, although its overall size was larger than most of its competition. The Gary Dyer-driven Mr. Norm's Super Charger entry is on the trailer. (Photo Courtesy Kramer Automotive Film/Print Library)

A young Don Schumacher piloted this early Stardust Charger. At this point, "The Shoe" was among the numerous young men (and a handful of women) who wanted to find fame and fortune in Funny Cars. (Photo Courtesy Kramer Automotive Film/Print Library)

body combinations during the year, which became the final season of major experimentation. For XS racing, the NHRA had already banned trucks (including a pair of popular West Coast Jeeps), roadsters such as Garlits' *Dart 2*, as well as non-production vehicles for 1967, leaving that category for modern-era coupe and hardtop body designs. Ford stayed deeply financially committed to this style of racing. The Ramchargers also adapted to the changing technology.

"Our 1966 Dart had been pretty conventional, with its Hotchkiss-type rear suspension and conventional leaf springs," remembers Tom Hoover. "The 1967 model was really a change, as Jim Thornton chose to use the ideas he had come up with when working on *Little Red Wagon* in 1964, when he mounted the driveline into its own sub-frame. We called this a torque rotation canceling design. By setting the driver's position rearward, we basically did the same thing, and that car worked beautifully. It went down the track like it was on rails."

AHRA embraced more variation, but often did so through its numerous classes (one AHRA race had 413 classes!), as did many of the independent events, which used various weight and fuel rules to classify cars. Ironically, by the end of 1967, the combination that Garlits' outlawed *Dart 2* roadster had innovated was becoming the standard, even if the car had to have a roof. These vehicles now had a slightly longer dragster-style wheelbase, lift-off/flip-up single-piece body, supercharged fuel engine, and the driver and engine set back as far as

The Rams experimented with exotic fuels and engine setback, but Tom Hoover was most proud of Jim Thornton's torque rotation cancellation suspension. The team had turned the injector "hat" around because it was not exposed to the open air. (Photo Courtesy Kramer Automotive Film/Print Library)

The American, *another altered-wheelbase car likely built from an earlier Super Stock car, is seen at the 1967 Super Stock Nationals. The car appears to have received both a product and a speed shop sponsorship, a rarity in this period. (Photo Courtesy Kramer Automotive Film/ Print Library)*

The Ramchargers were in the team's final year as a group of factory engineers turned racers. Mike Buckel piloted the Dart most of 1967, and a number of members campaigned the dragster in 1968 and beyond. He is seen here racing Dave Strickler's Corvette at Richmond Dragway. (Photo Courtesy Kramer Automotive Film/Print Library)

With trademark cigar in hand, Dick Landy is being interviewed for a 1967 television event. Chrysler's clinic programs helped make stars out of Landy and the Sox & Martin operation and opened many doors for publicity that normal drag racing efforts did not. (Photo Courtesy Landy Family Film Archive)

The two-car Landy race team arrives at Pomona for the 1967 Winternationals. The car on the rear trailer was a rare 440 body code Hemi Coronet; the real R/T is a 440 Magnum-powered model. (Photo Courtesy Landy Family Film Archive)

possible (although the driver was directly in front of or atop the rear axle rather than behind it).

After Garlits won Indy in his 426 Hemi dragster in 1967 (recounted in the sidebar on page 38, "Big Daddy's First 426 Hemi Efforts in Top Fuel"), the engine gained more followers. Through the year, Keith Black and Roland Leong tested a second *Hawaiian* dragster that showed promise, and, once competitive, Leong also joined the ranks leaving the 392-ci version behind. The choice for most Chrysler-bodied Funny Car entries was also the newer Hemi engine. At Indy, on the same day Garlits won, Gene Snow repeated his 1966 Eliminator win by beating them all in the new Super Eliminator category with his well-traveled injected C/FD Dart.

Supercar Performance Clinics

For the new year, the two big stars remaining in Chrysler's drag racing program, Dick Landy and Sox & Martin, were in Super Stock. They were also to begin what was some of the most intensive full-time employment ever registered by factory-sponsored racers of any style by running Supercar Performance Clinics. This was a series of midweek appearances scheduled for dealerships nationwide while the teams followed the racing schedule.

The idea of offering performance clinics oriented toward both owners and potential buyers had been financed because Chrysler management was truly interested in promoting its performance models. In addition to the personalities, these events included giveaways, door prizes, film showings, test drives, special races with local radio personalities, drag racing promotions wherever applicable, and more. It was actually a big success for promoting Chrysler performance, and several other manufacturers' brands followed suit before 1970.

Both teams had converted new vehicles to race-ready trim very early in the 1967 season, before the new SS/B

An interesting aspect of the Dodge that Landy raced was its lengthened rear wheel-well opening, something the Sox & Martin Plymouth did not have. This made slight wheelbase changes undetectable.

Note the differences in wheels and tires, as well. While Chrysler supported both teams, they also had their own separate associate sponsorships. Sox & Martin used Keystone wheels and Firestone tires.

Street Hemi package cars were finished. In late 1966, Landy was given a 1967 base Coronet 440 model hardtop that had been a special assembly-line build with a Hemi installed. Painted silver with a black top, this car was first raced at the season-opening events in California as a standard stocker with the R/T logos painted on it.

When the 440 Magnum-powered R/T built for the clinic program proved to be a lighter car than the Hemi, mechanic Mike Landy (Dick's brother) spent three days swapping all the Hemi gear from the rare early 1967 Hemi hardtop to that body, rebuilding it into a WO23 package clone while the team toured that spring. According to research by historian Erik Lindberg, who restored this car, Mike Landy said this change was worth about 75 pounds, an important consideration because Landy was a big man. Both cars were repainted at midseason to Landy's new deep blue/white top with a red and silver accent paint scheme.

"You know, for some reason, the 1966–1967 Hemi body was about 100 pounds heavier than the other B-Bodies were," says Tom Hoover. "The B-Body Hemi cars were good in 1964 and 1965, and in 1968 and 1969 those bodies became lighter again. Although they did not get back down to where the early cars were, it was still a lot better than in 1966 and 1967. To make shipping weight, the RO/WO cars were a lot of work."

Meanwhile, Jake King converted a 383-powered Belvedere II into the first Hemi GTX car the Sox & Martin team raced. In both cases, the lighter factory body construction was utilized to facilitate better weight balance than the conventional Street Hemi versions had.

Like Landy's WO vehicle, Sox & Martin received a standard RO car late that spring, which necessitated second drivers at the larger events, because the A134-powered 440 wedge clinic cars needed to be driven as well. Dave Strickler arrived to temporarily wheel the second Sox & Martin Hemi machine before Bill Jenkins persuaded him to come back to a Chevrolet. Jim Wetton, who had bought Landy's 1965 car in 1966, came onboard to pilot a second car on that team in early 1967. The automatic-equipped 440 models were used as part of the clinic drag race promotion, dealership display, and actual competition, where they could be fitted into either SS/EA (Super Stock) or B/SA (Stock).

Buddy Martin (middle) stands with the two Hemi-powered Belvederes at the Midwest Mopars in the Park event in Minnesota in 2013, the first time they were together since 1967. The RO23-code car (right) is in the collection of Clark and Colleen Rand; the GTX trim RO model (left) is owned by John Mahoney. Incidentally, Mahoney's car is wearing the RO hood from Arlen Vanke's 1967 race car, which was wrecked by a subsequent owner in 1968, soon after Vanke sold it.

After surfacing in the collector hobby several years ago, the RO23 Plymouth raced by Ronnie Sox has toured with Clark and Colleen Rand as a showpiece. Between this and the other examples, Sox was by far the most successful of the 100 or so racers who received the packages, winning the NHRA Springnationals with it in both 1967 and 1968.

As with prior packages created solely for racing, one of the major changes to the 1967 package cars was moving the battery to the trunk, which aided traction. Using a heavy truck example from the Mopar catalog helped even more.

The business office in the 1967 package was somewhat Spartan. Sitting on the bench seat, handlers Ronnie Sox, Dave Strickler, or Herb McCandless slammed through the gears while carefully watching the Moroso tach.

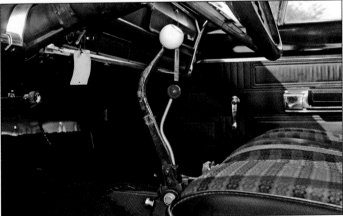

Sponsor Hurst supplied Ronnie Sox with shifters in 1967. From the outset, a number of prominent aftermarket companies realized the value of being associated with the Chrysler clinic effort.

Mike Landy often drove the wedge car for that team. Sox drove two cars or had Herb McCandless, Melvin Yow, or even Buddy Martin on the extra go pedal.

The Sox & Martin 1967 B-Body Hemi cars warrant a little more attention. The homebuilt Hemi GTX was a good-running car, but like the one Ronnie piloted on race day, it really needed the fresh-air/trunk battery possibilities that the RO package offered. Although it could be moved to SS/B with the scoop installed, it was not legal in Super Stock unless the VIN matched the one that the NHRA had on file. So the team added the parts and Jake King found the RO-coded race car VIN tag from the 1965 Paper Tiger altered-wheelbase hardtop at the shop.

Either the original Hemi GTX RS23J or this replacement VIN tag was put into the car's doorjamb tag location when the NHRA was teching the car. This identity problem was not an issue with the other sanctioning bodies or independent events. Still, the change left a lot of onlookers, even Mopar enthusiasts, wondering how the car could have GTX trim and the RO hood.

Current owner John Mahoney discovered the 1965 VIN on the key ring he received when he bought the team's 1967 GTX conversion car some time later and heard the story from crew chief Jake King himself.

Top of Super Stock

In 1967, the NHRA's SS/B and SS/BA classes were filled with several different cars, mostly Hemi and Max Wedge Mopars, while SS/A and SS/AA were the sole province of the 1965 A990 aluminum-head Race Hemi packages (the iron-headed 1964 A864 drag package was at a disadvantage). SS/C and SS/CA and the other lower three classes featured the steel-nose and low-compression Max Wedge packages, GTOs, 396-ci Camaros, and others. The new A134 440 wedge, single 4-barrel packages (only available in the heavy-bodied hardtop) was down in SS/E (Super Stock/Eliminator) and SS/EA, well below the 9.50 pound-per-horsepower margin.

That June, several of the new Hemi cars made their debut at the NHRA Springnationals in Bristol. Sox was

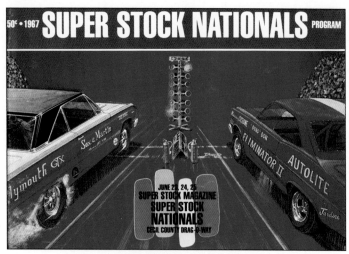

The popularity of the 1967 Chrysler Clinic Program, which was featured every month on a single page in Super Stock & Drag Illustrated, resulted in Sox's car being used as one of two vehicles sketched on the cover of the magazine's signature event program. Sox posted a runner-up to Dick Arons' Camaro at this event. (Photo Courtesy Mike Goyda, goyda.com)

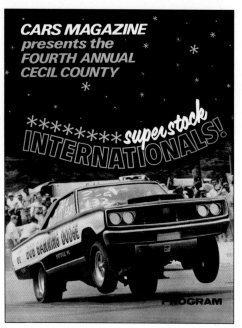

The Bob Banning Dodge-backed Coronet run by the team of Tom Sneden and Dave Reitz was popular on the East Coast ultra-stock circuit. Regional match racing organizations were birthed on both coasts and in the Midwest during this era. Cars were modified more for that purpose than for NHRA's handful of nationals-type races. (Photo Courtesy Mike Goyda, goyda.com)

able to win the SS/B class title. Then he won the overall eliminator on Sunday over Ron Mancini's SS/BA Max Wedge Plymouth. Sox also posted a runner-up finish at the three-day Super Stock Nationals at Cecil County Dragway to Dick Arons' Chevy the following month. At Indy, Chevy won when Bill Jenkins' Camaro beat Bob Brown, who was in a 1965 SS/A Plymouth. However, by that year at Indy and thereafter, drivers in the heavier automatic 1967 Hemi cars were handicapped when the NHRA understandably banned the controversial banzai start (see the sidebar "Banzai Summer" on page 94).

Still, one example of the 1967 breed in particular that deserves mention was not NHRA legal. It was the AHRA/ NASCAR Grand Stock entry of Tom Sneden and Dave Reitz that ran in the 3,000-pound Gas division. The duo had been competitive since the Max Wedge era with the car known as *The Bounty Hunters*, but to better promote the dealership, the car was simply lettered "Bob Banning Dodge" for the 1967 season. Beautifully finished and extensively modified under the NASCAR rules, this was a WO23 Dodge that literally stood out from the crowd, as Sneden pulled the nose into the air on every pass.

Thanks in part to Shirley Shahan's 1966 Winternationals win, female drivers also received attention in 1967. Shahan had a Wynns-sponsored Dodge for the new year. A special car went to a young female driver from Colorado named Judy Lilly. She ended up with a legitimate factory-built 1967 Hemi Plymouth post coupe that was refitted as an RO23. It was the only such Hemi package believed to have been built and conspicuously raced from the 1967 model series.

Unfortunately, little could be done to make the NHRA-legal RO/WO package competitive during the eliminator. The 1967 Mopars looked the part but struggled, and late in the season, Tom Hoover and the crew decided it was time for a fresh Super Stock package for 1968. That result was successful beyond imagination.

Although well-preserved examples of the 1967 WO/ RO packages survived, because of their lack of class competitiveness during and after the 1967 season, many were converted to Ultra Stock–type gas-burning modifieds on the AHRA and Midwestern United Drag Racers Association (UDRA) match race circuit or into bracket cars soon after. Their low production volume and potential streetability make them popular on the modern collector's market.

Today, Dave Reitz and Tom Sneden still race in nostalgia competition on occasion. They are seen here with tribute-style race cars during the 2014 Old Time Drags at Englishtown, New Jersey.

Shirley Shahan is getting ready to unload her Drag-On Lady Plymouth in June 1967 for the Super Stock Nationals. Shirley was very popular nationally by this time and had some associated media exposure in Hollywood as a result. (Photo Courtesy Kramer Automotive Film/Print Library)

Ed Miller: World Champion

Regardless of everything else, the main story of 1967 in Hemi door-car drag racing came not from Landy and Sox or thousands of dealership clinic attendees, but from a two-year-old car out of Rochester, New York, which took home the first NHRA Super Stock World Championship, a lot of recognition, and George Hurst's biggest-ever-in-any-class prize money check. This was Arlen Vanke's old 1965 A01/A990 Hemi Plymouth, now being campaigned by Ed Miller and Kip Guenther.

During 1966, Miller had piqued the attention of Bob Cahill because of his hard work. He even received some parts from Detroit after agreeing to keep the car running in Super Stock/A (Miller was one of the truly competitive shifting talents in the Hemi ranks) rather than convert it to A/Modified Production. The team gave the car a nice paint job and decided to tow it to the 1967 Winternationals. There, the Plymouth won the first SS/A class title, but lost in the overall eliminator finals on Sunday to an independently campaigned L79 Nova that was similar to the one Jenkins had been running the previous season.

Part of Eddie Valquez's success in his Chevy II was based on no prior record for indexing his runs. From the start, Super Stock participants were always leery to not topple their records, because you needed to compete based on that number. Every class winner and runner-up in SS/A, SS/B, SS/AA, SS/BA, and SS/CA at Pomona was a Chrysler, and they had to run hard to take home the class glory. On the other hand, Valquez was the only entrant in the SS/C class at Pomona, so he ran a soft 12.72 at 107.91 single to the win (in comparison, Dick Arons, one class lower in a new Camaro in SS/D, went 11.91 at 119 mph to win his class).

On Sunday, all Valquez had to do was leave first and be ahead at the finish. Ed Miller came up on the other side of the ladder the hard way and pumped off a string of low 11-second times. His 11.18 in the final was a breakout (more than .10 below the legal index) loss as Valquez played the finish line with the 4-speed stove bolt to a subpar 12.74. As small consolation, on the long ride home Guenther told Miller, "We lost the first one, but we'll win the last one."

Miller was actually more like the little guy NHRA talked about in Junior Stock than a factory hero. He laid bricks for a living and raced on a shoestring budget. He and Gunther literally wore out the Hemi engine fasteners tearing the engine apart and spent most of 1967 in match race trim chasing the NASCAR drag circuit. A chance to run a Division III point race at St. Thomas, Ontario, unexpectedly pushed their Plymouth up higher in the NHRA Northeast Division 1 (NED) standings as well. They had missed one division race earlier in the year and was allowed one from outside the home division.

During the summer, they also reset the NHRA SS/A record three times, and when they defeated Bill Jenkins' Indy-winning Camaro at the Land of NED's final points race at Connecticut Dragway, the low-buck team also won the division title over the Grump, 2,200 to 2,100. That earned the team a spot at Tulsa to chase the big money.

Seen here at a tribute dealership during Carlisle Events Chrysler Nationals, team partners Ed Miller and Kip Guenther were reunited when collectors Don and Mary Lee Fezell brought their restored Plymouth for the display.

When it mattered, this was the view that competitors had of the Miller-Guenther 1965 S/S Plymouth. As a result, the 426 Hemi won three straight NHRA World titles in 1965, 1966, and 1967.

Ed Miller shifts his way to $10,000 and the NHRA World Super Stock Championship.

Doesn't that tell you something?

Just more of the same thing we've been saying for years: if you want to be a winner, if your goal is to be first, you have no choice but to go *Hurst*.

Ed Miller of Rochester, New York said it better than we could on the last weekend in October at Southwest Raceway, Tulsa, Oklahoma. Ed came to Tulsa completely *Hurst-equipped* with a competition plus 4-speed, Line/loc, Reverse Loc/out and T-handle. He shifted his way through the toughest field of Super Stocks ever assembled, and he went home with the big money—the $10,000 non-contingent award for Super Stock Eliminator, presented by George Hurst himself. And Dick Arons of Detroit, the runner-up, proved that it's not only true for manual shifters. His 1967 Camaro is

equipped with Line/loc and a Hurst Dual Gate for automatic transmissions.

In fact, Ed Miller's big win in the World Points Final completed our sweep. Super Stock Eliminators at the 1967 NHRA Winternationals, Springnationals and Nationals were all *Hurst-equipped*.

Can we say any more, except if you're tired of being shutdown, sick of second class status, get down to your local performance equipment outlet and check out the full line of the Hurst products the pros use. Or write us and tell us what you drive and we'll send you all the facts about the winning combination for you. Hurst Performance Products, Warminster, Pa. 18974.

HURST

Part of Hurst's advertising campaign showing Ed Miller with a trophy and some of the contingency money the team won for its victory at Southwestern Raceway in Tulsa, Oklahoma, to end the season.

Ed Miller was no flash in the pan. His prowess with that 4-speed had given him the class titles at both Bristol and Indy in 1966, plus the Pomona class crown and event runner-up, and several point-garnering records during the 1967 season. He took the elapsed time numbers down to 11.15 and the MPH record up to 127.29. He converted the car to as low as 2,900 pounds to run the NASCAR series events.

Despite that, the Hemi that made Miller and Guenther $16,000 richer that weekend was worn out. It used a welded-up crank, and the rear of the block had been patched back together after a clutch explosion. In a tough field, in which even Stahl and Vanke could not get their 1967 cars qualified, Miller was seeded in with the 1965 model, but then he lost oil pressure on a Sunday morning check-out pass. It turned out to be a broken rocker arm that had let a lifter come out of its bore. Luckily, the team found the problem and fixed the car in time as the NHRA decided to run all the hotter cars first because of approaching rain.

That afternoon began with Miller beating Okie resident Don Grotheer (SS/B 1967 Plymouth), then Larry Cooper (SS/AA 1965 Plymouth), and finally Bill Jenkins' SS/C Camaro on a red light. In a light evening drizzle, Miller faced Dick Arons for the season crown. The Hemi car was indexed by the NHRA at 11.05 to the 396/325-hp Camaro's SS/EA 12.13 number. Miller, who was used to driving on the slippery 7-inch tires from the previous season, pulled ahead to take an early lead on the tricky surface. Then he won it all, 11.19 to 12.32.

The 1967 racing season was over, but new things were on the horizon. That fall, Dodge released a new 1968 version of the Charger, Plymouth released a budget muscle car, and the Super Stock Race Hemi engine was about to find its ultimate calling for the twentieth century.

In this vintage photo, Ed Miller and Dick Arons get off the starting line in a light drizzle as the final pair of cars run at the NHRA World Finals in Tulsa in 1967. Arons, from Detroit, was a formidable competitor, running his Camaro in SS/EA, but Miller overcame the slippery conditions to record a win, notoriety, and a big payday for the Hemi. (Photo Courtesy Don Fezell Collection, Photographer Unknown)

CHAPTER EIGHT

1968

Hemi Proliferation

Chargers, Road Runners, Super Bees and A-Bombs

Selling cars is the real reason any car company chooses to go racing. In retrospect, the Race Hemi engine's heritage took a milestone leap forward in 1968 as the company pulled out all of the stops in Super Stock drag racing. But Chrysler still needed to sell new passenger cars.

To justify building the Hemi as a production engine, Chief Engineer Bob Rodger had estimated selling 4,000 examples per year. However, the 1967 model year, which ended in August, had seen less than 1,500 units built across all three model lines in which the Hemi was offered. So before going back into the Race Hemi packages, let's look at how marketing played a role at the time.

Identifying the Market

Although profitable per unit, the upscale GTX, Coronet R/T, and Charger were all priced out of the range of many buyers. Noticing the exploding muscle car business, executives wanted increased sales. The idea was not to put a Hemi in every garage, but to sell products through dealerships other than, say, Mr. Norm Kraus' operation in Chicago.

After all, Grand-Spaulding Dodge was a hip place in a hip city, and Mr. Norm knew how to sell hot cars to younger buyers. For example, he paid for your plane ticket if you flew to the Windy City and left with a new car contract in your pocket. In fact, Grand-Spaulding even financed, built, and warrantied custom car packages (headers, cams, etc.) because it had the service personnel to do so. A number of moonlighting professional drag racers helped make these mechanical changes behind the scenes at Grand-Spaulding on a piecemeal basis. But beyond all of that, many (but not all) dealerships simply wanted to see the younger floor traffic that the hotter models brought in, and they wanted to sell that audience a car they could afford.

Robert Anderson, Chrysler-Plymouth Division Vice President and General Manager, was determined to figure out his company's market share. During early 1967, Plymouth had created a pyramid chart to define the performance marketplace. This showed four possible buyer groups, with the smallest at the top and the largest base at the bottom. The pinnacle group included the small number of actual big-name racers such as Sox & Martin and Petty Engineering. These were people who competed for a living and bought and did whatever it took to win. Also included were hardcore racers who may not have made a living at racing but lived for racing.

Selling Hemi-powered Road Runners proved that Chrysler had found a winning market combination, with more than 1,000 units built in 1968. Many ended up on the dragstrip, but a lot of others were used and used up on the street. Tony D'Agostino's restoration is more perfect than most assembly-line cars ever were.

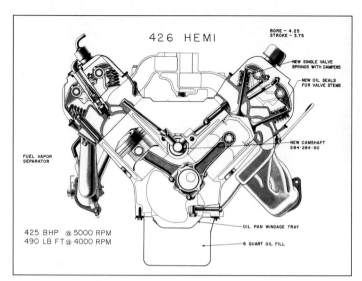

The Street Hemi received some minor changes in 1968, the most notable being the windage tray and deeper oil pan. Cam and valvetrain differences helped to tame the elephant as well. (Photo Courtesy Chrysler Group LLC)

The second group was the weekend drag racer, someone who wanted something to go racing with but was not into it full-time. He or she sacrificed to buy the right stuff. The company's Super Stock packages already covered most of this market share.

Third on the chart was the well-off image buyer, the person for whom the GTX and R/T had been created. This was the buyer who had the wherewithal to buy performance and wanted to have some comfort as well. After all, wives and girlfriends were funny about that stuff.

At the bottom, the largest group was the under-30 guys, with a job and perhaps a family, who watched racing with a passion but also had to watch their wallets. If that guy wanted a big-inch Mopar, the 383-ci Belvedere or Coronet was his budget limit. Or maybe he went down the street to look at a new 350-ci Chevelle, which at least had trim on it that received some attention at the drive-in. Money or not, image matters to car guys.

Chrysler's styling department selected this little black-and-white replica of the Warner Brothers "Road Runner" to illustrate the model name in 1968. More colorful renderings were used on later editions.

Enter the Birds and the Bees

So the plan was formulated to create a performance car for this market. The project fell primarily to Jack Smith and Gordon Cherry of Plymouth's midsize product planning group. The goal was a base model with heavy-duty equipment that could run a 15-second quarter-mile at 100 mph, cost less than $3,000, and have street appeal. The starting point was a reworked version of the 383 in the base Belvedere. Dick Maxwell came up with a plan to integrate the better 440 Magnum components into this engine, which was then re-rated to 335 ponies with little additional expense and tooling.

The 4-speed was standard equipment; the Torqueflite was optional. Just one engine option was available, the Hemi, and the suspension was fitted with performance parts as standard. The hood had some simple chrome callout trim and blackout treatment; otherwise, the car was crisply Spartan. Still, something more was needed to give this machine the kind of street credibility the average two-door Plymouth didn't display.

Thanks to thorough research and interviews by editor Cliff Gromer for *Mopar Action* magazine, the back-story about this car came out. The Madison Avenue suits at Young & Rubicon saw that Pontiac had the LeMans and came up with the moniker LaManche. After Plymouth executives watched a popular cartoon on Saturday morning television, however, they knew that *Road Runner* was the right name.

Once registered with the AMA as a car designation, they gave Warner Brothers a choice: Either license their famous character and get paid or Chrysler could legally design its own variant and Warner Brothers would get nothing. In the end, the Hollywood firm took $50,000 ($10,000 a year for five years) and also received additional money for an advertising campaign, which probably included those cool Dodge Super Bee cartoons as well. The company had hoped to sell 2,500 of them that first year. Instead, it sold 52,000 and pushed that number to more than 80,000 in 1969.

The Road Runner was a real trendsetter for the industry, and ended up on the racetrack with Hemi power. More than 1,000 examples were optioned that way in 1968, making it one of the highest-production bodies for the Street Hemi. Drag racer Lee Smith had one on the track, and so did Ronnie Sox. Richard Petty drove one on the NASCAR circuit, and a lot of young guys who wanted to go racing on either the street or the track found a way to come up with $714 to see that Hemi callout on the hood and own the engine that rumbled underneath. Although not a pure Race Hemi, guys who could skillfully tune this engine found the Road Runner to be a great way to win

Norm Nelson's USAC entry was colorful, making ample use of the notable cartoon in the racing environment. Here it's at the Indianapolis Raceway Park during the sanction's spring event. (Copyright CR Racing Memories 1410006, Ray Mann Photograph)

Dick Landy won NHRA's Winternationals A/MP and Street Eliminator in this 1968 Charger. This car was converted from an early-production standard Charger with an acid-dipped shell and fiberglass front end. It used the 1965 A990 Race Hemi engine and was also driven in AHRA's SS/E heads-up class. (Photo Courtesy Landy Family Collection)

trophies on Sunday afternoons or a quick $50 on Saturday night. And chicks wanted to hear that funny horn.

Missing the cue at first, Dodge realized it needed a similar model and created a slightly more expensive version around the Coronet called Super Bee. Released in early 1968, it used the special 383 (again, Hemi power was the only engine option). The Super Bee, plus the restyled Coronet and Charger R/T models, were the nucleus of the new Scat Pack, a promotional program for Dodge's best performance cars. Also included in the "hive" was the Dart GTS with the new 340 and 383 engines, but a street Dart could not be had with Hemi power.

They Eat Cobra Jets, Don't They?

Ford had been busy during the 1967–1968 offseason. Thanks to a push from *Hot Rod* magazine and a 1967 rebuild project that dealer Robert Tasca of Rhode Island's Tasca Ford had authorized around a 390 Mustang that needed a warranty replacement engine, the 428 Cobra Jet Mustang was created. When the 1968 NHRA season opened at the Winternationals on the Pomona Fairgrounds, Ford made a huge publicity splash with a batch of them in the hands of the company's best drag pilots.

They dominated the SS/E category of Super Stock that weekend as the NHRA left them factored at 335 hp (you know, the same advertised horsepower as the new 383 Road Runner). They won that one class, Al Joniec over Hubert Platt, and on Sunday Joniec downed Dave Wren's SS/DA Max Wedge 1963 Dodge for a clean sweep to the overall Eliminator title. Platt also ran one in C/SA, but he missed the final-round call for class to let Dave Kempton's Max Wedge win.

The Super Stock indexes had changed for 1968: Nothing was legal for SS/A or SS/AA yet (now listed at 5.99 pounds-per-factored-horsepower and under), and SS/F and SS/FA had been added to the fray. More than 100

The Charger proved to be a popular model. This one is at one of Landy's dealership clinic displays. (Photo Courtesy Landy Family Collection)

cars were classed into Super Stock at Pomona for 32 final spots, and Chrysler took 7 of the 10 possible class crowns between the B and F classes. Of the Hemi cars, Ed Miller won SS/B in his World Champion car, Tom Crutchfield's similar 1965 Dodge won SS/BA, and Sox won SS/D in the team's 1967 Hemi GTX.

The real action for Mopar fans, however, was in A/Modified Production (A/MP). Dick Landy raced a 1968 Charger that had been built in September 1967 as a non-R/T factory Hemi 4-speed. The body was acid dipped, with a fiberglass nose. It was created solely for the NHRA's A/MP class and was a true forerunner of what became Pro Stock. The hometown hero from Sherman Oaks took home the class crown with it, and he had also modified it to run in the AHRA's heads-up SS/E category. The Charger, in its second-generation body rendering, proved to be an iconic design for Dodge. At Pomona, Landy was also driving his new 1968 SS/EA 440-ci Dart and beat Gas Rhonda's new Cobra Jet with that car in both the class final and the first round of eliminations.

Pomona was the start of what became a very visible year for the Hemi in drag racing, but the cars that put Chrysler on the map that year were still being finalized. As with the 1967 Hemi package cars, they were not on the racetrack until May, but unlike the prior season, there was nothing street about them.

Dawn of the Factory Hemi A-Body

When the Barracuda and Dart had been completely restyled for 1967, space provisions had been made during development to potentially allow a big-block wedge to become a factory-available option. At the factory's request, Arlen Vanke reworked a set of cast-iron manifolds via cutting and welding for clearance and successfully swapped a 383 engine into a new Barracuda. Soon after, a production version was finalized. Mr. Norm's shop guys also modified a C-Body production exhaust manifold and installed a 383 into a Dart prior to any factory release. After taking it to Detroit to prove it could be done, Dodge followed suit with a 1967 383 GTS. Although it made the cars nose-heavy, the B engine became a midyear option in 1967.

To go one step beyond that, early in the 1968 model year, Norm took the plunge and ordered 50 new Darts with the RB-engine 440 Magnums and A727 Torqueflites. These models were coded with an *M* in the VIN tag and sold only through the Grand-Spaulding franchise. These cars were produced primarily to homologate the package for Super Stock, and the NHRA classified the package into SS/EA.

Hurst Performance converted these cars from standard 383 models at its facility in Madison Heights, Michigan. A handful likely ended up competitive in nighttime combat on the streets of Chicago and elsewhere against other custom rides, such as the Nickey Chevrolet 427 Camaros. Most, however, were turned into race cars like the one Landy used at the Winternationals. Manager Al

Smith of Grand-Spaulding Dodge filed the 50-name list of GSS 440 buyers with the NHRA on January 11, 1968.

In addition to putting the big-block under the hood, the 1967 body change also made it more feasible to install a Race Hemi into either the Barracuda or Dart. Once Dick Maxwell had given this project the go-ahead in late 1967, Tom Hoover assigned a capable young assistant, Robert Tarozzi, to work with Larry Knowlton and Dan Knapp at the Woodward Garage to create a prototype from a 1967 383-ci Barracuda. Tarozzi was gifted at calculating things such as weight balance and performance potential, and, using both hand math and a computer, he figured out exactly what the cars should be capable of doing before a wrench was lifted.

Several factors were paramount to their development: NHRA legality, cost, and shipping. Tom Hoover spelled these out at the time when he wrote a first-person narrative for *Hi-Performance Cars* magazine, which was later reprinted in Martyn Schorr's excellent *Mopar: The Performance Years* book. Tarozzi gave some further background in an extensive interview with me in 1993, which was published by editor Greg Rager in *Mopar Muscle* magazine. "The previous public Super Stock offerings could be driven on the street," Tarozzi recalled at the time, "so this was sort of the crucial point in terms of product planning. They were deciding to take the major step and just build an all-out race car that you couldn't register or put on the street."

Indeed, a primary challenge was reducing the weight to about 3,100 pounds for the 500-hp factor that the NHRA had now put on the 1965 Race Hemi engine package; it settled in at the very top of SS/B by about 6.1 pounds. For this reason, by using fiberglass extensively

This is the original 426 Hemi Plymouth Barracuda used as the test mule for the 1968 Super Stock Hemi packages. Bob Tarozzi and Larry Knowlton assembled it at the Woodward Garage, and Myron Serbay now owns it.

The cross-ram returned in the 1968 race package, but used iron heads instead of aluminum versions to keep it heavy enough for SS/B, whose minimum weight was 6.00 pounds per horsepower. The engine was factored at 500 hp, the same as 1964 and 1965 versions.

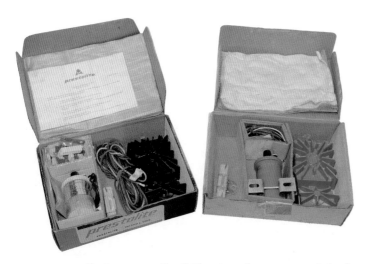

Factory-installed on virtually all Hemi package cars, original boxed Prestolite ignition kits are rare. The black box version (left) was used on cars through 1967. The 1968 cars used the blue box transistor (right). Both 1967 and 1968 cars used the factory dual-point distributor design but the kit limited the spark problems inherent to the point-style design. These examples were provided by Kramer Automotive.

This 1969 photo shows the layout of the original exhaust system, which was mandated by the NHRA rules to remain intact. There was not much to it. (Bill Tanner Photo, Courtesy Frank Wiley Archive, Kramer Automotive Print/ Film Collection)

in place of sheet metal, the iron heads could remain on this rendition of the Race Hemi. This also helped meet the issues of cost, as they could use the standard Street Hemi castings already being put together on the engine assembly line.

Tom Hoover recounted a further, more critical point: "At that time, I believe the tooling for the aluminum heads was gone; we would have had to redo that and it would have been very expensive. That was a much bigger factor than just getting the cars to weigh right for B-class. We also had to sell them for the 1968 season, so the timing needed for new tools just to make that head did not make sense, either."

Overall construction of these engines went back to Chrysler Marine & Industrial at Marysville where

the engine received a magnesium cross-ram with two 770-cfm Holley race carbs (R4235 and R4236), similar in design to those last used in 1965 on the A990 package. The compression was increased to the old 12.5 standard. As in 1967, the package also received the Prestolite transistorized ignition and viscous fan.

Because the cars were strictly for off-road use, no production-type exhaust manifold was needed. Hooker was given the job of fabricating the headers for the cars, which were, in turn, coupled to an exhaust system. This consisted of 2.5-inch pipe and blow-through glass-pack mufflers that ended in turn-down ends just in front of the rear axle (the presence of a physical exhaust system was still mandated by the NHRA rules). Knowing that drag racers have their own tricks, the Street Hemi cam remained in the block, and the stock oil pan was left in place for ease of shipping. It was highly recommended to replace it with a deep-sump race unit before running the car. All the preproduction testing was done with a deep-sump pan and Racer Brown camshaft.

John Bauman, who was the Chrysler go-to guy on carburetion and airflow, came up with a large,

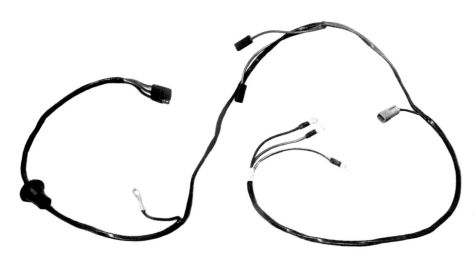

The Prestolite wiring harness was recommended until being superseded by the Mopar electronic ignition and distributor. If you're redoing an original car, however, note that the Chrysler version seen here (provided by Kramer Automotive) was not included in generic kits.

ROOSTER TALES: DRAG BOAT PROWESS

In Les Brown's garage, engines legal for H-class/later GP class were supercharged methanol-burning A102 types at the 426 displacement. Note that they are still using the K-head valve covers and used cast-iron heads. (Photo Courtesy Ray Jackson)

As expected, the same horsepower that was capable of winning races on land was put to use on water. In fact, one of the biggest and oldest boat racing events on the circuit was the Gold Cup races held on the Detroit River each summer. Once available in quantity, the 426 Hemi was pressed into duty in both the straight-line drag boat and oval-course water racing by several independents.

Racing boats are divided into two basic designs. The faster three-point hydroplanes are twin-hulled and ride almost atop the water. Just the outboard sponsons' edges and part of the propeller are submerged between the tunnel they create under the boat The deeper V- or flat-bottom designs use a handle or pedals to operate metal cavitation plates to help level or turn the craft. Racing is normally from a moving start in both disciplines.

The factory was not overtly involved in drag boat racing. But it had an ally in Keith Black, the West Coast power guru who serviced drag and closed-course boat racers on the West Coast before and during his ascent as the authority in blown fuel engine building. As with the nitro-powered land drag cars, those versions that burned fuel inevitably ended up with Hemi power.

Closed-circuit racing is on a surveyed oval course of a mile or more in circumference, and different classes race on these circuits. Some classes, such as the Gold Cup, race on a short course within a longer course. Rivers and lakes are the common venues for this type of racing, with five-lap heats to qualify for position and a top speed recorded before the final race.

Bill Sterett of Kentucky and the Miss Chrysler team in the Unlimited Hydroplane class were among the notables. Following the craft's debut in June of 1966, Sterett and his crew were plagued by various problems, but Keith Black's crew was called in to help. They had sorted things out enough by the summer of 1967 to not just win but dominate the Union Internationale Motonautique (UMI) World Championships (not Gold Cup) at Detroit that July, winning both heats and the event for a perfect 1,200-point score. Notably, this remains the only time an automotive-propelled boat has won an Unlimited Hydro event (most Unlimited competitors ran surplus aircraft turbines).

In 1968, Sterett turned to an aircraft design, won the 1969 Gold Cup at Detroit, and promptly retired from a sport that had become quite dangerous due to the increased speeds.

Les Brown had dominated the SK Runabout class for flat-bottom ski-boats and had been instrumental in getting the class started in 1959 with early unblown Hemi power. For a time, a 426 Hemi run by Duff Daily dominated the unblown 7-Liter Grand National class. Brown's single-engine SK flat-bottom named *Long Gone* was quite a step down from the Sterett unlimited hydroplanes, but that would change.

"By the 1970s, we were the only boat that ran a Hemi in the biggest, fastest Limited Hydroplane class, against about 20 big-block Chevies," remembers Ray Jackson, who crewed on *Long Gone*. Les Brown was the only one, with a single-engine H-class hydroplane, to receive factory backing from Chrysler, though it was only for a short time. "This was through Ray Nichels over in Indiana, and we got blocks and parts from them; that was where I saw the first set of 16-plug heads," Jackson says.

Based on the rules, the cast-iron A102 block was used at the standard 426 inches; when the rules were superseded by the GP class, it became a 500-ci limit. Les and his son/crew chief Ron Brown used a blown-alcohol design for the most part, but also ran a couple of races using nitromethane and had a blown-nitrous combination for a while as well. By then the boats had become lighter, competition was tighter, and the engine's physical weight became an issue.

"The Hemis weighed more, but they put out more," adds Jackson. "I mean, when we put the nitrous on it, Ron used a pretty ingenious method. He centered the switch in an old valvespring and put that under the throttle pedal; the driver was at almost full throttle and felt the resistance. You really needed it coming out of the corner, and once he pushed that down and got to full throttle, the nitrous hit that thing. It sounded like it was going to rip the back of the boat off!"

Later, pilot Kent McPhail set a Grand Prix Class 5-mile heat record on a 1.67-mile course of 105.700 in 1981, still using the 426-ci displacement against much larger competitors. *Long Gone* won the 1982 Grand Prix Class National High Point Championship with McPhail as well. One of those boat engines, a 1970 NASCAR mill from Nichels, is now in Ray Jackson's street-driven 1965 Belvedere. Ron Brown ended up as crew chief on *Miss Budweiser*, whose turbine-powered efforts gave it six Gold Cup titles.

This is Long Gone *at speed. (Photo Courtesy Ray Jackson)*

"Near the end, almost when Les retired, one more guy came into GP with a Hemi in an older Lauterbach-design boat, with the driver behind the engine. It went fast on the straights, but didn't turn worth a darn," according to Jackson.

During a Hemi car reunion in 1993, engineer Bob Tarozzi revisited his seat in the original factory mule. His careful calculations made the cars competitive almost immediately.

aggressive scoop. Measuring 4 inches high, 34 inches wide, and 24.5 inches deep, this new design was tall enough to allow fresh air that had not been tumbled across the turbulent boundary layer on the top of the hood to enter the pair of cross-ram-separated offset carbs. The scoop held enough air volume to meet any engine demand. In the *Hi-Performance Cars* magazine story, Hoover admitted it had been about 18 months in development. Bauman's subsequent testing in this matter resulted in a scoop design with a raised lower lip to block out the boundary air layer entirely. This ended up on the 440 Six Pack street cars released the following model year.

From Tarozzi's calculations, the plan was to get as much weight as possible moved off the front half of the car despite the 750-pound engine. The hood with scoop and front fenders would be fiberglass, with the doors and front bumper stamped from lighter-gauge steel (not acid dipped as sometimes stated). The doors would also use special lightweight glass from Corning with a piece of seatbelt strap used in place of a roll-type mechanism. A button-snap would hold it closed. The fixed rear-quarter

windows were also of the .090-thick glass. Inside would be the lightest seats Chrysler made (for the A100 Dodge van) with hole-sawed nonadjustable aluminum mounting plates. There was no provision for a rear-seat passenger.

When it was all done, almost 380 pounds had been removed to get the cars to just more than 3,000 pounds.

The men worked over the winter at the Woodward Garage to build the prototype, machining what was not available off the shelf. An export-design four-piston-caliper 4.5-inch manual disc layout went under the front end, using 14 x 5.5 rims and D70-14 tires. There was no room for a power brake booster and hardly enough for the master cylinder. The car used the standard rear Hemi drums that were already on the differential (which was selected based on transmission choice); this differential was the standard B-Body width.

For clearance in the A-Body wheelhouse, positive-offset 15-inch steel rear rims were added to the package, with 7.75 x 15 tires. If you wanted a radio or heater, you were in the wrong business, and once again there was no sound deadener, body seam sealer, or warranty. Indeed, a special "Not for Highway Use" disclaimer decal was placed in the doorjamb between the two hinges, although a handful of these cars eventually found their way onto the street.

Tarozzi took special pleasure in calculating the proper rear spring rates and weights prior to construction. He had the suspension lab work up some calculations, did some figuring, and verified the results on a computer. The resultant spring had excellent load and proportioning, to the extent that the package did not rely on additional control pieces to prevent axle windup. A special multi-leaf package was created to those specifications just for this car.

SOX & MARTIN PRESENT THE PLYMOUTH SUPERCAR CLINIC

Ronnie Sox ran this Road Runner in the early part of the 1968 season. Herb McCandless also drove it, but it was never an overly competitive car. This handout card shows Ronnie and Buddy Martin at the start of the 1968 season.

Tommy Erwin was at AHRA's first Spring Nationals at Bristol, Tennessee, to see the brand-new Sox & Martin Hemi Barracuda coming into the pits. This June event is considered the first place the cars appeared formally, although Dick Landy's Dart was seen at the Hot Rod Magazine drags earlier that season. (Photo Courtesy Tommy Erwin Archive; University of South Carolina 018__1968)

Once installed with proper driveline parts, the mule car weighed and behaved pretty much as Tarozzi had predicted. As the weight was wanted in back, the standard-weight rear bumper, and OEM steel deck lid were used, and a heavy truck battery was mounted in a metal tray behind the right rear tire. Heavy-duty shocks took care of the rest. Up front, the special K-member engine support for these bodies was installed with spacers between it and the unibody structure, which lowered the engine about an inch.

The Hemi was to be dropped in from above rather than installed from beneath, as happens on the assembly line. However, the elephant engine's physical width had to be addressed and Tarozzi figured out changes for each side of the engine bay.

First, the passenger-side inner fender and upper control arm mount were reworked so the valve cover could be taken off without unbolting the engine mounts and raising the powerplant. Fabricators modified the shock mount by cutting through it, heating it, bending it, and then rebrazing the fix. It was rather crude in appearance but it worked. Also, a special plate was created to offset the brake master cylinder and move it outboard on the driver's side to gain clearance for the back of the valve cover. Because the master cylinder still needed to be unbolted to service the engine, flexible brakes lines were installed.

Testing and Production

According to original paperwork in David Hakim's collection, Dick Maxwell sent the proposed plan to the NHRA's Bill Dismuke on December 7, 1967. In it, he gave the basic information and suggested the cars would be optioned to use either the cross-ram or inline Street Hemi intake and noted that the rear wheel openings would be modified for 10-inch tires. They were again called business coupes because they would feature just two seats.

A response from Dismuke on the matter dated December 27 noted that the package was acceptable, but that the tires could not extend out of the top-third of the wheel well, and that NHRA would require 50 of each example (cross-ram and inline intake models), should the engine package be optional. In the end, the Darts had some rear wheel opening trim work done, and the offset 15-inch rims kept the tires tucked in tight; the Barracuda design had enough clearance already. The inline manifold option was dropped. The only option available at the time of purchase was the driveline.

Before production was finalized, extensive testing was performed in January with the mule Barracuda at Irwindale Raceway in California. From those tests, B&M created and built a new race converter based on the A-Body's weight for the Torqueflite models. This car featured a reverse valve body, Hemi high-performance engine parts, and a 4.86 Sure-Grip rear gear in the 8¾ rear housing out back. The 4-speed models received the slick-shift treatment, a cast-steel bellhousing, and 10.5-inch clutch, and they were backed by the Dana 60 truck differential with 4.88 gearing.

Because he had a background in road racing, Tarozzi was the test driver at Irwindale. He immediately discovered the K-frame changes had resulted in some handling issues. Under power with soft rear slicks, the car wanted to dance around due to the amount the nose had been raised, so he recommended that a new steering arm be created as well. This idea did not take hold until after the cars were under construction. The package was finalized, and Brian Schram in the product planning department began the parts procurement process for the race car program. The groundwork had been solid; the only big change following the test was for the updated steering arm.

Building the A-Bombs

Although the NHRA made noise about cars being assembly-line built, interpretation on how final finish was done was pretty open. As mentioned, for the 440 Darts, the company had used a conversion service offered by Hurst Industries in Madison Heights, Michigan. Hurst was now contracted to build the Hemi cars and subsequently created a temporary conversion facility in an older industrial building in Ferndale to do the work.

The 383 models for 1968 were batch-built at the Hamtramck, Michigan, assembly plant in two groups, one

This is a restored example of one of Dick Landy's Hemi Darts. The Landy operation raced versions of this body with both 440 and 426 Hemi power in 1968.

on February 18 and one on May 21. They left the plant incomplete; without engines, transmissions, front-end sheet metal, and in code 999 special primer paint. Towed individually about 8 miles to the Hurst plant by a standard hook-style wrecker, they were mechanically finished and then taken to a nearby plant parking lot for distribution.

At Hurst, the front-end engine installation changes were accomplished, the Hemi engines installed, and the OEM doors replaced by special units. On the Darts, the rear wheel well openings were modified for additional tire clearance using a template to cut and fold the metal back. The gel-coated fiberglass parts went on last, and the cars, now a combination of gray metal and black fiberglass, were soon on their way to new owners, many of whom drove to Detroit to pick them up personally.

On February 14, 1968, Dodge dealers were given the option to order these cars through confidential bulletin #12. With the initial batch of cars off the assembly line and brought to Hurst on February 18, Plymouth followed suit with a public press release dated February 20. Unlike other manufacturers, there was no need to have a private phone line to Detroit to qualify to buy one of the special packages, but the first cars went to factory-favored drivers before the remainder were sold to regional offices and dealerships.

The announcement for the Plymouth models, distributed by National Sales Manager R. D. McLaughlin, ended tersely and stated that any customer orders required a signed disclaimer that they understood that the cars were not highway legal and were sold without warranty. The actual Dodge paperwork for that warranty disclaimer, in the Chuck Comella paper collection, shows it needed to be signed by both the ordering dealer and the car's purchaser. Incidentally, Comella purchased his Dart late in 1968 with an engine that had been blown up at the dealership, and he did not race it until almost 1970.

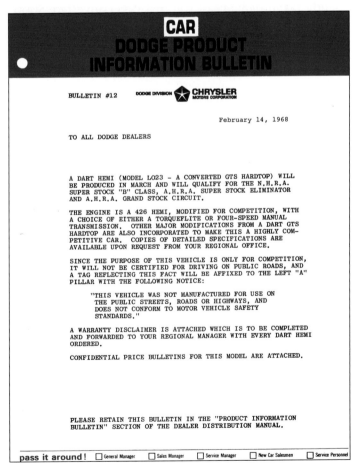

CAR

DODGE PRODUCT INFORMATION BULLETIN

BULLETIN #12   DODGE DIVISION ◆ CHRYSLER MOTORS CORPORATION

February 14, 1968

TO ALL DODGE DEALERS

A DART HEMI (MODEL LO23 - A CONVERTED GTS HARDTOP) WILL BE PRODUCED IN MARCH AND WILL QUALIFY FOR THE N.H.R.A. SUPER STOCK "B" CLASS, A.H.R.A. SUPER STOCK ELIMINATOR AND A.H.R.A. GRAND STOCK CIRCUIT.

THE ENGINE IS A 426 HEMI, MODIFIED FOR COMPETITION, WITH A CHOICE OF EITHER A TORQUEFLITE OR FOUR-SPEED MANUAL TRANSMISSION. OTHER MAJOR MODIFICATIONS FROM A DART GTS HARDTOP ARE ALSO INCORPORATED TO MAKE THIS A HIGHLY COMPETITIVE CAR. COPIES OF DETAILED SPECIFICATIONS ARE AVAILABLE UPON REQUEST FROM YOUR REGIONAL OFFICE.

SINCE THE PURPOSE OF THIS VEHICLE IS ONLY FOR COMPETITION, IT WILL NOT BE CERTIFIED FOR DRIVING ON PUBLIC ROADS, AND A TAG REFLECTING THIS FACT WILL BE AFFIXED TO THE LEFT "A" PILLAR WITH THE FOLLOWING NOTICE:

"THIS VEHICLE WAS NOT MANUFACTURED FOR USE ON THE PUBLIC STREETS, ROADS OR HIGHWAYS, AND DOES NOT CONFORM TO MOTOR VEHICLE SAFETY STANDARDS."

A WARRANTY DISCLAIMER IS ATTACHED WHICH IS TO BE COMPLETED AND FORWARDED TO YOUR REGIONAL MANAGER WITH EVERY DART HEMI ORDERED.

CONFIDENTIAL PRICE BULLETINS FOR THIS MODEL ARE ATTACHED.

PLEASE RETAIN THIS BULLETIN IN THE "PRODUCT INFORMATION BULLETIN" SECTION OF THE DEALER DISTRIBUTION MANUAL.

pass it around!   ☐ General Manager   ☐ Sales Manager   ☐ Service Manager   ☐ New Car Salesmen   ☐ Service Personnel

The press release dated February 14, 1968, for the Dodge Dart program stated the non-warranty/non-street legal information for potential buyers. (Photo Courtesy David Hakim Collection)

As mentioned earlier, a handful of the Hurst cars ended up on the street. This Dart is owned by Daryl Klassen and is tagged. He has made some accommodation for the less-forgiving highway environment, such as better air cleaners.

Steve Comella launches Chuck Comella's Dart at the 2014 Gatornationals. Chuck bought the car with a blown engine in it from the dealership in 1968. It is one of the very few original Hurst cars still being raced today.

In the end, approximately 150 examples were built through the Hurst method: 70 of the Plymouth body code BO29 Barracudas and 80 to 84 of the Dodge body-code LO23 Darts. Part of this difference was due to the fact that Grand-Spaulding Dodge ordered 22 Darts itself, as Mr. Norm wanted to have a variety available for his customers. Plus, he had orders from several noted Midwestern Dodge campaigners. Tragedy almost struck when a fire broke out at the Grand-Spaulding dealership garage while 18 of them were under conversion into race cars for delivery. Thankfully none were lost.

This is not to say there were no problems. Owners who purchased 1965 model Super Stocks quickly found out that these were not similar to the "take off the trailer and go" packages. List price was initially stated as $5,495; dealer wholesale was reportedly $4,200 to $4,400 based on delivery charges. Author Jim Schild has found MSRP retail figures of $5,214 for the Plymouth and $5,146 for the Dodge. These Darts and Barracudas really did need to be blueprinted before competing.

In addition to the cam and oil pan swaps, one major issue was with the color-anodized hex-head cap screws used in the cross-ram intake. The three sizes were very similar in length and had been color-coded so they could be easily distinguished by sight. However, the anodizing process made the gold screws fragile. Their heads simply broke off at any uncertain moment and they could be ingested into the combustion chamber with very bad results. This was discovered as the racers picked up the cars, and a couple of engines reportedly blew up while being loaded onto trailers.

Dave Koffel, a racer from Ohio and a metallurgist by trade, had just come to work for Chrysler and was given the job of addressing this problem, getting parts out to racers, and making sure that any cars yet to be delivered

were changed over. He remembers that he also had to figure out what to do with all the heavy OEM doors that had been removed from the assembly-line cars.

Due to the evolving handling issues, the replacement steering arm was shipped to some owners who had already taken delivery of the first cars converted. Shortages in the fiberglass parts supply chain resulted in a few Darts delivered minus hoods or fenders; those parts were then shipped later.

Bombers from Burlington and Lots from Landy

Again, Sox & Martin built the team's first A-Body Hemi by hand. *Super Stock & Drag Illustrated* magazine editor Jim McCraw traveled to Burlington, North Carolina, to watch Jake King assemble the team's first Hemi Barracuda, which had begun life as a 1968 383 model and was scheduled for its first clinic appearance at the New York Auto Show the following weekend. It is not known

This is an original Sox & Martin 1968 Barracuda now owned by Clark and Colleen Rand. Several of the Hemi Barracudas this team raced still exist. This one is now painted the same as when Sox raced it at the 1969 World Finals, which he won.

The engine was fitted into the bay by moving the master cylinder toward the passenger's side using a plate. At Tarozzi's directions, employees at Hurst also dimpled the passenger-side shock tower to allow access to the valve cover and header bolts. (Photo Courtesy John Stunkard)

Here is the relocated master cylinder and plate.

whether this car was first converted by Hurst or was a full Sox & Martin shop conversion from a real BO29-tagged Formula S body and Hurst simply supplied parts in the interest of time. The car was first tested in May at Cecil County, with Tarozzi and others on hand.

Sox & Martin was *the* biggest component of whatever was being done by Plymouth's drag racing program, and in addition to the clinics, the team was fielding several cars at each event. The new SS/B Barracuda basically replaced the 1968 Hemi Road Runner that had been put together early in the year; that car was not raced extensively because it had no fresh-air provision. The other

Inside, you can see just how basic the interior package was: two small bucket seats and a few extra gauges. Note the drilled aluminum seat supports.

Race Hemi still in the stable was the homebuilt 1967 GTX, now running in SS/D.

Herb McCandless was integral to the Sox & Martin operation through the Pro Stock years and in Mopar circles was known as Mr. 4-Speed. He was now usually in some vehicle for the team on race day: the Hemi Road Runner or the clinic program 1968 440 GTX (whose weight pushed it down into SS/F). A clinic 340 Barracuda could also run E/SA in Stock Eliminator, and *Hot Rod* magazine staffer Jim McFarland drove this car to runner-up honors at the 1968 Winternationals.

Landy likewise had a Hemi Dart in his shop that was blueprinted for SS/BA, in addition to the SS/DA 1967 Coronet, his SS/EA M-code 440 Dart, and the clinic program's SS/FA 1968 Coronet R/T. However, the new Hemi Charger was his most notable entry of the season, immortalized by several color magazine features. The NHRA A/MP-AHRA SS/E machine was a full-tilt race car that was closer to Ultra Stock on the NASCAR or UDRA heads-up circuits, and used the cross-ram intake and aluminum heads from 1965.

Indeed, in 1968 the factory decided that the car Landy drove would run in the more radical Street and Modified Eliminator classes, while Sox would contend for the crowns in legal Super Stock. It is sometimes suggested that Dick Landy didn't win much in Super Stock. That was partly because that was not where he always raced, even though the Landy team usually ran one of its Darts in competition after those cars arrived, often under the tutelage of Bob Lambeck.

The trunk in the 1968 model again featured a heavy truck battery mounted just behind the passenger-side rear tire, where torque from the engine could be used to the greatest advantage.

Restored examples of the as-raced 1968 cars have become popular, with many being converted back to vintage authentic appearances after a career in racing. This is the old Speedwin Automotive Engineering Dart that was often seen in advertising in Cars magazine at one of the York U.S. 30 reunions in Pennsylvania.

Both the Landy and Sox & Martin programs were in great demand by the dealership and show car circuits; to get around, air travel had become a must for the star drivers. Part of the reason for having so many cars was that there were usually vehicles on tour at all times during the racing season. Full-time employees worked both in their shops and on the clinic tour; these teams had become the business professionals of drag racing.

The clinics proved to be so popular that they were expanded into several regions with new presenters during the 1968 season. These were not the same deals that the two big-name teams had; they were mostly contract programs for parts, appearance money, and expense money. Still, it was an honor to be one of the clinic demonstrators. Dodge added a full clinic program for Bill Tanner out of Lenox Dodge in the Atlanta region, plus other contract racers doing mostly local clinics. The Plymouth group now included Sox & Martin plus contracted racers Arlen Vanke, Ed Miller, Dave Koffel, Wiley Cossey, and Don Grotheer who, like Tanner, received a full factory deal.

On with the Show

Due to adjustments in the rules for qualifying and breakouts, an anonymous writer in *Super Stock & Drag Illustrated* magazine stated wryly in late 1967, "P. S. Disconnect your brake light switch and put new brakes on your racer. You'll probably need 'em this year." The result was exactly that; in many handicap class eliminator races, locked-up-tire smoke was visible as cars tried to not go below their index, which now resulted in disqualification, even of the winner.

After the mandatory 30-day waiting period, the Race Hemi A-Bodies first showed up at the NHRA 1968 Springnationals in mid-June. This event had moved from Bristol to the Madison Township Raceway Park in Englishtown, New Jersey, after the Tennessee track switched to the AHRA sanction for the new season. The NHRA used a system of low-qualifier plus class winner to create a 32-car field. Sox throttled them with a hot 10.54 low best on the base 11.05 SS/B record in his new 'Cuda and then took the class title as well with non-breakout driving skill. This was an ongoing challenge for Chrysler in NHRA racing, as Sox had two possible "ins" (Low ET and Class), which potentially left out another Chrysler on race day.

The West Coast's Wiley Cossey drove his 1967 Hemi RO-package car to the SS/C crown to put Jenkins' Camaro out of the program in class. Hemi cars also took class wins in SS/BA (Larry Cooper's Dart) and SS/CA (Joe Avrey's 1967 Plymouth). Other Hemi cars were seeded via their qualifying efforts, and enough new SS/B and SS/BA A-Bodies had hit below the fresh record indexes that even Jenkins' *Grumpy's Toy* was kept on the trailer for Sunday's eliminations.

For the eliminator on Sunday, however, the .10-break-out rule was in effect: go quicker than the record minus .10 second and you were disqualified, period, even if it was a heads-up challenge between identically classed cars. Brake-smoke pandemonium ensued, as every driver tried to gauge performance and the finish line. Then in round two, Sox had a slick literally spin off the rim while racing Hubert Platt's Mustang. Melvin Yow had been advancing in the team's SS/D 1967 Hemi GTX, however, and Sox overtook that car.

By the semifinals, it was all Mopars at E-town: Sox's year-old Hemi GTX beat the Landy team's SS/EA 440 Dart

The new Hemi Dodge Darts also came out for the AHRA Spring Nationals. Tommy Erwin captured Dick Smith's virtually stock-appearing example on the weigh scales, still with steel wheels. (Photo Courtesy Tommy Erwin Archive; University of South Carolina 019_1968)

The 4-speed Rumble Bee was another early runner, backed by Cogdill Motor Company. Whether at rest or under power, the reshaped rear wheel opening is very evident. (Photo Courtesy Tommy Erwin Archive; University of South Carolina 044__1968)

driven by Bob Lambeck, and Don Grotheer's new *Cable Car* SS/B 'Cuda trailered Avrey's RO Hemi Belvedere car to set up the final.

Sox moved to the lead, Grotheer chased him to the lights, and both drivers were under their indexes. Sox was least offensive with an 11.20 on the GTX's 11.39 SS/D index, while Grotheer arrived there first by running 10.82 on the 11.05 SS/B number. Although technically both were out, NHRA Director Jack Hart stepped in, declared Sox the winner, and another $4,000 was on its way to Burlington, North Carolina.

Sox had actually begun to establish the Hemi Barracuda in the record books even at this early date. At Bristol's first AHRA race, held earlier in June, *The Boss* 'Cuda had won a special heads-up Super Stock bracket on Saturday night, beating Winternationals champ Al Joniec's Mustang (now using the NASCAR tunnel-port equipment) with a 10.68 in the mountainous altitude on Saturday. In Sunday's Grand Stock handicap race, Sox again put them all on the trailer to beat Dan Smoker's 1965 A990 Plymouth in the final.

As mentioned, the first Sox & Martin Barracuda was hand-built by Jake King and it was truly a blueprinted machine even at this early date. During the following season, Sox went on to show how good a package Hoover and company had designed, despite new ZL1 and L72 427-ci Camaros from Chevy and some serious competition from both Ford and AMC.

The Big Go and World Finals

Over Labor Day at Indy in 1968, when all the West Coast teams also showed up, it was a real invasion in SS/B, but qualifying was something of a debacle. After Englishtown, the NHRA decided that to prevent brake-lights and sandbagging, the lowest elapsed time recorded in the

class elimination finals (winner or runner-up) would now be the new National Record and subsequent racing index. Also, there would be no breakout rule during Monday's final round (the .10 breakout was in effect until the final). Moreover, that number would be left as the new record following Indy.

It seemed like a perfect plan, except that nobody wanted to hammer that index regardless, and either under factory edict or personal will, the brake-light folly continued. The factory had an open test session at Muncie Dragway on Tuesday for guys to help get ready for the big event; tech at Indy started the next day.

The SS/B record stood at 10.83 Thursday morning and showed it was ripe for picking when Sox came off the trailer with a blistering 10.42 to take the top qualifying spot. During class, Sox and Wiley Cossey ended up in an all-Barracuda SS/B final, when Sox, already in the field, was told by the factory to red light so that Cossey could run it soft and be guaranteed a spot on Monday as the SS/B class winner. Sox, ever a competitor, showed his displeasure by leaving on the second yellow and then running it out the back door to a 10.55.

Mary Ann Foss (née Jackson) is seen at Indy in 1968 alongside the new Go Hummer II Dart. A number of female drivers ended up driving Hurst Hemi package cars. (Photo Courtesy Pit Slides Archive, quartermilestones.com)

Seen here at Dallas in 1969, Gary Ostrich was the class winner in SS/BA at the 1968 U.S. Nationals. He was able to save the index in the final as already-qualified Jack Werst deliberately lost so Ostrich did not need to run flat-out for the class title. (Photo Courtesy Ray Mann Archive, quartermilestones.com)

Arlen Vanke won the U.S. Nationals in 1968 to become the first driver to pilot a Hemi A-Body to a win in Super Stock. Don Grotheer had posted a runner-up to Sox's 1967 GTX at the Springnationals in Englishtown six weeks earlier. Akron Arlen is seen here at Indy during early eliminations on Monday. (Photo Courtesy Ray Mann Archive, quartermilestones.com)

Foul or not, that fast number would have been the new hard-to-meet index, so Sox didn't cross the scales or go to teardown. The fastest SS/B car on the planet was quietly withdrawn from competition and sat in a hotel parking lot soon after; Sox eventually drove the team's class-winning SS/D 1967 GTX on Monday, the same car he drove at Englishtown for the win. Incidentally, the GTX was already sold, to be delivered to its new owners at the end of this event.

Racing for the SS/BA title (which had an even softer 11.06 record) were two other Barracudas. Gary Ostrich won class when Jack Werst, the factory warranty rep from Philadelphia known as "Mr. 5 & 50," deliberately rolled off onto the track apron in the final to eliminate his already-qualified entry so Ostrich did not need to hit the number to win. This was the racing politics of the era, but the drivers were not always willing participants, not even Werst, whose paychecks were signed by Chrysler.

In Monday's finals, trap speeds as low as 62 mph followed top-end tire smoke, but several drivers, including Sox, Ostrich, and John Hagan, still lost on breakouts. Six Mopars and two Chevrolets were left by the Super Stock quarterfinals.

Working his way up one side of the ladder was Arlen Vanke and a new SS/B 'Cuda, which made it into the final round by beating Jenkins in the semis. He would be racing Wally Booth, whose Detroit-based SS/E 396 Camaro took down Dodge contract racer Dick "Barney" Oldfield in the Good Guys Dart in the other semifinal. For the fame and money, with Booth clocking a losing 11.44, Vanke put a Race Hemi A-Body into an NHRA winner's circle for the first time with a 10.64. As a direct result of that race, both drivers' national records were hit as well, which kept some of the better 4-speed cars out of the World Finals in Tulsa.

At Beaver Springs Dragway in 2006 Bill Stiles launches in his original 1968 Barracuda, now restored, which was a heavy hitter on the Division 1 circuit in 1968. Unfortunately, racing politics played a role during his trip to the 1968 World Finals in Tulsa and he was disqualified on a minor cylinder head infraction after resetting the national record he already held.

That season-ending event in Oklahoma also dealt in Super Stock politics. Bill Stiles had qualified on top with a 10.95 in his Barracuda on the SS/BA 11.06 index (a record he had set earlier). When he went to back that number up for a new record, he registered a rear-wheel start that sent the timers to an extreme 10.66. Perhaps providentially, his heads were conveniently determined illegal in teardown despite having not been changed since the start of his engine program.

Grumpy Jenkins, who was the first alternative, was now back in the program in his SS/C Camaro, which was also convenient, because Chevrolet Product Planning rep Vince Piggins was getting a special manufacturers' award from Wally Parks at this meet. All Bill Stiles earned was a long ride back home to Pennsylvania.

Jenkins' Camaro lost to Judy Lilly's SS/BA Barracuda in round two, but Lilly lost on a breakout to the SS/D Jenkins Competition 396-ci Nova that Ed Hedrick was driving. In the semifinals, Jenkins himself drove the Nova to

Considered one of the most beautiful of the 1968 Hurst-built cars, this is John Hagan's Barracuda from Minnesota. This photo was taken at the NHRA World Finals in 1969. (Photo Courtesy Ray Mann Archive, quartermilestones.com)

Former sprint car racer "Big Al" Graeber issued this postcard in 1968 to promote his new Charger, burning nitromethane on a nighttime pass at York U.S. 30. He may have done this exhibition solely for a publicity photo, as he is not wearing fire gloves. Al had been part of the Hemi FX revolution since 1965, having quit open-wheel driving because of its dangers.

a win over Don Grotheer, the last Mopar standing. The Grump faced off against Dave Strickler's 302-powered SS/F Z28 in the all-Chevy final, a race that Strickler won to earn the 1968 Super Stock World Championship. The Grump's 1967 Camaro, the former Indy winner now modified for match racing with an L88 Corvette engine and running in A/MP, lost to Fred Hurst's new A/GS injected Hemi Barracuda in the Street Eliminator division final, leaving Jenkins as bridesmaid in World Championship action yet again.

Fuel Racing

For racers of nitro-powered combinations, Garlits' 1967 Indy victory had been a huge boost for the 426 fuel engine. The main thing that kept a lot of dragster owners and drivers in their 392-ci designs was economy, being comfortable with more familiar tune-up combinations, and perhaps also mere stubbornness. When Garlits did it again in 1968, winning both the Springnationals and Indy, Top Fuelers began to make the switch to the late-model engine.

Although conversions in the dragster ranks were slow but steady, a vast majority of the Funny Car campaigners, at least those with Chrysler body styles, had already moved to the 426 architecture. Parts were abundant, performances were equal or better than what else was available, and increased potential had arrived in the form of better tires and more serious speed equipment. One shift in the nitro car ranks during 1968 was the use of slipper clutches and direct-drive units in place of worked-up Torqueflites. Coupled with new tires from M&H and Goodyear, speeds for the Funny Cars were pushing into the 190s by the end of the season.

By far the most popular Dodge body for Funny Car racing was now the new Charger, which could be had in standard width and, by 1969, the match race–type

mini (narrowed) format. Several teams made the transition to this design, and also began doing minor home-made aero work, mounting the rear window flush and flush-mounting either a fake grille or a piece of clear plexiglass over the OEM inset covered-headlight design, and a rear deck spoiler. A few notable Chargers during 1968 and 1969 with the changes included the popular *Mr. Norms* and *Chi-Town Hustler* fuel cars from the Midwest, the *L.A. Hooker* and *Super Chief* examples of the West Coast, and the new Bob Banning gas-burner and *Tickle Me Pink* (Al Graeber) home-built nitro entry in the East.

Gene Snow had a new 1968 Dart built early in the year, but he replaced that body with a Charger shell. Blown on nitro, the car is remembered as the first car to legitimately surpass the 200-mph barrier. Snow coupled a direct-drive Crowerglide setup with the sea-level air at the Gay family's Houston area racetrack on August 17 to go 200.88. He backed it up with several additional runs in the following months.

Fred Goeske's Road Runner was a one-off body created at the insistence of the Southern California Plymouth Dealers Association, which backed his efforts. This is the cover of the 1969 Cavalcade of Stars publicity folder. (Photo Courtesy Terry Ross/Mike Goyda)

In the Plymouth ranks, the Barracuda was the weapon of choice at this time, driven by up-and-coming drivers such as Clare Sanders (*Lime Fire*), Rich Siroonian (in Big John Mazmanian's entry), Don Schumacher (*Stardust*), and Larry Reyes (*Super 'Cuda*). Fred Goeske, still with backing from the Southern California Plymouth Dealers Association, had a one-off 1968 Hemi Road Runner Funny Car on fuel; this car became part of the new Coca-Cola Cavalcade of Stars Funny Car circuit in 1969, but was too big to be successful in open competition.

In addition to former gasser standouts, such as Big John, dragster pilots who wanted to get in on the Funny Car popularity and bookings also put cars together. Notable was the Tirend Activity Booster–sponsored Barracuda of Tom "the Mongoo$e" McEwen, which he debuted in 1969. McEwen, Don Prudhomme, and Plymouth did not know what history would do for them yet, but that $ symbol in Mongoose was a foreshadowing of the next big thing in drag racing.

One team not in a new 1968 Charger or Dart Funny Car was the Ramchargers. The group had toured excessively during the previous five years, had helped spearhead the evolution of the FX and Funny Car classes, and ran one of the fastest dragsters on earth, yet still maintained a 9-to-5 corporate grind. Times were changing, and the commitment to run safely and successfully had become ever more expensive and time consuming. Besides the time now required to race, Mike Buckel had suffered a broken foot while jumping from the team's on-fire Dart at Detroit Dragway late in 1967; it was no longer a simple experiment.

The dragster guys led by Dick Skugland and Dan Knapp spun off into their own group and opened a retail engine building service; they continued to make history. Tom Hoover and Dick Maxwell were still involved in the management of the Super Stock program with its associated politics, which was work enough.

Following the buildup of the 1968 A-Body Hemi, the factory's Woodward Garage adjunct did not last much longer, as its management and focus were turned over to longtime Detroit associate Ted Spehar. For Mike Buckel and Jim Thornton, it was time to hang up their helmets and be normal Chrysler engineers again. The team quietly disbanded as weekly vagabonds, and the duo that had helped make the *Ramchargers* stockers such a feared team never went back into the door-car ranks either. Once you had been part of the nitro circus for that long, gasoline was just for washing parts.

Back on the Banking

The Daytona 500 looked as if it would be close for the first time in years. Like the Charger, the midsize Fords had been slickly restyled for 1968 and were being marketed under the name Ford Torino and Mercury Cyclone GT. On paper, the cars seemed to be equally matched in terms of dimensions. The Ford wedge engine was benefiting from ongoing refinement with the tunnel port replacement parts, and the Hemi was allowed dual inline carbs for the first time. A special dual-plane manifold hosting a pair of Holley carbs was released for this reason. News had already leaked that Ford was now developing its own 429-ci engine with hemispherical heads, but that was still a season away.

The 1968 Charger looked fast standing still. Designer Bill Brownlie and his stylists had masterfully blended the sheet-metal curves into a tapering design, that, frankly, looked sexy. The front fenders swelled slightly, were tucked closer through the door section, and then widened again across the rear section. Light, scalloped indentations were mirrored side by side on the hood and doors. Round taillights, body-marker lights, and a flip-top chrome gas filler mounted on the driver-side fender only added to its aggressiveness. It was popular and Charger found 92,000 buyers that year.

Dave Koffel, long a fixture in Sportsman drag racing, ended his active career in this injected Barracuda, which won three A/XS titles in 1968. He went to work for Chrysler that same year. (Photo Courtesy Ray Mann Archive, quartermilestones.com)

By virtue of his season title, USAC racer Don White won the right to display the big #1 on his new Charger in 1968. The styling changes made the car very successful on the street, and with guys such as Don, a winner on the dirt. Note the rock shield to prevent windshield breakage. (Copyright CR Racing Memories 1410008, Ray Mann Photograph)

Installing dual 4-barrels on the production Street Hemi didn't persuade NASCAR to homologate it. However, a short-lived inline dual 4-barrel layout in 1968 was allowed. The unique manifold was cast to mount two Holley carbs, but it showed minimal benefit over the bathtub model. These examples were provided by Kramer Automotive.

In part due to aerodynamic considerations, circle-track engines used cowl-fed air instead of the open-face scoops found in drag racing. This version provided by Kramer Automotive was used with the scarce twin-Holley 4-barrel layout.

Two styling cues stood out: The blacked-out vertically slatted grille featured covered headlights sunk into the nose, and the rear window sloped at a much steeper angle than the two rear cab pillars on either side; this was known as a flying buttress design. This design feature had been used on some GM models as well, and it served not only as a styling treatment, but allowed for a larger trunk opening on fastback designs. These two defining elements made the new Charger into an unruly stallion on the NASCAR circuit in 1968.

Author Frank Moriarty, in *Supercars: The Story of the Dodge Charger Daytona and Plymouth Superbird*, recounted a great deal of information on the aerodynamic effort Chrysler pursued in earnest starting in 1968. Quite interestingly, two of the men involved came out of rocket science. John Pointer had been involved in the hypersonic styling of missile noses with the Chrysler Missile program; prior to his employment in the Special Vehicles Group, he hadn't spent much time thinking about speeds below Mach level. Bob Marcell had come from space-oriented reentry vehicle projects at the University of Michigan.

Once in Highland Park, the two men joined a Special Vehicles Group team led by Larry Rathgeb, who was in charge of the company's stock car development program under the supervision of Dale Reeker. Fittingly, the Huntsville, Alabama, facility that Chrysler used for government aerospace research also served as a summer base for the circle-track guys, who also included George Wallace, Dick Lajoie, and John Vaughn.

Thanks to Vaughn's effort, the company had rented the use of two wind tunnels. Wichita State University had a small version for work using 3/8-size models. Aircraft builder Lockheed had just built a new tunnel measuring 16 by 23 feet in Marietta, Georgia. Full-size cars could fit into that one. Engineers had already begun work at these facilities to find out more about how drafting (the process of two cars tucked in nose-to-tail) functioned. When the Charger, which had been computer-estimated at 184 mph but had lost badly to the Fords at Daytona in 1968, proved to be a handful, this effort took precedence. Indeed, at the Florida race, Al Unser had finished fourth in Cotton Owens' car out of Spartanburg, South Carolina, but the next 1968 Dodge entry was Butch Hartman, 20 laps behind in sixteenth place.

It was quickly discovered that the inset grille worked just like a hood scoop. The air trapped going through it had to escape somewhere, and most of it came out from

Although very stylish, the 1968 Charger in NASCAR proved to be a real handful due to its inset front grille and flying buttress recessed rear window. Al Unser drove Cotton Owens' #6 to the fourth-place finish at the 1968 Daytona 500. Neither he nor Donnie Allison in #66 ever raced in these car numbers again. (Copyright CR Racing Memories 0612023, Ray Mann Photograph)

On the ARCA tour, Iggy Katona and his #30 were also champions coming into 1968. His 1968 model Charger is seen at the 1969 Daytona ARCA 300, and he also ran this car at the first Talladega ARCA race, held on October 26, 1969. (Copyright CR Racing Memories 0600303, Ray Mann Photograph)

The new Dodge Charger was stylish enough for Hollywood movies and more than 90,000 members of the public. However, the deep-set grille proved to be a problem on superspeedways. Steve Fox owns this unrestored Hemi. (Photo Courtesy John Stunkard)

under the car. The result was an unreal 1,250 pounds of lift at 180 mph; the front wheels did not want to point the car anywhere but straight. The rear window design was worse. As air rushed over the models, the yarn tufts used in the tunnel to show how wind was moving over the car surface stood straight up in the air. This was actually a low-pressure lift area on a car that already had no deck spoiler of consequence. Driving a Charger at race speed required skill and perhaps some foolhardy courage.

There are images of 1968 Chargers racing throughout the 1968 season, but very few made winner's circle appearances. Indeed, a look at the NASCAR records from 1968 shows Dodge racers in 1967 models at a lot of events. However, Dodge only had four wins that year. Two of them came from Bobby Isaac, now in the Norm

Krauskopf K&K Insurance entry, using the Harry Hyde–tuned 1967 Charger. Isaac did well enough week to week so that he was runner-up in the points standings in 1968. The two drivers who shook off their fear and pushed new 1968 model Chargers to the front on the superspeedways both won at Charlotte. At the World 600, the winner Buddy Baker came in first in the #3 Ray Fox entry. The fall race went to "Chargin' Charlie" Glotzbach out of Indiana in the Cotton Owens #6 car.

A front spoiler helped a little; lift dropped to "just" 500 to 600 pounds, but at the expense of drag. During a test session at Daytona that spring, Pointer sketched out a solution that actually solved the two big issues: a flush grille and a flush rear window. As it turned out, the 1968 Coronet grille was a simple change with no

The Charger 500 was the first answer to the problem. A street version is seen here on the banking at the NASCAR track in St. Louis, shot from the window of an adjoining Plymouth. The cars were built in the fall of 1968 to be homologated for NASCAR competition at the start of 1969.

Don Garlits was given a new Charger 500 to help promote the model for 1969. NASCAR required 500 examples; today, that number is believed to have actually been just under 400 units instead. (Photo Courtesy Garlits Museum Collection)

Richard Petty finished third in the NASCAR points with his Hemi Road Runner, but was frustrated as the Ford packages continued to dominate during the 1968 season. At the end of the year Plymouth had no plans for an aerodynamic restyling for 1969, so Petty switched to Ford. (Copyright CR Racing Memories 0702026, Ray Mann Photograph)

additional tooling beyond bracing. A sheet-metal plug and new glass mounted into the recessed flying buttress area pulled the rear window flush to the C-pillar edge. A new deck lid was needed as well, albeit a very small one.

As NASCAR now required a six-month window from announcement and a minimum of 500 built units before a model could be allowed to race, in June 1968, the Charger 500 was announced as a 1969 model. It was equipped identically to the Charger R/T, with standard performance hardware and the 440 Magnum for power; the Hemi was optional. Creative Industries, a company that supplied spoilers and hardware to Detroit's auto manufacturers, was contracted to produce all the Charger 500 changeover parts. They also agreed to take on the Charger conversion work.

The Charger 500 was a race-oriented vehicle and built for function. Members of the styling group were probably not overly thrilled to see their carefully cued body lose some of its curves, but the name of the game, as Dodge Vice President Bob McCurry stated, was win. That fall, a number of Hemi Charger 500s were given to magazines as 1969 model road test cars to help promote the program. If it all worked out, this Charger would be ready to take no prisoners in February 1969.

Also by this time, Pointer and Marcell had done preliminary sketches for yet another advancement scheduled for 1970; they had also independently come to the same basic conclusions. This car would have a nose much more aerodynamic than anything ever seen on a midsize vehicle, as well as address the ongoing issues of rear downforce. When the initial meeting of the Special Vehicle Group was called for these possibilities, a representative from Plymouth was invited to attend. He declined, saying his boss told him not to bother; they had Richard Petty and King Richard was able to drive whatever Plymouth had.

Petty actually had a better year in 1968 than most drivers have in their entire career. The Road Runner looked like a flying brick, but it did have a flush grille and flush-mount rear window. After Rathgeb and Petty Enterprises finished touching up the edges (it was in the wind tunnel at the same time as the Charger), the Plymouth was mostly able to run close to the Fords. Petty won 16 races and finished third in points. However, the telling story was that of the tracks 1 mile or longer. On those, he won only at Rockingham; the other wins were at places such as Hillsboro, Virginia, and Fonda, New York. That was skill, not speed. And, Petty was the only Grand National winner for Plymouth during the 1968 season.

When the Charger 500 was announced, Petty began talking with Plymouth about its NASCAR plans. He knew the redesigned Dodge had an advantage, and Ford had already announced a restyling that would result in the new, slicker Torino Talladega and Cyclone Spoiler II models. Dodge already had a full slate of drivers, however, and Plymouth would not have stood for him changing corporate brands. Late in 1968, despite the high points finish, Richard Petty did the unthinkable and switched to a Ford for the 1969 season.

After all, the fastback Fords and Mercurys were now packing new horsepower availability plus a distinct aero advantage. David Pearson was able to get his second championship in three seasons in 1968, this time in a Blue Oval product. The USAC and ARCA crowns went to A. J. Foyt and Benny Parsons, respectively. Ford guys. Still, whatever the Charger 500 might do in the following year, the rocket scientists were putting together unheard-of ideas. Coupled to the drag packages now populating the dragstrips, 1969 gave the Race Hemi further notoriety.

CHAPTER NINE

1969

Winged Wonders and Players

Arrival of the Dodge Charger Daytona

B ob McCurry was mad. The 1969 Daytona 500 had just ended, and Dodge had still failed to gain a title in the Great American Race, despite the one-two-three Dodge finishing effort in one of the Daytona qualifying races by Bobby Isaac, Charlie Glotzbach, and Paul Goldsmith.

On the final (200th) lap, LeeRoy Yarbrough had used the classic slingshot technique to put his 1969 Torino Cobra into victory lane in a very close finish over Chargin' Charlie Glotzbach and the Cotton Owens' #6 Charger 500, with three more Fords hot on his tail. The fixes provided by reworking the Dodge model into the sleeker Charger 500 variant had not done the job, and for the vice president and general manager of Dodge, anything less than that Daytona title was like kissing your sister.

Ford's newest driver, Richard Petty, had already put a conventionally trimmed Torino into the winner's circle at Riverside International Raceway, the only road course left on the Grand National circuit. The Torino Cobra was how Ford referred to its new aero-styled Talladega model bodies, which first arrived at the Daytona 500. Although Yarbrough's aforementioned win catapulted his career,

McCurry was probably not thinking much about him. He was thinking about just one thing: Dodge in a victory circle as soon as possible.

The drawings and ideas that aero scientists John Pointer and Bob Marcell had come up with independently in late 1968 as fixes for and possible use as a 1970 Charger NASCAR model were already under experimentation. Now this project was going to be accelerated. Larry Rathgeb of the Special Vehicles Group and Dodge product planner Dale Reeker started up the corporate ladder to see if they could get approval to put together something this radical as a street homologation package for racing. Chief Engineer Bob Rodger told them to go for it. McCurry took one look at the sketches and exclaimed how ugly it was, but then asked if it would win. Rathgeb told him yes. McCurry took a moment, cursed, and told

After losing at Daytona, Dodge's Bob McCurry pulled out the stops to begin development on the new Charger Daytona. This example is on display in Talladega and was a factory re-creation of #88, but it is also the real ex–Bobby Isaac car used for the Daytona's development work.

The name of the game is " WIN. "

A picture of Bob McCurry was sized to 4 x 5 by Chrysler to be taped to the dash of a Dodge race car. This unused example came from the Harry Hyde paper collection at the Wellborn Musclecar Museum. (Photo Courtesy Wellborn Museum/ Hyde Archive)

The grille's small forward-edge opening was a problem due to the lack of airflow into the radiator, especially at idle. The problem was not as serious at superspeedway speeds.

The design of the wing's twin uprights had a large influence on the way the cars handled in traffic. Road tests at the time celebrated how they worked when passing truck traffic. This restored 440-powered street car is owned by Tony D'Agostino.

The front-fender blister scoops were added by John Pointer to adjust for the downforce that the aerodynamic package created.

them to get started; he would run interference on the other levels of management to make sure they could get it done as quickly as possible.

The track after which Ford had named its newly restyled Torino was still under construction in Alabama, and it was taking every penny Big Bill France had to get it finished. It became the most radical purpose-built racetrack in America, with 2.66 miles of racing surface and banking at 33 degrees, 2 degrees steeper than Daytona. Dodge was determined to have the new model ready in time for the track's first event, scheduled for that September. Because the bigger goal was to win Daytona in 1970, that moniker was placed on the Dodge project: Charger Daytona.

In March, work was formally authorized and began in earnest. Pointer and his guys were in Chelsea, Michigan, at the sprawling Chrysler Proving Grounds. As a testbed,

Pointer was given a car that NASCAR had tossed out after the 1968 Firecracker 400 in Daytona. The 1968 bodies had been repositioned over the floorpans to begin with, and this Charger featured a design evolution that had the forward portion of the rockers shaved an additional amount. This car was adjusted back to legal height and given a Street Hemi for the initial design work.

The reshaped nose was fabricated from aluminum and angle iron the previous January. The bills were already coming from the wind tunnels, where an aero crew led by Bob Marcell was busy trying things that Pointer had come up with.

"In terms of leading the early 3/8 wind tunnel studies, John Vaughn is the guy who put that part of the program together," says Doug Schellinger, who researched the era extensively. "Vaughn contracted with Wichita State and later Lockheed for the full-scale tunnel tests. He was with Chrysler's aerospace arm from 1960 to 1968 and had done prior work relevant to Saturn V, including some of the design parameters of Launch Complex 39 at Cape Kennedy."

The width of the rear uprights was as important as the height because it functioned as a vertical stabilizer.

This view of D'Agostino's Charger shows the flush rear window, the narrow deck lid, and the wing design.

So it really was rocket science. With tweaking by Marcell and Pointer from this starting point, the team settled on a long version of the front end that stretched 18 inches from the bumper support. It had everything the car needed for speed, plus enough depth to add flip-open headlights to the substructure of the nosepiece. Care was taken on its width and the leading edge angle, coupled with a lower lip spoiler and a small mesh grille opening.

The wing was a different story, but also had production considerations. Any flat deck-mount spoiler could not have offset the new benefits that the nose added, so Pointer began working with a foil-type wing. With input from engineer Gary Romberg, the style settled on was based on the Clark-Y airfoil used for lift on aircraft. On the car, it was instead inverted atop a pair of vertical uprights for downforce.

In earlier tests, Pointer discovered the optimal nonadjustable deck wing height was around 12 inches off the deck; at heights 15 to 17 inches, downforce benefit was negligible. However, by making the horizontal Clark-Y crossover wing adjustable, the wing's angle simply created the downforce, not using the body of the car as lower level spoilers and deck lip spoiler designs do.

There was a further consideration on the issue of height. The street owner still had to be able to access the trunk. So, in the end, with the uprights pushing skyward, the height was almost 2 feet off the deck at 23 inches. In this development process a secondary benefit was found: the design of the uprights.

On April 13, 1969, the press had been invited to the Chelsea Proving Grounds to see what was coming, as Dodge again needed a six-month production announcement lead before NASCAR would allow a body adaption. A meeting of the Automobile Competition Committee

for the United States (ACCUS) was also scheduled at the end of the month, and it was likely that minimum vehicle construction figures would change. A fairly exact street car prototype was on hand, painted white. The race car for press day was the modified ex–Bobby Isaac 1968 Charger with a nose fairly close to what had been designed, but using a pair of high, spindly uprights supporting the foil and mounted at the very rear of the car. Painted red and lettered to look like the #71 K&K Insurance car that Nord Krauskopf campaigned with Isaac and Harry Hyde, it gave media wonks a preview, but actually did not reveal some of the more significant findings.

The vertical uprights actually became as important as the horizontal foil that bridged them. By working closely by phone between the wind tunnel and the proving grounds, engineers came up with the idea of streamlining the upright, which became an experiment in creating the perfect center of vehicle stability. Race drivers needed to have a car that could be driven, not simply stuck on the pavement at the mercy of airflow. By the time the positioning was finalized, the wing was no longer simply placed at the rear but carefully situated on the rear quarters to center the car's downforce pressure directly ahead of the car's physical center of gravity.

With this balance, the driver was not at the mercy of simple aerodynamics but could steer it. In addition, it was very stable from the sides. If the car began to kick sideways, more of the vertical upright surface was exposed to the air speeding past it, and it straightened back up. Larry Rathgeb's frank assessment was that it was ideal.

With Reeker working again with Creative Industries on how to carry out the construction details for the street Daytonas, testing began on the race package using two of the top guys from Dodge's racing program, Charlie

Race-prepped, NASCAR mandated the wing be solidly attached to the car, as seen on the Bobby Isaac #71 at the Wellborn Musclecar Museum.

Glotzbach and Buddy Baker. Like Glotzbach, Baker had been driving for Cotton Owens in 1969 and once joked that he had the "number 2 size hat, number 14 size shoe" that made him a perfect test driver.

The truth was the duo proved in the real world what the development team had come up with, and they drove stock cars faster than anyone before. If the factory wanted a 500-mile test run done, they'd do it; all in a day's work. Six lanes wide, the banking at Chelsea was a steady incline from level to 31 degrees, but the track was a simple oval and 5 miles long. If you had the guts to hold it wide open, it was longer (and smoother) than anything on the NASCAR circuit.

The first actual test of the Daytona body was held at Chelsea in July, with a NASCAR-prepped Charger 500 from Nichols-Goldsmith on hand for comparison, plus

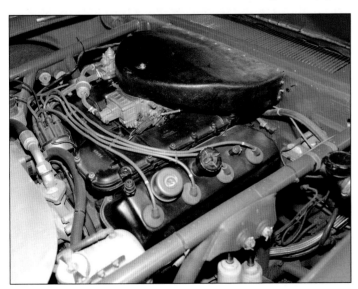

The engine in the Isaac car. The paired shocks and coolant layout was designed to take the abuse of 500 very fast miles.

a bunch of onlookers. The initial announcement of the plan for the Daytona had been to gain 5 mph on the superspeedways. When calculated at a ratio of 17 hp per mph, this would have required 85 hp, or a 15-percent reduction in drag. After the hundreds of thousands of dollars now spent, the new car was just about that much faster than the Charger 500, at 194 mph.

Years later, Rathgeb and team member George Wallace recalled the reason for such slight improvement was actually because of corporate cloak-and-dagger efforts. Reportedly, a small Holley 4-barrel had been fitted to the Daytona's Hemi engine to provide a bit of a smokescreen as to what had been developed, particularly during this first test that everyone was watching. Calculating the possible results on paper, Chrysler insiders knew it would be much better on the track.

Baker and Glotzbach knew that as well and showed it during the following month with the right NASCAR-legal equipment on the car. Although never verified, Chargin' Charlie reportedly punched a hole on the straights at the Chelsea track at an unheard-of 243 mph. He and Baker wistfully wished they could put stands up right there and run a race at the Chrysler test facility. Indeed, even at well in excess of 200 mph, the car was stable. Buddy Baker made just one partial lap with the deck spoiler off to see how the nose worked alone and came back pale faced and white knuckled.

When testing moved from the Michigan facility to Daytona soon afterward, the racing surface itself presented problems. At one point early on, instrumentation in the car showed Glotzbach was lifting off the throttle due to the bumps he encountered. He said he could not see. On the advice of Larry Rathgeb, he ended up standing on it, actually closing his eyes, and pointing the car where it needed to go until it settled back down to get open-throttle data. This was a harbinger of the future; the tracks were not up to the new car's capabilities.

As the Talladega race approached, Creative Industries had been handling the construction of the production models. The parts were finalized and created, and

This is Bobby Isaac's Daytona Charger. This example is the same car that was used to set records at Bonneville, and its modifications may have been a bit more extreme.

Here are two Race Hemi distributors (both provided by Kramer Automotive): The one on the right uses a conventional slotted cam/oil pump drive base. The left model and drive gear use a much larger base for circle-track duty.

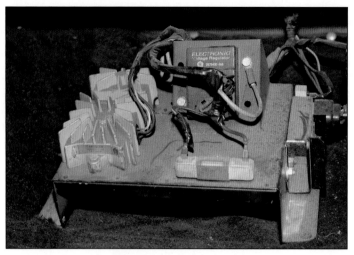

The ignition equipment in the Isaac car was mounted in the passenger-side footboard area where it was easily accessed.

the requisite 503 Daytonas were built as Charger R/Ts at the Hamtramck plant and then converted at the Creative Industries facility, a leased production plant on East Ten Mile Road. Someone from NASCAR even came and counted them.

The novelty of the extreme design was great enough that the cars sold pretty well as soon as the dealerships took delivery of them; reportedly, actress Raquel Welch owned one briefly. Testers at *Car Life* magazine joked that no matter what they said, Dodge would have the last laugh, and Bob Rodger issued statements regarding how the aerodynamics program benefited future highway vehicle design. Editor Jim McCraw at *Super Stock & Drag Illustrated* believed that the cars would "still be wild years from now." With a base price of $3,993 for the Charger Daytonas, not much higher than a similar Charger R/T, the company reportedly lost $1,500 on each one. Seventy of them came with Street Hemi power; the rest were 440s.

Two other visible changes to the car for better airflow were wide chrome trim pieces mounted to the windshield pillars and two rearward-facing scoops above the wheel openings on the front fenders. The latter were a source of media and enthusiast controversy over the years, but they were actually added by Pointer during development. Knowing that increased downforce would result in a lack of tire clearance, he included them simply to make room, and his decision had nothing to do with the brakes or air pressure under the nose.

One interesting footnote in history involved Glotzbach, Smokey Yunick, and Ford. On August 10, 1969, Chargin' Charlie was in a Torino Talladega for the Dixie 500 in Atlanta. Smokey Yunick, whose best efforts were

with Chevrolet, was listed as the owner. It seemed that this was done to give Glotzbach a chance to feel how the Talladega worked. He started sixth and finished fourth. Fords took the top five spots at the event and his piloting of this Ford effort was possibly in hopes of plucking another A-grade driver from Chrysler.

Dark Days at 'Dega

But Atlanta was not Talladega, and Talladega, a Creek Indian word for border, was going to test the will of men and machines before things began on September 14, 1969. Dodge's swift cars were capable of running on the massive banking, but an issue with the curing of the fresh surface was playing havoc with the tires. Both the Chrysler and Ford racers had huge problems. Despite this, the layout allowed for possible record-setting speeds.

"The problems with the track surface at Talladega were not unknown leading up to the event," says researcher Doug Schellinger of the Daytona-Superbird Club. "Chrysler had tested the Daytona at the track in late August, and a number of the top drivers took laps with speeds in the high-190-mph range. Larry Rathgeb's lap charts show a comment from Goldsmith, who came out of retirement to make some laps, about the track being 'just a rough SOB in one and two.' Even Bill France took a couple of easy laps in the car, but Bobby Allison actually stated in the test paperwork he thought the track was coming apart."

Early in the weekend, Rathgeb and Ronney Householder came to an agreement to enter the actual engineering car they had used at Chelsea in the event under a Ray Nichels affiliation as car #88. The truth was, as a Chrysler engineering vehicle, racing it was a no-no from the factory standpoint. Glotzbach, who was driving the

Buddy Baker and Charlie Glotzbach were the drivers chosen to test the new Charger Daytona at the Chelsea Proving Grounds. Baker piloted Cotton Owens' #6 once the race cars were available. (Copyright CR Racing Memories 0301012, Ray Mann Photograph)

In a wing at speed, Chargin' Charlie is seen in #99, which was the factory entry fielded by Nichels-Goldsmith. Dow was the sponsor in 1970. (Copyright CR Racing Memories 0501003, Ray Mann Photograph)

"real" Nichels Daytona, was asked to make a couple of laps in it to keep it legal for qualifying. Householder instructed Rathgeb to tell Glotzbach to keep it under 185. Chargin' Charlie took one warm-up lap and then let it all hang out: 199 mph. Householder was livid, but Rathgeb put Charlie back in it a second time, and he took the pole with the car at an unheard of 199.466.

During that August, the drivers had organized a collective that they called the Professional Driver Association (PDA). This was to address the immediate issues of safety plus grievances about payouts, pensions, and other things that were often anathema to Bill France and other race promoters. Richard Petty was the top guy at the PDA, and as time for the race drew closer, it became obvious that the new facility would be a catalyst for labor strife. Not without reason, though.

The cars were eating tires within five laps and some drivers were complaining of dizziness from high-MPH vibrations. France, who had invested huge sums of time and money into the track, was adamant that the show go on as scheduled. Petty, as well as many of the other drivers and team owners, threatened to walk out. Eventually 30 big-name cars and trailers pulled out on Saturday afternoon. This included Glotzbach and Baker; Firestone also left because of the tire problems.

"On the Friday before the Talladega 500, both Goodyear and Firestone flew new tires in," Schellinger recounts. "There was a late-afternoon test session with Glotzbach in the Nichels #99 and Donnie Allison in the #27 Banjo Matthews Talladega. It was high drama with the crews and factory personnel on pit road gathered around the cars when they came back in.

"Glotzbach had gone out and proceeded to break the right upper control arm on the rough track. Allison's tires fared no better and had chunked in a matter of a few laps. The end result was that Firestone simply withdrew from the event. Regardless of manufacturer, the tires had

a chance to last at reduced speeds below 195 mph. When pushed to the limit, they failed."

Glotzbach vacated the seat of the #99 Nichels Engineering Daytona to honor his commitment to the PDA. Schellinger notes there was no Dow sponsor in 1969 and Chrysler stood behind the drivers, whatever they wanted to do. Because of his obligation to Chrysler, Nichels stayed and Householder told a promising young driver named Richard Brickhouse to take over the car. With a factory deal at stake and the chance at a top-class ride, Brickhouse withdrew from the PDA and stayed to drive.

Bobby Isaac had qualified his new Daytona in second place at 196.386 and he had not joined the PDA group. Harry Hyde was sponsored by K&K Insurance, which backed the NASCAR series; he was also associated with Chrysler. The Hyde/Isaac team also stayed. The engineering #88 had been withdrawn, so these were the only two wings. Bill France had a minor contingency with a number of Grand Touring Sportsman drivers on hand for a Saturday race who stayed over on Sunday and filled out the final racing program.

Brickhouse drove the #99 Charger Daytona home to victory when Isaac ran into some problems early on

USAC star Don White raced his Charger 500 in 1969; the troubles at Talladega did not affect him. (Copyright CR Racing Memories 1410009, Ray Mann Photograph)

that put him a lap behind. Brickhouse also found the top groove was easier on tires than the lower levels of the fresh track, and he ran several laps at 197 mph before Chrysler told him via pit board to slow down to prevent a blowout that could wreck the car.

To this day, the drivers involved in the PDA walkout have maintained that it was necessary at that moment, but it was a close call for NASCAR. The following month, Bill France gave Bobby Isaac, Nord Krauskopf, and Harry Hyde each a solid-gold Rolex watch. He told them that they had saved NASCAR because the sanctioning body would have gone bankrupt if it had needed to refund 64,000 Sunday tickets. Harry Lee Hyde told me that his father proudly wore the watch almost every day to work until he broke a link on the band. When the jeweler charged him $3,000 to fix it, that watch was put away in a safe place.

And Beyond

The next big superspeedway test was Charlotte, as the wings were intended solely for superspeedway use. However, Donnie Allison won in his Torino, with three Daytonas hot on his tail. Although the Daytonas were faster than the Fords, tires remained a pivotal issue due to the car's great downforce, something that had not been fully considered in the development phase.

By this time, tire development technology was ongoing not just among companies, but among steel-belted radials, fiberglass (polyglas) composites, and the old rayon standby, with associated issues of cost and longevity being challenged by speed and tractability. In hindsight, there may not have been any point in the history of auto racing when the crucible of needed technological improvements made street products better.

The Fords won again at Rockingham, which had just been redesigned with banking. Bobby Isaac finished the year with a win at the new Texas International Speedway on December 7, 1969. Unlike Talladega, this track had a low-grip surface. After leader Buddy Baker crashed during a caution, Isaac put the #71 K&K machine into the lead to give the Charger Daytona a second 1969 victory. The company gave him a new Challenger R/T as part of his winnings.

Now Plymouth Makes It

Although the Plymouth Superbird is a 1970 model, plans were made to build it while the Daytona project unfolded. The cars were required to be finished and available for public purchase by December 31, 1969, because of changes the government had already made regarding concealed headlamp operation (that would go into effect on January 1). Although the cars did not race in 1969, this is a good place to cover their construction.

"Plymouth had been offered the chance to do an aerodynamic car at the same time as the Daytona," says Schellinger, who owns the Ramo Stott Superbird. "They hesitated and fell subject to the increased homologation numbers for 1970."

Just after the Charger Daytona announcement in April 1969, ACCUS met and changed the mandates for production homologation. Now, instead of 500 units, it

Bobby Isaac posted the second win for the Daytona at the season-ending race at Texas International Speedway. Its less-abrasive track surface was much more conducive to the tires of the era than Talladega's pavement had been. Here he is seen with Bobby Allison's #22 car and James Hylton's #48 Ford. (Copyright CR Racing Memories 1410001, Ray Mann Photograph)

NASCAR's rule on dual 4-barrels for the Hemi ended quickly, but development for the program progressed far enough to create this unique inverted tunnel ram (provided by Kramer Automotive). Two carbs did not fit onto the bathtub intake.

The inverted tunnel ram featured a large plenum area and runners that pushed upward to create the sonic length for atomized fuel to resonate into the cylinders. It is not known if the unit was ever used in NASCAR; its application was likely in the USAC and ARCA. This example was provided by Kramer Automotive.

required either 1,000 cars or one example for every two dealerships, whichever was greater. This ruling effectively ended Ford's overt participation in aero racing, and when Ford president Semon "Bunkie" Knudsen was abruptly replaced by Lee Iacocca in September 1969, the company's involvement in big-dollar auto racing ended as well. Iacocca killed virtually all Blue Oval programs by the end of the following year.

In the meantime, Plymouth wanted Richard Petty back, and after speaking favorably in private with "the King" in June 1969, the company made a commitment to both a wing car program and a corporate realignment that entailed major changes in its racing program. Petty Engineering also received the race car distribution business that had been part of Ray Nichels' firm for years, a huge coup that had repercussions in the stock car racing world. Still, the man most associated with the Hemi in circle-track competition was returning home.

To meet the requisite numbers that NASCAR adopted with the ACCUS ruling, 1,935 'Birds needed to fly. Plymouth had hoped it would be a simple mating of the Day-

tona nose to the upcoming 1970 model design, but that was not to be. Instead, it was back to the wind tunnel again. The nose had to be reworked, and after considering the options, Plymouth used the hood and front fenders off the just-restyled 1970 Coronet to achieve better continuity with the nose change. As the result of a minor reworking of the rear window opening, all production Superbirds were built with a vinyl top to cover the handiwork.

Unlike Dodge, where Bob McCurry, a former college football team captain, told styling to go pound sand if they complained, Plymouth stylists were involved from the beginning of the Superbird. For starters, the stylists wanted the nose's leading edge to be a little higher, which increased drag. Also, due to cost considerations, the rear window and quarter panels could not be radically changed to get the same fastback effect as on the Charger Daytona and the Fords. As a result, the Superbird was never as slick at speed as the Daytona, and, assisted by the factory, the guys at Petty Engineering did a lot of real-world on-track testing with it after the car's design was finalized. One major positive change during development was a wider, more angular wing support, which helped high-speed stability even more. When the cars were completed, the wing support was decorated with a special Road Runner Superbird logo.

Creative Industries was still involved, as the company supplied a lot of the special aero equipment, but the cars themselves were built in batches on the Lynch Road assembly line using special instructions and then transferred to the Clairpointe pilot assembly plant for final conversion. At full capacity in November, about 50 'Birds a day came off the line. Of these, actual option production breakdown numbers are sketchy. Most were 440 4-barrels, about a third used the new 440 6-barrel package with three Holley 2-barrels, and approximately 100 were Street Hemis. Unfortunately, many 'Birds languished at dealerships for months, a few for years, after they were released. The formal announcement came in December that Plymouth by Petty was back for 1970.

Plymouth needed to create almost 2,000 Superbirds as 1970 models before the end of 1969 due to mandatory federal changes in headlight laws. Here are a Street Hemi Superbird and a 440 Daytona on the banking at Bristol Motor Speedway during a special exhibition in 2003 sponsored by Year One.

Players and Payers: Manufacturers Step Up

Drag racing was not sitting still in 1969, not by a long shot. The 1968 Hemi A-Bodies were out in force, and other competitors were attempting to make their mark as well. Vince Piggins of Chevrolet Product Promotions had used the COPO program usually reserved for fleet builds to get around the General Motors 400-ci limit on the Camaro. Of the resulting 1969 427-ci models, most were sold either through Don Yenko of Pennsylvania as street cars, or through Fred Gibb's franchise in Illinois. Gibb used the COPO process to buy stripped-down cars for racing. He worked closely with drag racer Dick Harrell, whose close association with Jim Tice's AHRA organization in Kansas City aided this relationship.

The iron 427-ci L72 engine was installed using COPO 9561, mainly for Yenko in Chevelles and Camaros, but other dealers who had the know-how could also order them.

Gibb used COPO 9560 to create aluminum-block versions, coded ZL1. These replicated endurance engines that had been developed in the Can-Am open-wheel series during the years Chevy was "not racing." Only 69 of these cars were built, and while good in theory, the package did not hold up under Super Stock legal scrutiny during the season.

Bill Jenkins settled into 1969 with an iron version that ran in SS/D, and he used an actual aluminum 430-ci Can-Am block for match racing.

Ford needed to homologate its new Boss 429 engine in 1969 for NASCAR as well and selected a street model of the Mustang for its installation. Kar Kraft did these conversions and built Boss 429 Mustangs in limited quantity in 1969 and 1970. These vehicles were not designed with science for drag racing. Ford marketed them as street models, and the street-designed intake manifold and camshaft did not allow the large-port engines to breathe well.

As a result, few of the several hundred Boss 429 Mustangs released to the public ended up on the strip. However, in keeping with past methods, a handful of

The Red Light Bandit *Dart of Bill Bagshaw is preparing to make a run at Dallas in 1969. Bagshaw was able to put together a Dodge deal with the help of a friend at* Hot Rod *magazine when Shirley Shahan left to race for AMC. (Photo Courtesy Ray Mann Archive, quartermilestones.com)*

lightweight examples were specially built as race cars for specific drivers such as Hubert Platt, Al Joniec, and Dave Lyall (as were two Mercury Cougars for Don Nicholson and Ed Schartman). The well-traveled SOHC was sometimes the engine of choice simply because of its familiarity during the busy racing season. Mickey Thompson and Connie Kalitta did the workups on the new Boss engine in the nitro classes.

AMC came calling in Sportsman drag racing as well. Bob Tarozzi had now come to Hurst as a contractor and had used the same basic calculations from the Hemi A-Bodies to help American Motors create an AMX to be used in drag racing. Well balanced and using a 390-ci engine, the cars showed promise and fit into the NHRA's class structure under SS/D and E. Dart racer Shirley Shahan left the Dodge program that spring to race one. Her Dodge contract deal went to another California racer, Bill Bagshaw, who had come from the gasser classes with an early Corvette he called *Red Light Bandit.*

Racing Around the Nation

As had been the case in the past, the upstart AHRA saw the writing on the wall and, after the exhibition races of 1968, established a professional heads-up door-slammer category named SS/E. In the truest sense of competition, the class had a simple slate of rules: a flat weight, a flat displacement, and gasoline fuel. With AHRA events from coast to coast by then, big-name racers were on hand to show off at places such as Lions in Long Beach, California; Bristol, Tennessee; West Palm Beach, Florida; and Detroit, Michigan.

The NASCAR drag racing series had been canceled at the end of 1968, so now there were only two national sanctioning bodies, as well as a handful of regional series.

The NHRA maintained its Super Stock division as before, but this was now augmented by a number of Super Stock circuits across several divisions. Division 1 and Division 7, on opposite coasts, were very active by 1969. Coupled with the amount of racing equipment on hand, the opportunities presented by match races, and growing notoriety in the press, it was becoming more and more possible to race door cars for a living, preferably with some kind of bankroll from Detroit.

Campus unrest and vehement political discourse was in the news during this time, and racing was not immune to controversy either.

The Hemi Fights for Equality

Winning. When it comes to competition, very few drivers and participants went to the effort needed if there was no possible success. Indeed, racing from the factory

Rich Thomas is at the 1969 AHRA World Finals; note the little spoiler that had become a popular add-on to the cars not racing in the NHRA. The age of Pro Stock was on the horizon. (Photo Courtesy Ray Mann Archive, quarter-milestones.com)

perspective is a showcase of skill, ability, and technology. Sometimes it's combined with random opportunities to be victorious, but most often it is the result of good planning and a level playing field. However, when push comes to shove, rules are viewed to be the outside limit of what one might get away with. In the late 1960s, Chrysler had some issues when it came to the NHRA's enforcement policies.

During every year that the Race Hemi was produced for drag racing, Chrysler met the mandated requirements for production. This was at no small expense, and the company did not fudge the production numbers. The Race Hemi cars were well designed and as a result they were factored at 500-rated hp across the top categories in Super Stock (the A-Bodies in SS/B-BA and the aluminum-head 1965 A990s in SS/C-CA). The 1967 RO/WO cars were now

This prototype Six Pack intake for Hemi use (provided by Kramer Automotive) was created by Chrysler Engineering and was reportedly on Tom Hoover's personal car. The design would have been on the stillborn A279 ball-stud Hemi program. The Six Pack became a noted part of the A134 440-ci wedge engines.

in SS/D (against Jenkins' COPO Camaro), while Street Hemi models were primarily in E or F.

The B- and C-class Chrysler Race Hemi entries were always a threat on race day, but the mild changes and large size of the 1967 cars put them at a disadvantage against the smaller makes in the D class, and they could not make the published weight break. SS/E and lower classes were not Race Hemi focused, although Street Hemis and 440 combinations raced there. In fact, the 1968 runner-up at the U.S. Nationals, Wally Booth, sold his Camaro and raced a 1969 Hemi Super Bee in SS/EA most of the 1969 season.

Representing the factory and its racers, Dick Maxwell, Tom Hoover, and Bob Cahill felt that the NHRA was giving the other manufacturers more leeway in terms of construction and homologation requirements. Several letters survive that were addressed to Competition Director Jack Hart, tech boss Bill "Farmer" Dismuke, and Wally Parks. In the letters, points were made about horsepower factoring, production methods, etc. In late 1969, Hoover sent one long discourse that used scientific measurements to show this lack of parity and that the various combinations of Fords were favorably factored by 13 to 18 percent over the Street Hemi, Race Hemi, and AMX 390 (most of which were purpose-built race packages).

For instance, one sticking point had been regarding the 1968 Winternationals, at which Ford had been allowed to race in Stock with the Cobra Jets (addressed twice, once in a letter by Cahill to Parks on March 6, 1968, and again on April 11 between Maxwell and Dismuke). In August 1968, Hubert Platt's 4-speed Torino (the transmission was listed as not available in Ford's production paperwork) was the subject of two letters by Maxwell in rapid succession. One of them ended tersely, "How are we doing, Farmer? Did we make our point yet?"

More Cars, More Classes

Chrysler could live with the Hemi having a high-factored horsepower number, but the company worked throughout the 1969 season to ensure that the class records remained advantageous. After all, one other big change came in 1969. The NHRA had now expanded the category through SS/J, meaning that there were 20 possible class winners for the final 32-car program.

As a result of new weight breaks in 1969, the steel-nose/hood-scoop version of the 1964 A864 drag engine became visible in competition as well. This hardtop body had not been built in any quantity and had never before been involved competitively in national event–level drag racing. In earlier years, it would have been classified with the lighter aluminum-nosed models.

A letter sent to the NHRA by the Reedman Corporation Chrysler-Plymouth dealership in early 1966 included a window sticker and info on at least one Plymouth so built. It is now known that some, several dozen actually, were created that first year. The new class change allowed a 1964 Race Hemi to fit into SS/C and SS/CA (aluminum nose) and SS/D and SS/DA (steel nose). It also made up for the fact the NHRA had basically outlawed the entire 1964 Race Hemi model run for most of the 1960s because all of the A864 drag package cars had been equipped with aluminum panels.

"We saw all those cars as a way to have more Chryslers in the fields," says Tom Hoover. "It was simply more ways to win by getting more cars qualified."

Race Hemis Rule

Those SS/B and BA 1968 A-Body models were doing just fine in their sophomore year, considering how much competition they had. Arlen Vanke now had two Barracudas and took one to the AHRA Winter Nationals heads-up Super Stock Eliminator (SS/E) crown at Beeline Raceway in Phoenix to start off the season. A week later, Don Grotheer overcame all contenders with his SS/BA *Cable Car* 'Cuda at Pomona to give Plymouth a second 1969 Winter Nationals win, beating Jerry Harvey's SS/IA Cobra. Harry Holton, a longtime West Coast racer, made it three Hemi wins in a row when he took the Super Stock title at Bakersfield with his Dart.

Interestingly, Ronnie Sox and Dick Landy raced each other twice at Pomona, but not in Super Stock. Both

Don Grotheer's restored Barracuda wears the scheme he added after his big win at the NHRA Winternationals in 1969. The original car is now in Chuck Smith's collection. Here, Don (left) and Chuck (right) stand next to a tribute that Don owns; the original car is behind them.

Dick Landy won Top Stock at the 1969 AHRA Spring Nationals with this Hemi-powered 1969 Charger, classed in Formula/Stock (F/S) 5. (Photo Courtesy Tommy Erwin Archive; University of South Carolina 083__1968)

had A-Body cars in A/Modified Production, which Sox won with a .07 record-dropping 10.53. Landy's hot 1969 Charger then beat Sox's AHRA Winter Nationals Top Stock–winning 1969 Hemi Road Runner for the B/MP class title at 11.01, lowering that record by .24 as well. After class runoffs, Landy's Dodge then returned to the Pomona winner's circle for a second time in 1969. The B/MP Charger took the overall Street Eliminator title, running a blistering 10.80 in the no-breakout final against Jim Thompson in Bob Riffle's Anglia gasser.

Sox was back in Super Stock when the 1969 NHRA Springnationals were held, having been moved to a new track in Texas, Dallas International Motor Speedway. In the final, *The Boss* SS/B 'Cuda beat Barrie Poole's Mustang for the S/S crown, going 10.63 in the final to slightly bump the record. None of the Chrysler cars ran in the MP classes here (Landy's Hemi Charger was in SS/F, and Don Carlton was driving the Sox & Martin 1969 Road Runner in SS/E), and when Bill Jenkins' A/MP car was tossed on a rules infraction, Dyno Don Nicholson won Street Eliminator in a 1965 SOHC A/FX Mustang.

Also at Dallas, Jenkins brought a ZL1 Camaro for SS/C, but Bill Dismuke ruled it ineligible because Chevrolet could only show 46 units sold of the required 50 (the ZL1 had a sticker price that topped $7,000 in 1969 and were very hard to sell as a result). Ron Mancini and Dave Wren showed up in SS/DA with the first of the steel-nosed 1964s in NHRA competition.

The following weekend in AHRA Top Stock action at Bristol, Landy took home another Street title in the 1969 Charger, but Jenkins won the Super Stock Eliminator class. This was the solid beginning of Pro Stock, but a lot of experimentation was going on elsewhere.

Ed Miller won an East Coast heads-up circuit crown in his Barracuda using cumulative points, finishing at the AHRA fall race held at the new track in Rockingham,

North Carolina. Jenkins dominated the Super Stock Nationals with his Can-Am–engine–Camaro, which garnered points over a three-day period. With Nicholson in the vintage Mustang and Ed Schartman in a new Maverick, it was an interesting mix. Indeed Jenkins, Schartman, and Sox all chose to compete in B/Gas at the 1969 Nationals. Sox raised some eyebrows in the pits when the hood came off to reveal eight short-stack Hilborns.

The 1969 Mopar Nationals

Indeed, the long months of summer led to the U.S. Nationals at Indianapolis, and perhaps the grand finale of factory involvement in the Super Stock category. By now, the NHRA had legalized Jenkins' SS/C ZL1 Camaro and he was likely to be a threat in what had formerly been all-Hemi territory. The NHRA had again tried a rules change in the division to maintain parity at the Nationals.

For 1969, each Super Stock competitor was allowed four runs. The two quickest cars were then qualified from those runs. The lowest elapsed time of those two cars was that class' index on race day. With no legal cars running in SS/A through SS/AA, technically, it meant the 36 fastest cars on Sunday raced on Monday (18 pairs from each class between SS/B-BA and J/JA), with all-new indexes set during qualifying to maintain parity; in return, there were no breakout rules.

The Race Hemi camp consisted of the A-Bodies running in B and BA. Also, the CA cars from 1965, which had been joined by Wally Booth in Ted Spehar's new *Iron Butterfly* 1964 Dodge, plus the 1964 steel-nose scoop cars of Mancini and Wren ran in DA. Reports at the time hinted that the following events were completely spontaneous. However, the truth was that neither Chrysler nor its racers wanted to tip their hand so early on Friday afternoon. One by one, the teams began to leave as if

Noted car builder Tom Tignanelli created a number of experimental-type gas cars. Perhaps none was as unique as this lift-body Charger he ran that received a Daytona-type nose before coming to Indy in 1969. (Photo Courtesy Pit Slides Archive, quartermilestones.com)

they were returning to the motel (the racers did not keep their cars at the track overnight in this era).

This was not a boycott similar to the one PDA hosted at Talladega two weeks later. It was a protest. However, using an American Express card, Dave Koffel rented Tri-City Dragway in Hamilton, Ohio, about two hours east of Indy. Each B, BA, and CA car was given three flat-out runs, with a couple of guys watching the clocks. Because only two cars per class were allowed to race on Monday, it was agreed that only the two quickest would come back to qualify at Indy. The plan was to keep those class indexes nice, soft, and right where they were when the event began.

In B, it was Sox and John Hagan. In BA, it was Grotheer and Bill Tanner's Dodge (which humorously had a CASE tractor logo on the scoop to identify it as different from the Six Pack logo on the new Super Bee). The CA guys were Jim Hale and Booth in Spehar's *Iron Butterfly* (which had been Tina Spehar's 6-cylinder street driver only a month earlier).

Iron Butterfly *was a 1964 sedan that Ted Spehar had converted from his wife's street car, with an aluminum front-end and iron-head Race Hemi. Wally Booth drove it at Indy, and then Dick Oldfield (seen here at Dallas) took over. (Photo Courtesy Ray Mann Archive, quartermilestones.com)*

As part of the expanded clinic program, Bill Tanner's Dart was now the beneficiary of factory support. The Case logo on the hood scoop was a humorous dig at the recently released Six Pack for the wedge engine. (Photo Courtesy Frank Wiley Archive, Tanner PR image, Kramer Automotive Print/Film Collection)

On Saturday morning, just a half-dozen of the many Hemi cars came into the lanes for qualifying. NHRA officials were not happy, but there was not much they could do.

After class teardown, 6 cars, including 1 Hemi, were bounced, leaving a short 30-car program. It consisted of 14 Fords, 13 Chryslers (7 Hemis and 6 wedges), and 3 Chevys; the only AMC class qualifier had also been tossed. Even without a breakout rule, in the first round, only 12 cars were quicker than the qualified numbers, including Booth, who went 10.70 on the original 11.08 CA record.

Just one Ford, driven by Roger Caster, was left by the end of round two. With no breakout enforcement, there was no holding back. Round three saw Wren's SS/DA Plymouth go 10.92 to beat Bob Lambeck in Landy's wedge, Sox at 10.54 over Caster, and Tanner *losing* on a holeshot with a 10.43 in BA to a 10.88 from Mancini's 1964 DA Dodge. In the semis, Mancini fell to Sox, who hit 10.40, and Wren went 10.90 to beat Grotheer, who fouled away a 10.44.

After several years of frustration on Labor Days past, Ronnie Sox won Super Stock at Indy when Dave Wren's driveshaft fell out 15 feet off the line. The icing on the cake was that, with nobody in the other lane, Sox's slowing 10.89 also saved the SS/B record, which was a healthy 10.61 leaving Indy.

On Tuesday, the NHRA called a meeting of the principals from all the manufacturers and the leaders of the Super Stock Drivers Association to end the index wars. The AHRA season-long SS/E class and the Experimental Super Stock (X/SS) division at the Super Stock Magazine Nationals at York had shown them that heads-up door-slammer racing was the way it ought to be. With suggestions and input from all involved, before long, the NHRA finalized the rules for its own head-ups class in 1970, which was called Pro Stock.

Get the Grump, and Good

There was no doubt that Bill Jenkins was fast, and he had saved the SS/C index at Indy. After the results of the 1968 World Finals, Chrysler wanted to make sure that competitors were in the proper classes, and not let anybody else just walk in. Sox had saved SS/B and no other Hemi indexes had been hit. That left SS/C stick as a problem. Soon after Indy, Dick Maxwell called Arlen Vanke.

There was one final points meet left before the World Finals that year, a cool-weather race called the National Dragster Open at National Trail Raceway outside of Columbus during the first weekend of October. To make a difference, Vanke needed a 1965 A990 car legal for C, built solely to "stump the Grump." Maxwell helped

round up the parts and sent them to Ohio, while Vanke secured a barely used A990 Plymouth and began to work his magic on it. That meant blueprinting a good 1965 aluminum-head engine, putting the car together including installation of a manual transmission, and getting it ready to hit the number. And no Mr. Nice Guy stuff; Vanke intended to decimate the record.

Record runs took place on Saturday; to get one, the car needed one under-the-record run plus a backup within 1 percent on the same day. For two weeks, Vanke and his team worked 18 hours a day and had the car finished at the last minute; they towed it into the Hebron, Ohio, track on Saturday morning. Akron Arlen caught a quick nap while a couple of the crew guys drove it around inside the track to get the virgin driveline broken in.

Just after noon, Vanke rolled into the record lane, dumped the clutch, but fumbled for second gear; the new clutch linkage had bound up against the headers. After a little work with a ballpeen hammer on the pipe, the car, now the center of attention, returned. The engine roared through first and second, but now the third-gear shift was a problem, as one of the blocker rings inside the transmission had broken.

The sun was setting, and there was no time to get it back out again for record runs and a backup. The late Dave Duell, who was part of the crew working on the car, told me that Jenkins had been a spectator in the crowd and left for home smiling that evening knowing SS/C was still his plum at 11.31.

Nobody told Vanke it was over, though. Without sleep, he took the car back to Akron, fixed it, and returned Sunday to run eliminations. The breakout rule was in effect for the eliminator: go too fast and you're out. The final-round record rule was in effect as well: If you went flat-out in and won in the final of Super Stock, that number was the new record.

The 1965 Dodge that Arlen Vanke put together to reset the SS/C record in dramatic fashion is seen here in the pits at its debut. At Hebron, Ohio, in October, it reset the record by .7 second. (Photo Courtesy Pit Slide Archive, quartermilestones.com)

The actual Sox & Martin car that won it all in 1969 appears in Chapter 8. This example was created as a tribute to the team's greatest effort in Super Stock by longtime Hemi racer Bob Reed (left). Ronnie Sox (right) drove this modern version as a twenty-first century match racer.

Vanke began to march through a field of very tough Division 3 racers, five rounds' worth, and came to the final against Dewey Cook in a 1965 A990 CA entry. For the first time since it was built, the Plymouth Hemi came to life unchained, and Vanke was merciless on the shifter. In the traps, it roared to a 10.61 besting the national record by a huge .7 second. Remember, Sox had held the current SS/B record to a 10.61 at Indy. Torn down for tech, it was found to be legal. Mission accomplished.

The 1969 NHRA World Finals

Super Stock at Dallas, which had also become the new home of the NHRA World Finals, found a lot of racers going flat-out, and the record book took a beating on Saturday as the guys planning for Pro Stock took one last ride in Super Stock. Sox took the B number down to 10.29, while 1965 World Champ Joe Smith, substituting for Don Grotheer, took BA to 10.36. With Vanke's 10.61 holding in C, new driver Dick Oldfield drove *Iron Butterfly* to a 10.75 in CA, while Ron Mancini did likewise in DA with a 10.92.

Bill Jenkins and Dave Strickler showed up with two 427 Camaros equipped with TH400 automatic transmissions (Bill's ZL1 in CA and Dave's L72 in EA), but the NHRA disqualified them both for the simple reason that neither car had ever shown up at any prior event in automatic trim. Strickler parked his ride while Jenkins reconverted the ZL1 back to the Muncie box but had no luck touching Vanke's record. Due to all the Fords in the lower classes, the lone Chevy to qualify in Super Stock was Ed Hedrick in the Yenko shop's yellow SS/E L72 entry, automatically seeded-in from Division 1 based on points.

On race day, Ronnie Sox began a march to the front for prizes that included a special $5,000 jackpot bonus that George Hurst had put up for any championship-winning driver who had already won Indy the previous month. Mopars went rounds, and the two semifinals were three

against one. Sox beat the sole-remaining Ford of Barrie Poole, running a close 10.20 (almost .10 under the new 10.29 record) to win.

Then it was Mancini against Oldfield, both in 1964 Dodges, and both had run identical 10.83s in the previous round, yet they were a class apart. Mancini's DA car was considered a shoo-in. However, when the cars approached the starting line, the *Zoom-O* Dodge began smoking and then its transmission exploded in spectacular fashion, putting fluid and shrapnel all over the ground.

The engine in the Reed/Sox match race car gives ample evidence of the level of modification being practiced as the evolution in Super Stock occurred. It also provides a glimpse at today's sophisticated SS/AH Hemi Challenge competitors.

Ron Mancini's 1964 Zoom-O Dodge at the World Finals in Dallas. Later that day, the car had a tremendous transmission failure. (Photo Courtesy Ray Mann Archive, quartermilestones.com)

Paula Murphy prepares to make a run in her 1969 Barracuda at the AHRA World Finals at Tulsa in 1969. At this point, the NHRA was very cautious about licensing female drivers in the fuel-burning classes; Paula was one of a handful breaking the barrier. (Photo Courtesy Ray Mann Archive, quartermilestones.com)

"I was standing right there," remembers Tom Hoover. "It let go, and it was sort of heartbreaking to see Ronnie out for that reason. People said it was the converter, but it was actually an overrun sprag failure. If that broke, the front drum could spin to about 14,000 rpm."

So Oldfield singled into the money round, but Sox was not going to be denied now. He ran 10.23 to put the SS/B record even lower, with Oldfield close behind, hitting the SS/CA record down a tick to 10.74. Almost $10,000 in prize money from Dallas, plus the joy of victory in three of the four 1969 NHRA national meets, went back to Burlington. Sox and a cast of other stars were now done with it all, heading for the brave new world of Pro Stock.

Fuel, Fires and Flight

The Hemi, both the 426-ci and its earlier 392-ci rendition, remained popular in the dragster classes, while supercharged and injected versions of the 426-ci continued as the de facto power for Chrysler-bodied Funny Cars. The year 1969 was big for the nitro cars, but not always for the right reasons. Although the NHRA acquiesced with a Funny Car eliminator at its three national events, the organization had still not found a way to make the Funny Cars into a stand-alone class (again, the AHRA already had both a fuel Funny Car and an injected Funny Car division).

The NHRA program suffered a black eye when Gerry Schwartz was killed at the spring race in Dallas. The Funny Cars garnered further notoriety in August when veteran driver Huston Platt, brother of Hubert, lost control of his Camaro at Yellow River, Georgia, during a match race and killed several spectators. Nevertheless, cooler heads prevailed and the North Hollywood sanctioning body announced there would be a new Funny Car

Tuner Austin Coil squirts fuel into the supercharger injector of the Chi-Town Hustler Charger at a match race in Sacramento in 1970. Pat Minnick was the driver. (Photo Courtesy Jon Steele Archive, quartermilestones.com)

The restored Chi-Town Hustler is in Greg and Kathy Mosley's collection. It is credited with inventing the smoky burnout.

Eliminator class when the NHRA's new 1970 Super Season began. The cars were that popular.

An exciting new phenomenon was the smoky burnout. It came about as a part of the process tuner Austin Coil wanted driver Pat Minick to use to heat up the tires on the *Chi-Town Hustler* Charger out of Chicago. Changes in dragster science had eliminated the once-popular rooster tails of smoke. The *Hustler* guys wanted to make sure there was hot rubber traction at the launch, much as the gold-dust rosin of previous years had been worked into the surface via multiple, hard, burn-through launches. The result was to create a literal smoke bank with the tires.

Coil later admitted that he had some regret about the spectacle, as the outstanding performances the car made were often overshadowed by its showmanship. Regardless, smoky burnouts became part of the Funny Car business. The dragster crowd chose to emulate it by doing burnouts themselves again, sometimes using traction compounds that ignited into flames.

Front-engine dragsters were no laughing matter, however. The clutch and driveline settings that had eliminated tire smoke and resulted in better performances (the entire 32-car field at Indy was below 6.80) had parts spinning at unreal speeds; when something let go, it could be devastating. Explosions became even more tragic at the 1969 Nationals at Indianapolis. In the first round, John Mulligan, a popular driver who had won the Winternationals, clocked the low ET of the event at 6.43 but rode out a horrible fire and four barrel rolls. His injuries from the burns were severe enough that he died from them the following week.

Toward the end of Monday finals, between the semifinal and final rounds, several drivers attempted to take home Top Speed of the Meet, including Jim Paoli, who had fouled against Kelly Brown in the semifinals. Loading up a dose of hydrazine in the lanes, Paoli launched and then came apart in the lights, the clutch discs and parts flying into the normally safe grandstands. Paoli escaped unharmed, but four other people were injured, one critically.

A report at the time stated that RFI, the major fuel supplier at the event, had been adding benzene to its nitromethane prior to sale, and this resulted in false hydrometer readings. The hydrometer is a tool that measures the specific gravity of a liquid, telling the racer what percentage of nitromethane was in a given test batch; methanol was then added to create the right balance. According to Steve LeSueur, who has been a race fuel dealer since the 1970s, this would have had serious consequences.

"Benzene actually quiets the nitro explosion, allowing the fuel to burn. It is an exciter in terms of lighting the nitro, but is not affected by pressure changes like hydrazine is. Over the years, we put just about every oxygen-bearing compound we could find with nitro, trying to get it to light better," LeSueur says.

And if those fluid gravity readings were incorrect as suggested?

"A bomb. You'd have a higher-than-realized nitro percentage with a fuse," says LeSueur. "Indy 1969 was the swan song for hydrazine. It is my belief that those explosions were from hydrazine, not any benzene mix." A magazine report from 1970 stated that there had been 22 blower explosions during the 1969 Nationals.

The Ramchargers race team continued on, and in 1969, with Leroy Goldstein as pilot, the feared dragster began winning. The engine-building business was growing by leaps and bounds, and the team took its car to victory at both Phoenix and Bristol on the AHRA Grand American tour. After that sanctioning body acquired the former NHRA Tulsa track for its season finale, Goldstein drove to yet another final round. He faced off with Steve Carbone in the *Crietz & Donovan* entry.

In the lights, the back of the engine exploded; Goldstein rode out the fire and made a trip to the hospital for burns around his eyes. Otherwise uninjured, he came back to celebrate the team's point-accumulated AHRA Top Fuel World championship, but it was the team's last in a slingshot. Dodge's new Challenger was on the horizon, and when 1970 dawned, the Ramchargers were back in the Funny Car. And in the record books, again.

Fire was a serious problem. John Mulligan, seen here in 1968 at the World Finals, was badly burned at the 1969 NHRA Nationals in a huge round-one engine explosion and crash; he died in the hospital a week later. (Photo Courtesy Ray Mann Archive, quartermilestones.com)

CHAPTER TEN

1970

The Super Season and Superbirds

Hemis Make History in Clashes Everywhere

It was the dawn of a decade. The NHRA's new "Super Season" for 1970 was the most prolific in the history of the racing organization to date. The four current events (Winternationals, Springnationals, Indy Nationals, and World Finals) were augmented by three additional races.

These were the Gatornationals in Florida, the Summernationals (in York, Pennsylvania, that one year only), plus a new post–World Finals race at the almost completed, multimillion-dollar Ontario Motor Speedway in California. That event was the Supernationals, sponsored by Mattel Corporation's Hot Wheels.

For fans of the Funny Car, Hot Wheels had already stepped up in another big way for 1970. Competitors Tom "the Mongoose" McEwen and Don "the Snake" Prudhomme had a chance to meet with key personnel at the popular toy company, and Mattel recognized that the duo could be a key asset in product promotion of their popular miniature die-cast car replicas. The only real change was that the McEwen/Prudhomme team primarily raced fuel Funny Cars, something that the Snake had not done before. After forming a corporation, Wildlife Racing Enterprises, the two found other companies

willing to sponsor them as well. An important one on that list was Plymouth.

Plymouth's new Rapid Transit System, a promotional program for performance models, had been announced for 1970, and it too was looking for a way to market new models, two in particular. One was the newly introduced fastback A-Body, the Duster. It was available for street use with the 340 as its largest engine; the red fiberglass replica that McEwen raced had a supercharged John Hogan–built Hemi underneath the shell. The other new model was the E-Body platform Barracuda; the top rendition was the Hemi 'Cuda model. Prudhomme raced a yellow replica of that design with a blown Keith Black Hemi engine under the hood. (Dodge's similar new E-Body was the Challenger.)

The well-funded team toured extensively, almost as much as the factory clinic crews. In 1970, they appeared at 60 events, including racing, and made Mattel-generated stops at shopping centers and retail stores to promote the toy line in the same way

Hot Wheels were hot in 1970. This is Don "the Snake" Prudhomme's new 'Cuda at the NHRA Nationals, with veteran driver Jay Howell at the controls. (Photo Courtesy Ray Mann Archive, quartermilestones.com)

The 1970 Winternationals where Prudhomme's counterpart, Tom "the Mongoose" McEwen, is in the staging lane with his brand-new Duster. The Hot Wheels deal had been McEwen's idea and catapulted the sport into pop culture significance. (Photo Courtesy Pit Slides Archive, quartermilestones.com)

Don Prudhomme looks up while working on his 1970 Barracuda, a car that became iconic in drag racing history. (Photo Courtesy Jon Steele Archive, quartermilestones.com)

Sox and Landy promoted racing products. It was a major coup for the sport, and it established the Snake & Mongoose franchise in both the sport and popular culture.

Although Prudhomme still campaigned his fuel dragster (and raced to another victory at the 1970 Nationals with it, putting Jay Howell in the 'Cuda), many other former dragster campaigners had made the switch to Funny Car, including Roland Leong. After a less-than-stellar start in 1969 when driver Larry Reyes crashed the team's new car in its debut, the *Hawaiian* Charger came back to that same event, the NHRA Winternationals, and won it all in 1970.

Tom McEwen poses by a dealership-supplied 1970 'Cuda. The duo toured extensively in 1970; they were the epitome of cool. (Photo Courtesy Jon Steele Archive, quartermilestones.com)

According to research by editor Phil Burgess of *National Dragster*, by May 1969, Leong and Reyes had rebuilt the crashed car into a narrowed mini Charger. They won somewhere around $5,000 in one weekend at three independent Funny Car races, and then match raced the remainder of 1969 before returning to NHRA to post the aforementioned victory. New driver Butch Maas repeated the feat for Leong in 1971.

Like Prudhomme, Leong relied on horsepower by Keith Black Racing Engines. Larry Reyes also posted runner-up honors to Leonard Hughes' new 'Cuda at the first Gatornationals at the end of February, driving a second team car for the Louisiana-based Candies & Hughes team with Leong tuning.

Among dragster racers making the switch were Leroy Goldstein and the Ramchargers Racing Engines team. They were in the Funny Car battles of 1970 with a new Woody Gilmore–built Dodge Challenger, and they also tackled the record book head on.

Into the 6-Second Zone

The Ramchargers dragster engines had been run on the edge. However, author Dave Rockwell recounts that the new Funny Car responded well with somewhat mild tuning at first. After Goldstein, nicknamed "the Israeli Rocket," had adjusted to sitting encased by fiberglass in the team's new chassis and fresh engine combination, they began to run the car a little harder.

On June 14, the car won the NHRA Springnationals in Dallas with a solid string of 7.0 runs, besting Gene

Ramchargers *ran as fast as 7.03 in winning the NHRA Springnationals in June. The Challenger became the first car to run in the 6-second zone the following weekend, but burned to the ground at Detroit in July. The late Leroy Goldstein was the driver. (Photo Courtesy Jon Steele Archive, quartermilestones.com)*

Snow in the final with a 7.03, so the 6-second barrier was there for the taking. It became a question of who would do it first. A week later, Goldstein showed up at New York National Speedway on Long Island for a multiday Funny Car race. The evening event at near-sea-level air was a perfect testing laboratory. After solid efforts on Friday, Phil Goulet tuned the car for a heavy load of fuel. Goldstein drove it to three consecutive times of 6.98, 6.97, and 6.96 on Saturday night to make history.

Writer Gray Baskerville, in recounting the 1970 season for the *Hot Rod* magazine *No. 10 Yearbook*, made note that the automatic transmissions had truly given way to the two-speed/clutch combination in the faster Funny Cars. Along with other chassis refinements that made the cars more like their dragster counterparts, this change allowed the Ramchargers to push the envelope, and broke the barrier wide open. By the time the circuit was back in California that November for the Orange County Manufacturer's Meet, an annual Funny Car extravaganza, there were 21 runs in the 6-second zone, and speeds were pushing 220 mph.

This power came at a cost, however. Two weeks after the outstanding performances on Long Island, the *Ramchargers* Challenger was running back home at an eight-car show at Detroit Dragway and clocked a 6.96. The second run was at a close 6.99, but Goldstein was already very busy hitting the fire bottles and getting the flame-engulfed car stopped. He emerged uninjured, but because of its magnesium parts, the trick Dodge burned to the ground. The team had to really thrash to get another one ready in just two weeks to keep its lucrative summer match race bookings.

Funny Cars: Indy, Snow and Twin-Plug Heads

Then came Labor Day and the Big Go, that year's U.S. Nationals. Don "the Shoe" Schumacher debuted a new car built by fabricator John Buttera. This professional team with two entries and Hemi power built by Ed Pink set the stage for victory with consistency and a willingness to push the equipment hard. When it came time to run for the money on Monday afternoon, the

Don Schumacher does a burnout in his 'Cuda in 1970. "The Shoe" went on to win Indy over Labor Day and had two cars in attendance, with Cliff Zink driving the other one. (Photo Courtesy Jon Steele Archive, quartermilestones.com)

Ramchargers were in the other lane against Schumacher. The Detroit team was again Low Qualifier (the fifth time in six Indy Nationals) and had throttled the field with a series of runs in the 6.80s, more than .10 faster than any of its competitors. Goulet had tuned the car for an unheard-of 6.70 lap, but the track could not take the power and Goldstein was up in smoke at the start to give The Shoe and his Chicago crew the biggest title of the NHRA season.

But it was Gene Snow, the winner of the first NHRA Summernationals, the World Finals, and the Supernationals, who finished off the history books for NHRA Funny Car racing in 1970. As the season wound down, he took his new *Rambunctious* Challenger to NHRA's

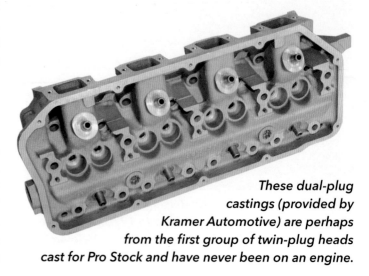

These dual-plug castings (provided by Kramer Automotive) are perhaps from the first group of twin-plug heads cast for Pro Stock and have never been on an engine.

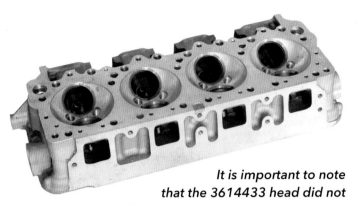

It is important to note that the 3614433 head did not receive the port redesigns that came to some of the future versions after more flow testing had been done. This example was provided by Kramer Automotive.

World Championship, and his efforts on the AHRA Grand American trail earned him that season-long crown as well.

One other development in the nitromethane classes that arrived in 1970, thanks in part to the Ramchargers team, was dual-plug Race Hemi heads. This was an innovation used once before by Chrysler, way back in the dark days of World War II and the XIV-2220 engine.

Regarding the dual-plug development, Tom Hoover gives a little more insight: "It is important to note that the Chrysler race group had a limited consulting relationship with BRM, the British engineering firm, through which Bob Cahill and I had several conferences primarily with Anthony C. Rudd, their chief engineer. Tony Rudd had been a development engineer at Rolls-Royce, where he worked on the Merlin World War II aircraft engine, and Tony suggested twin plugs for the Hemi.

"We sent them a 426 drag Hemi, which they evaluated with two plugs and got an output improvement. Next, after we went to the crank-trigger ignition during the *Motown Missile* program [to reduce spark scatter], we found that the 426 Hemi's high-speed output was essentially the same with the B plug position 'only' at 37 degrees advance when compared to using twin plugs at

their max power advance of 33 degrees advance. However, the engine's low-speed behavior was much more civilized with twin plugs, which was helpful during burnout and launch.

"The current-generation Hemi had twin plugs from its beginning. I suggested two plugs, the squish, combustion chamber, and placing the cam higher up in the cylinder block to the Chrysler design team when they consulted with me in 1998 regarding the new Gen III Hemi design."

In supercharged fuel racing, where the amount of nitro used could cause the plug to become wet and lose fire, it was a needed improvement, although it was not commonplace for some time. Dan Knapp modified the first ten sets of heads for Chrysler Engineering. He also created a set for the Funny Car, using twin magnetos that had a separately adjustable spark lead. These new parts were already on the car when it clocked an ET/Top Speed best 7.14 at 209 mph in April 1970 at the AHRA Grand American race at Lions Drag Strip.

That same race became notorious for another reason. In the Top Fuel final, Don Garlits was up against Richard Tharp and had a huge driveline explosion right on the starting line. This not only sliced through the chassis and put parts into the nearby grandstands with injuries, but also cut off half of Garlits' right foot. Following this and the emotionally painful death of John Mulligan and other friends, Garlits determined during his convalescence that he would rebuild with the engine behind the driver.

Others had tried this with small success, but they were not Don Garlits. Still, he returned at midseason in 1970 to drive the same slingshot in which he had been hurt. He had sold it to his crew chief Tommy T. C. Lemons, who had repaired it. This was the last year of professional racing

Innovator Gene Snow and his new Rambunctious *Challenger won both the IHRA and NHRA season titles in 1970. (Photo Courtesy Ray Mann Archive, quartermilestones.com)*

Don Garlits was maimed in a driveline explosion in April 1970. However, he recovered quickly enough to pilot a Top Fuel dragster before the end of the year. (Photo Courtesy Jon Steele Archive, quartermilestones.com)

that Big Daddy drove with the supercharger inches from his face and his rear end hanging over the differential.

Pro Stock: The Gang's All Here

Following the 1969 World Finals, and with input from all parties, the NHRA came up with a formula for the Pro Stock class. The rules were quite similar to those that had been allowed in Modified Production. The weight break was a flat 7.00 pounds per inch (i.e., 426 inches x 7.0 = minimum weight of 2,982 pounds), and a minimum weight of 2,700 pounds for vehicles of 1968 and newer construction.

Engines had to be from the same manufacturer as the car and in the factory location. They could have any internal modification, a maximum of two 4-barrel (or four 2-barrel) carburetors, any transmission, and any differential. Replacement body panels could be used for the fenders, hood, and deck lids, but the remainder of the car needed to be of factory steel construction (including the front bumper and doors). Partly in deference to the aluminum Can-Am short-stroke engines of Jenkins, a 45-percent front wheel/55-percent rear wheel maximum weight balance was also mandated. To jump-start the class, the NHRA created an optimistic minimum record index of 9.75.

Of course, teams did whatever was needed to meet the letter of the law. Regardless of the rules, chemical milling, or acid dipping, to lighten the steel body shells and the minor wheelbase changes that were often part of running Super Stock continued (stock wheelbase and no acid dipping were in the rules, but somewhat unenforceable).

As with several Dodge teams, the Landy operation had a new Dart Swinger in Pro Stock trim. A package was released to update the 1968 Hurst Dart bodies with new quarter panels and trim. (Photo Courtesy Pit Slides Archive, quartermilestones.com)

Still, there was not a lot of change at the start of 1970, as the cars were quite similar to the AHRA and match race packages of 1969. Entries for the 32-car fields were very large that first season (90 Pro Stock cars showed up for Indy), but it was basically a true professional category.

Dick Landy began the season with a new E-Body Challenger. One of his 1968 Darts was reconstructed as a second entry using 1970 Swinger body panels. Racer Larry Griffith's paperwork collection includes an invoice dated February 2, 1970, showing the 30 parts required to do this. Because there was little change between the 1968 and 1970 Dart designs, it was simply a case of exchanging trim and sheet metal. Griffith's opinion is that five teams made this change.

A 1970 Landy Hemi Charger in SS/EA was available for clinic and Super Stock work. A Hemi-powered 1969 Dart (the former AHRA heads-up entry) was raced in B/Modified Production. The Dart gave Landy his first title of 1970 when he won Modified Eliminator at Pomona for the second straight year, beating the Thompson & Riffle C/Gas *Rod Shop* Anglia in the final. He followed his Pomona Modified win with a win in his Challenger at a Bakersfield Pro Stock show, which ran as part of the March Meet the following month.

Incidentally, Landy began working with the new 16-plug heads in Pro Stock before anybody else, except the factory development crew. According to a story in *Super Stock* magazine, the NHRA temporarily banned them from Pro Stock, but the design was reinstated by that summer.

Plymouth Conquers Drag Racing

Like the Snake & Mongoose team, Sox & Martin had exciting new 'Cudas and Dusters. Ronnie Sox was in the team's 1970 Barracuda, while Herb McCandless piloted the team's new Duster once it was available that spring, both with the latest Jake King–tuned Hemi power. King now stayed at the shop most of the season, preparing engines for those cars as well as for a growing customer base. According to Buddy Martin in a period interview, 20 turnkey race cars and 50 engines had been built by the middle of 1970. Martin actually purchased all the tools (engine pump, wheel scales, etc.) needed to do the measuring for legality, both for their growing shop and to take to match races if needed.

McCandless' Duster was considered a marketing project for complete $10,000 Sox & Martin–built race cars. Also that spring, the team had a promising local driver named Don Carlton from Lenoir, North Carolina. He drove the old 1969 Barracuda that had raced in heads-up AHRA SS/E competition (now legal as an NHRA Pro Stock

Herb McCandless piloted the second 1970 Sox & Martin entry, this Duster. He won the NHRA Nationals in it, and he is seen here racing Sox at the new Supernationals late in the 1970 season. The car was totaled in a highway accident while returning from this event. (Photo Courtesy Ray Mann Archive, quartermilestones.com)

entry). The team added a hood-scooped 340 Duster for clinic work (it had a legal NHRA Super Stock 1968 'Cuda), and they even put together a Superbird for NHRA SS/E class. Sox & Martin Parts Manager Joe Fisher drove that car during its occasional appearances.

The 3,840-pound Street Hemi Plymouth was a unique car in that it met the new SS/E weight break by a mere 10 pounds; Fisher took it to the class speed record almost immediately at 124.83. It did not have a hood scoop (or the fender scoops found on the production cars), and the wing may have been somewhat heavier to get the static weight toward the rear wheels. The Street Hemi used a typical amount of "Jake King science," topped by a new large-plenum Edelbrock Rat Roaster supporting the twin inline OEM Carter AFB carbs. The fact that Petty Enterprises was nearby in Randleman may have played a role in some of the unique parts on this car.

Don Grotheer, the other half of the Plymouth clinic crew, had a new 'Cuda as well as clinic cars. Bill Tanner and driver Melvin Yow started the year with two well-tuned 1968 Darts in Pro Stock but had a Challenger and a converted Swinger like Landy's by the middle of the season. Of the many other Hemi cars in 1970, foremost was Arlen Vanke's new Duster. In this car, Vanke ran up a dominating five-race sweep of all the tough points meets in Division 3.

Don Grotheer was at York as well. This event was the 1970 Super Stock Nationals, and Grotheer had his new 'Cuda ready to go. (Photo Courtesy Pit Slides Archive, quartermilestones.com)

Others started the way Tanner had, and a large number of 1968 Hurst-built A-Bodies were converted to run on Pro Stock specifications while 1970-era cars were being constructed. Although these could probably be converted back to NHRA Super Stock, most of the drivers wanted the heads-up racing, as well as the lack of technical committee oversight on engine changes in Pro Stock. Indeed, a week-long rainout before the AHRA Grand American race at Long Beach where Garlits was injured allowed Plymouth contract racer Ed Miller to find some quirks

Classed into SS/E and with Joe Fisher driving, the Sox & Martin Superbird went to York in the summer of 1970. Note that the car has no fender scoops. (Photo Courtesy Pit Slides Archive, quartermilestones.com)

At this point, Grotheer was already testing with dual-plug cylinder heads. The early distributors were offset by 90 degrees. Also note the twin coils and paired firewall-mounted ballast resistors. (Photo Courtesy Pit Slides Archive, quartermilestones.com)

in his well-traveled heads-up Barracuda. As a result he was in the AHRA's Pro Super Stock winner's circle when that race was over.

The biggest challenge for most competitors was changing from the Torqueflite 3-speed transmission to a manual 4-speed. The faster cars needed the narrower RPM band offered by the 4-speed, but few could shift like Miller, Vanke, or Sox. It was into this crucible that Ted Spehar's new job became visible to the general public.

Make Mine a *Missile*

Ted Spehar was likeable and competent. After contracting with Bob Cahill to run an outside development arm for Chrysler in 1969, he sold his Sunoco gas station near Woodward Avenue and rented a small group of buildings in Royal Oak, Michigan. Working closely with Tom Hoover, Tom Coddington, and others in Chrysler's engineering department, this operation helped eliminate the frustrations posed by administrative oversight and union shop labor at Highland Park. It also gave the group a way to do quiet, effective work. Already, the growing requirements of upcoming emissions controls were taking precedence over performance work in the factory environment of all Detroit companies. If you could get in the door (most couldn't), Spehar's skunk works shop was the place to be if you loved Chrysler door-car racing.

Dick "Barney" Oldfield moved from upstate New York to work for Spehar and serve as a test driver. The race group built a new Challenger for development work. This car took its name from a nickname Vanke had given one of Spehar's previous projects: *Motown Missile*. It was a testbed for whatever ideas the engineering and race group wanted to try, with the resultant info relayed to the racers who ran Chrysler products. During the early

1970s, the dual-plug heads, a crank-triggered ignition, lightweight parts, manifold and hood scoop designs, and more were all on the docket for *Missile* development and kept drivers busy.

As had been the norm, testing was an A-B-A affair. Run a baseline (A), make a change (B), and rerun the baseline (A). One benefit of George Wallace's work in the NASCAR group was a calculation chart that adjusted for changes in barometric pressure and air temperature. By using a small weather station and some math prowess, actual levels of performance could be correctly ascertained even as the test day's weather conditions changed.

"George Wallace was a genius-level master of vehicle performance prediction calculation," Tom Hoover recalls. "He had predicted the Hyper Pack slant-6 we took to the 1960 Daytona road course lap time within 1 mph! However, he didn't build the eight-channel in-car data acquisition system we used in the *Missile;* that came from the shop in Huntsville, Alabama. Ron Killen brought the system to Cecil County when we tested the 6-speed ClutchFlite design.

"I then recruited Ron into our race group in Detroit where he became our data acquisition/electronics guru, leading to our doing real-time data collection. This helped lead to some of our high-RPM electronic ignition improvements, the crank trigger, our exhaust blow-down fixture, etc."

As mentioned before, Hoover and the crew really wanted to develop a Torqueflite transmission for the *Missile* that could run with the 4-speeds. The premise had already been developed to an extent in the gas classes when B&M mated a clutch in place of the torque converter, calling it a ClutchFlite. This adaptation was used to launch the car with more RPM and driver control, and shifting was done through the normal manual-reverse valve body.

Humorously lettered for "Barney Oldfield," Dick Oldfield prepares to get the new Motown Missile *down the track during a* Popular Hot Rodding *meet in Michigan in the summer of 1970. When the car did not break due to the number of experimental parts on it, it flew. (Photo Courtesy Pit Slides Archive, quartermilestones.com)*

A ClutchFlite transmission is getting ready for the Missile *during the formative stages of development. Eventually, a 4-speed was put into the car for racing, and Don Carlton took over as driver. (Photo Courtesy Larry Knowlton Archive, Wellborn Musclecar Museum)*

The 'Flite's stock 2.45:1 low-gear ratio did not help, so plans were made to try some unique parts. One actually used a pair of Torqueflites mounted together to create a 6-speed. Although Oldfield did the weekday testing with this project, the team also wanted to put this car into the racing environment. After all, in true Ramchargers fashion, the team could race and get paid for it.

By the time the NHRA Summernationals arrived at York, Pennsylvania, in the heat of July, the latest factory mule was refined enough to allow Oldfield to take the top qualifying slot at 9.93 with a regular ClutchFlite.

The previous three NHRA races had seen two victories by Bill Jenkins' Camaro, beating Ronnie Sox in the finals at both Pomona and Gainesville. The cars capable of winning were just cracking the 9-second margin at first. Sox and his new 'Cuda then went all the way at the Springnationals in Dallas, beating Wally Booth's returning Camaro to give Sox an unbroken string of victories at that event every year since 1967.

At the Summernationals, the low-qualified *Missile* went rounds but lost to Dick Landy in the semifinals. Coming up the other side of the ladder was the #2 Sox & Martin machine, the Duster piloted by Herb McCandless. At the time, the full tree was still in use in all categories, and Mr. 4-Speed was one of several drivers (including Oldfield) who were frustrated by red-light starts that day. That allowed "Dandy Dick" to give Dodge a second Pro Stock title that first year, in addition to his Bakersfield win.

Fans of the new class eagerly awaited the Big Go at Indy and they were not disappointed when entries showed up from around the nation. The work in the category had resulted in almost weekly performance increases, and 9.70s had already been part of the better events. Before the racing began, the coveted Best Engineered honors went to a brand-new Challenger that debuted at this event, the new *Red Light Bandit*.

Technology Refined

Bill Bagshaw began 1970 racing his 1968 Dodge Dart, which had been a major player in the West Coast Super Stock circuit. In the spring, he received a new factory Hemi Challenger that was being returned from a defunct dealership as well as an identical body-in-white (a factory shell pulled from the line before parts were added) that had been acid dipped at AeroChem. He had rented one-half of a large shop in Southern California to do this work. When he went to sign the lease, Ron Butler was there to sign for the other half.

Originally from New Zealand, Butler had been working for Carroll Shelby and had been part of the crew that helped field the team's successful sports car efforts at

Beautifully restored by Bucky Hess for John Gastman, this is Bill Bagshaw's Red Light Bandit, *the first drag car built by Ron Butler. It won Best Engineered at Indy in 1970 and is seen here at the same track in 2012.*

places such as Le Mans. He had just come under the Ford cost-cutting knife and was going to open his own fabrication shop. He had never been to a drag race.

As the two men talked, they began to see the potential of applying some of that knowledge to drag racing. For Bagshaw, it gave him somebody skilled at fabrication and race car construction; for Butler, it was a paying job and a fresh start.

As the two vehicles became one, Butler used every lightening trick he knew, getting the car under 2,700 pounds. He drilled out metal shavings from any part, and moved the rear axle slightly forward (this was possible because the factory had sent a new K-frame with the mounting points set a little forward from stock). A monster truck battery in a steel-plate box helped get weight toward the rear, as did a square steel tube full of lead mounted to the rear roll-bar supports.

The roll cage was also a big part of this car, as Butler used triangulation to tie the entire structure of the unibody together: forward-mounts to the front suspension, two vertical uprights at the center, and two rearward bars into the rear of the car, creating a steel tent inside the body. This made *Bandit* perhaps the stiffest car in the class. Coupled with the other innovations, and an engine by Joe Allread, the car was ready for its debut at Indy. Bagshaw went a few rounds that day and was also the Division 7 Pro Stock champion for 1970.

Overall, this effort was state-of-the-art for engine racing in general. It is not to say that people already in drag racing would not have found these things on their own, any more than NASCAR racers who were constantly refining body, chassis, and suspension technology. But Butler's fresh ideas and attention to detail were superb, and *Red Light Bandit* set a new standard.

On Track at Indy and Beyond

Without the high jinx of Super Stock regarding indexes and class strategy, the main thing in qualifying for Pro Stock was figuring out whom you raced on Monday. If you were fast enough to get into the 32-car fields of the time, you wanted to be in the top half or at least someplace between twelfth and sixteenth, because the field was split into a front half/back half eliminator: 1 versus 17, 2 versus 18, etc. The big hitters were at the front, and you were usually cannon fodder if you ended up between positions 17 and 22.

Although a large number of Chevrolets were on hand attempting to make the show, Chryslers were in abundance at Indy and made up more than half the final program with 17 entries. Don Nicholson was low qualifier in his SOHC Maverick at 9.90. After two rounds, the quarterfinals found no Chevy entries, two Fords, Mel Yow in Tanner's Dart, Bagshaw's new Challenger, and four Dusters.

Yow and three of the Dusters (Vanke, McCandless, and Ed Hedrick in Bill Stiles' new car) advanced, and Vanke and McCandless met in the final. It was the closet Pro Stock final of the 1970 season (reaction times were not yet recorded). The two ran just .002 apart, 9.981 for the Sox & Martin Duster to 9.983 for Akron Arlen.

After his win, McCandless ended up racing Ronnie Sox at the remaining two events during early rounds, but Vanke went to the final at each of those races, only to see Sox take the win and make the headlines. This included the winner-take-all World Finals in Dallas to give Sox the first NHRA Pro Stock World Championship and the big-money Hot Wheels Supernationals. For its effort, the Sox & Martin team took home approximately $80,000 for the season.

One of the team's cars was in every NHRA Pro Stock final round that season. Sox amassed enough points on AHRA's ten-race Grand American circuit so that by the time the tour had arrived back in Rockingham that fall for a second event, he had already locked up the Pro Super Stock Eliminator crown and the $10,000 that went with it. The only real dark spot was a highway accident that destroyed McCandless' Indy-winning Duster at the end of the season.

Super Stock Stalemate

After several seasons of trying to find a workable formula for Super Stock, in 1970, the NHRA finally settled on a variation that remains in place today. The new A-AA category was now 6.00 to 6.49 pounds per horsepower, basically giving the 1968 Hurst cars their own class, which nobody touched for decades. The rest of Super Stock settled into the previously used half-second increments through H at 9.50 and up, with I and J classes being dropped for that year, which left 16 classes. Although the sanctioning body again increased the number of classes as the 1970s progressed, the half-pound increment breaks remained the standard.

The new 1970 'Cuda and, for a short time, the Dodge Challenger R/T featured this engine-mounted Shaker hood scoop. The unit was directly mounted to the engine and protruded through the hood.

The Boss, Ronnie Sox, at Dallas for the NHRA World Finals, which he won to attain the very first NHRA Pro Stock World Championship. It was his only one. He also won the 1970 AHRA Super Stock title that season. (Photo Courtesy Ray Mann Archive, quartermilestones.com)

Since 1967, the class had used a five-year rule on body designs. Therefore, in 1970, when the margin moved to 1965, the 1964 models were again parked, even though the NHRA eventually dropped that mandate. A lot of Hemi guys were ready for something new, and they got it when the 1970 E-Body packages arrived.

The Plymouth Barracuda was a completely new design; the just-introduced Challenger raced for Dodge. What is not often talked about is that the E-Body parts were not as interchangeable in the way other Chrysler body platforms were. The Barracuda, whose performance variant was now the 'Cuda (a name first used corporately in 1969), had a wheelbase 2 inches shorter (108) than the new Challenger (110), a change that likely cost a substantial sum because of additional tooling for two different substructures. However, a good deal of the B-Body equipment was adapted to these vehicles as a cost-control measure. Because Dodge wanted the market share of Cougar rather than that of Mustang, both cars were almost as wide as the B-Body midsize designs, but made use of some of the most aggressive styling to come from Detroit in this era.

Models in 1970 were available in two-door hardtop and convertible designs. Dodge offered an SE (Special Edition) option with a smaller rear window and upscale interior components. The Dodge performance model used the R/T designation, as did the Charger and Coronet. Stripes and spoilers were offered on performance versions of the E-Body, with a special 340 Six Pack edition created of each to homologate special parts on the cars for a push into the SCCA's emergent Trans-Am sports car series that year.

The big cool option on the E-Body models was a new fresh-air hood scoop called the Shaker. Ford had used a small scoop of similar function on some 1969 models, but the Chrysler version was a wide, curvy unit with two forward-facing openings. With the hood scoop attached atop the carburetor system, and sealed for rain drainage with a rubber lip and steel base, the idle of a Hemi or similar high-compression engine made it quiver. That effect stopped as soon as the RPM smoothed out.

The Shaker unfortunately caused Dodge the same sort of problems in NHRA race legality as had the heavy 1966 models. At the time the Challenger was released, final safety testing was still being completed. Unlike with the 'Cuda, the base of the hood was right against the windshield with venting beneath it (no outside cowl area separating them). This meant there was no crush area to prevent the hood from sailing right into the driver's compartment in the event of a head-on collision. The underbracing for the Shaker hood was not designed to fold up, and Dodge had to withdraw its Shaker from the market in late 1969 due to possible liability. It was not retooled until very late in the 1970 model run. Because the performance hood had merely stylized blister openings, Dodge did not have a true fresh-air scoop until it announced in April that the specialized all-fiberglass version from the aforementioned 340 T/A models was now offered on R/T models as well.

The Hemi-powered Road Runner and GTX received a new version of fresh-air induction via a hood-mounted door that operated off engine vacuum; a toothy reflective "Air Grabber" decal adorned its sides. The Hemi Coronet models again used the twin-scoop Ramcharger layout that had debuted in 1969. It operated via a dash-mounted linkage cable, while Charger continued into 1970 without an engine fresh-air option.

The chrome dome now retired, Plymouth added a new fresh-air package to the new 1970 Road Runner, which operated on engine vacuum to open a hood-mounted door.

A knob on the dash allowed you to bare the fangs of your Hemi using the aptly named Air Grabber scoop. Few guessed that the muscle car era was soon to end.

Super Stockers in Action

The 1970 Hemi 'Cudas were raced by some teams in SS/D and SS/DA in place of previous Hemi package models. A number of competitors who chose them were happy to get away from the tough competition in the top SS/A and SS/B classes. Moreover, several of the Hurst cars had been wrecked at speed, and some were already in the hands of second owners. Sox & Martin's busy shop in North Carolina became almost a clearinghouse for the 1968 A-class cars, especially as Pro Stock took off.

The 1965 Hemi cars were in B class. C class was sparse but becoming a domain of Chevrolet Camaros with the 1964 cars now ineligible. The 1967 Hemi cars fell back into SS/D-DA with the new E-Bodies. E class remained a place for various makes, including heavier Street Hemis. Frankly, what hurt the new E cars in the DA class was a very strong 11.14 clocking by John Petrie's Hemi at the York Summernationals, resulting in a new index record number few could match (Petrie was protested immediately and found totally legal in teardown).

The Hurst models had won every Super Stock race crown on the 1969 NHRA tour. With six events and the Supernationals now on the schedule, plus so many good drivers leaving for Pro Stock, it became interesting to see how the older factory specials faired. With Detroit selling power aggressively, other competitors joined the fray. The most interesting was a 454 Chevelle convertible out of New Jersey.

Get Ray Allen

Tom Kling and Ralph Truppi had a stack of records to show that they could make horsepower. When they realized that the advertised shipping weight of a new Chevelle convertible powered by the 454 LS6 was at 8.03 pounds per factored horsepower (NHRA-rated 465), right at the top of SS/EA, they and their driver, Ray Allen, put one together with help from a performance-savvy dealership, Briggs Chevrolet. Running a 1969 Hemi GTX convertible in the same class, Chrysler employee John Tedder won SS/EA class titles at the first three events of the year (Winternationals, Gatornationals, Springnationals), and then Allen showed up and hammered the record to 11.33.

Allen was also a good enough driver that he dominated the Division 1 points standings, which led to a showdown at Indy with Philadelphian Jack Werst, who, like Tedder, worked for Chrysler. The plan to stop the LS6 was a Superbird that could have created real problems if it actually won.

"We had built the car in about four weeks, made a couple of test laps with it at Atco, and went to Indy,"

In period racing paint, this is what the old Jack Werst Superbird looks like today. This car was raced for a time and has been in the collector hobby since second owner Ken Jennings passed away.

recalled Jack Werst regarding the "get Ray Allen" Superbird. In a word, this was perhaps the biggest-ever "ringer" that Chrysler ever attempted to race in competition, and its only goal was to take Ray Allen out in the EA class runoffs before the final.

The Hemi engine was bigger than stock and was set back in the chassis. The wheelbase was reworked. Jack recalls it had a 300-pound wing in the back and had a super-heavy back window, plus a light nose cone. Everything had been in the acid tank: the hood, front fenders, doors, and body. According to Werst, "It was originally a stick-shift car, and the clutch pedal was still in it."

In the end, the "outlaw" didn't get anything. As Allen marched through class, Werst had no choice but to red light in the third round. Knowing the rumor mill was churning about the car since the event began, nobody was going to look at the car any closer. Leaving his Pro Stocker sitting unattended in the pits, Werst took the wing back to the motel. He raced the Atco points final with it, again not getting a chance to run against Allen. The 'Bird was sold with a legal engine not long afterward.

"The guy who owned it later realized it was something special when he ordered a set of headers for it from Hooker and they didn't fit," Werst says now with a laugh.

A much more legal Superbird was raced by Tim Richards, the future Joe Amato dragster tuner who had also built Werst's transmissions during the banzai era. This wing ran with some success that season, taking the SS/EA class win at the 1970 Summernationals.

But the Summernationals was also the site of the Hurst cars winning again, now in SS/AA. A pair of Mustangs had raced for the SS crown at the Winternationals, and a Camaro driven by Ed Hedrick won at Gainesville over Tedder's SS/EA Hemi GTX in that final. That same weekend, Herb McCandless drove a 1968 'Cuda (being sold to Billy Stepp by Sox & Martin for a Pro Stock effort) to the event's Modified Eliminator crown. In the Super

Stock finals at the Springnationals in Dallas, John Elliott's Mustang beat Bob Lambeck in Dick Landy's 1970 SS/EA Hemi Charger.

So, when the tour rolled into York, it was anybody's game. Ron Mancini, his explosive *Zoom-O* 1964 Dodge parked, was now in a 1968 Dart sponsored by Gratiot Auto Supply in Detroit.

He mowed down the field with the Dart via a series of 10.40s. At the Indy Nationals he proved this was no flash-in-the-pan effort by winning Super Stock again, giving Chrysler's package cars their third Indy crown in a row. After winning class (the final program consisted of just 16 cars, all class winners), the Dart went four rounds to meet Lou Downing's AMX in the final.

These two races were the 1968 Hurst Dodges' first NHRA national event titles in Super Stock. In addition to Landy's earlier efforts, Larry Griffith (in his Dart) had been the UDRA's champion in 1968, 1969, and, with new 1970 Swinger skin, 1970.

However, Allen's Chevelle really turned on in the last two months of the season. He went to Dallas and won the World Finals (as well as the 1970 Super Stock Championship) and the Supernationals, pocketing an estimated $40,000 for the season. The car garnered a huge amount of both fame and controversy decades later when it sold for $1.3 million at auction in 2006.

Drag Racing Elsewhere

Of course, Hemi power was dominant in other classes beyond Pro Stock and Super Stock: Top Gas, Competition Eliminator (especially any short-wheelbase altered on fuel), Modified, and AHRA's Formula class Stockers. McCandless won that group's GT-1 title in the Sox & Martin entry, the only real Hemi 'Cuda the team ever built into a race car for its drivers.

Among the supercharged fuel burners, Chrysler Hemi-powered drag cars won all six professional categories between the NHRA and AHRA that season. Sox and Snow doubled-up in Pro Stock and Funny Car, respec-

The Charger Daytona finally gave Bob McCurry and Dodge their long-awaited season title and also gave Dodge the manufacturers' title. (Copyright CR Racing Memories 0502029, Ray Mann Photograph)

tively; 392-ci racers Ronnie Martin and John Wiebe did likewise in Top Fuel.

Couple Mancini's wins with Sox's dominance and the high visibility in so much of nitro racing, as one might imagine, there was eventually a backlash. A lot of weekend racers were in Chevrolets, and a lot of technical inspectors had a penchant for the brand.

What happened during the following seasons was not quite the result of Chrysler pushing too hard, although frankly, Chrysler factory involvement likely played a part in negative decision-making at some of the highest levels of racing's sanctioning bodies. The success was more the result of having created a superior and, as important, readily available engine design. Although the fuel categories were becoming Hemi-only via simple economics by the end of 1970 (Chevrolet stalwarts Dick Harrell and Jim Liberman among those swapping for 1971), the rest of the dominated classes could be "fixed" with a pencil. Hey, when you can't beat 'em, outlaw 'em . . . .

NASCAR: A Little Bit Goes a Long Way

In August 1970, veteran technical journalist Roger Huntington wrote a lengthy feature for *Stock Car Racing* magazine regarding improvements to the 426 Race Hemi architecture over its six years of competition. He recounted that, during this same time period, Ford had spent millions on the SOHC Boss 429 and tunnel port advances to the 427 wedge, yet the Hemi maintained its competitive

Herb McCandless won the AHRA GT-1 crown with the team's second E-Body, the only real production Hemi 'Cuda that the Sox & Martin team raced. (Photo Courtesy Ray Mann Archive, quartermilestones.com)

Bobby Isaac won the 1970 Grand National championship. He did a good deal of it on short tracks with this conventional non-aero styled 1970 Charger, now enshrined in the museum at Talladega.

position despite seeing very little in terms of visible modifications. This was credited primarily to the foresight that had gone into the initial development work in 1963 and 1964, but moreover to ongoing tweaks both in and out of the factory.

For short-track success, the bathtub intake was a key factor, and at the 14-inch intake runner length, it was perfected to give spectacular results at 4,500 to 6,000, the RPM range used when exiting flat-track or tightly banked corners. Indeed, Huntington stated that the engine yielded a 102-percent volumetric efficiency rate at 5,500, meaning that there was more ready air-fuel mixture available through sonic tuning than the cylinder displacement could possibly use.

In addition to the civilizing effort Tom Hoover mentioned in Chapter 6, for 1970 the blocks were made stronger with additional material in the main bearing bulkhead area and the use of 9/16-inch main cap fasteners; this carried into the Street Hemi castings that year. One major benefit of the casting work in 1970 was that the heads were cast with the same-size ports as before, but material was added to the outside area by reducing the casting core dimension. This put a good deal of additional metal in the portable region.

So rather than reworking the heads with expensive new tooling, Huntington noted that Chrysler gave NASCAR builders a set of templates to optimize a larger port design by hand. Hand porting was also used to create a much more effective exhaust port that had been developed; it was rounded like a D across the upper surface.

This casting core process was also used on the so-called U/O heads for the 340 Trans-Am program. The OEM port architecture was unchanged, but it could be opened up far more than on a conventional 340 J head.

The (No) Need for Speed

Ironically, the big engines in NASCAR soon began to give way to that very same small-block technology starting in 1971. In mid-1969, at the same time ACCUS ruled

regarding special car production minimums (which became effective immediately for new releases), it announced adopting a 366-ci (6-liter) displacement limit in the future. This implementation was delayed primarily due to the expense to competitors, but a first step was to start handicapping the existing big-inch powerplants. When the Grand National circuit rolled into Michigan International Speedway for the Yankee 400 in August 1970, small-opening restrictor plates were placed under the carburetors for the first time.

This was actually an outgrowth of some of the issues that the drivers had been concerned with prior to the 1969 Talladega walkout; the desire was to try to maintain competition by slowing the entire field. During one of the 125-lap Daytona 500 qualifying races in 1970, a Charger Daytona piloted by rookie Talmadge Prince had crashed and he had been killed by the side impact from a competitor.

Many veteran drivers were actually glad when rules resulted in slower speeds. The restrictor plate attempt at parity, however, was among the combined factors that caused the Race Hemi to falter as a winning combination. You can't starve a racehorse . . . .

Wings Over Daytona

Sunday, February 22, 1970, dawned bright and sunny at Daytona Beach. It was the grand finale of NASCAR's Speedweeks tradition, and 103,000 people

Rookie driver Talmadge Prince was tragically killed on lap 19 of the first qualifying race at Daytona in 1970 in the #78 Dodge. (Copyright CR Racing Memories 1406004, Ray Mann Photograph)

Pete Hamilton proved to be the most proficient super-speedway driver in the Chrysler wing cars, taking home crowns at both 1970 Talladega events and the Daytona 500. (Copyright CR Racing Memories 0602023, Ray Mann Photograph)

filled the stands to capacity. Most of the Fords in action were from 1969, as restyling to the Torino and Spoiler for the new year had been detrimental to airflow. Cale Yarborough took the pole in the Wood Brothers #21 Mercury, but he was out with a blown engine before lap 32. For the main event, no less than 15 Chrysler wing cars, 10 Dodges, and 5 Plymouths joined the year-old Talladegas and Cyclones.

Of course, for fans of the Plymouth brand, seeing that #43 back on a blue Race Hemi–powered car provided great satisfaction. Actually, two blue-and-red Superbirds were at the event from Level Cross, North Carolina, the second one sporting #40, a number the team never used before or after 1970.

For the second car, Petty Enterprises selected a promising pilot from Massachusetts named Pete Hamilton, who had begun racing in 1962 at the age of 20. He had been the 1968 Grand National Rookie of the Year and spent most of 1969 in the NASCAR's Sportsman Grand American pony car division.

New Plymouth Trans-Am series driver/owner Dan Gurney drove a second Petty wing (actually the factory Superbird mule the Petty team had used for testing) at Riverside to start the season, took the pole, and finished sixth.

Hamilton then took over as the pilot of the team's second car. The plan was to run a partial season, mainly in superspeedway action with Maurice Petty as his crew chief; Hamilton started 15 events with the team in 1970.

Unexpectedly, Richard joined Maurice in the pits just seven laps into the race when the Hemi in #43 uncharacteristically expired; Hamilton had started ninth and stayed out of trouble the rest of the day. The team made

a critical call in the later laps when Richard Brooks spun out with his Superbird.

By then, the two main contenders were Hamilton and David Pearson in his Holman-Moody Ford. Both came in for a two-tire stop; then the Petty team brought Hamilton back in on the next lap for two more fresh tires while still under the caution. The added traction was enough as Hamilton soon made up the difference and Pearson almost spun out with two laps remaining, having to fall back. Pete Hamilton won the Daytona 500.

Unfortunately, for Bob McCurry and the Dodge guys, this showing was the same old story. Following the two lead cars were three Charger Daytonas driven by Bobby Allison, Charlie Glotzbach, and Bobby Isaac. As history shows, the Charger Daytona never won the Great American Race, but two months later, Buddy Baker made history with one in a different way.

The 200-mph Record

For Buddy (whose full legal name is Elzie Wylie Baker, Jr.), it was a chance to be the first to cross a certain threshold. Records rarely stand forever, but nobody can take away being the first to accomplish something, which is the reason people know names such as Neil Armstrong and Charles Lindberg.

Realizing the publicity value of the first 200-mph record, Dodge public relations man Frank Wylie set up the plan and made things ready for a run at this barrier in late March at Talladega, although officially the factory was coming to Alabama for a transmission test. Baker, in the 88 engineering mule, and all the aero guys from Special Vehicles Group (George Wallace, Larry Rathgeb, Gary Congdon, Larry Knowlton, and Fred Schrandt) arrived

Buddy Baker became the first stock car driver to top 200 mph, doing so in the Chrysler Engineering #88 Daytona. Chrysler built this period-exact tribute for display at the museum in Talladega.

This pit board, now in the Wellborn Musclecar Museum, was shown to Buddy Baker when he made 1970 a year for the history books by topping 200 mph during a test session at Talladega.

in Talladega, as did Frank Wylie and a film camera, plus NASCAR VIPs, including Bill France.

Despite poor weather, as soon as the track was dry enough to be safe, the test car began making laps, creeping up to speeds of 191, then 194, and then 198. After each handful of circuits, Baker came in, and the team made minor adjustments. He went out again and gave more feedback. By the time the sun was in the western sky, the car was on a fine-tuned edge as he pulled out for his sixth multi-lap session. On his thirtieth lap of the day, timing equipment set up by Wallace rang up a 200.096 time.

In the late afternoon of March 24, Baker pushed the car further, to a 200.447 time. This time was superseded by Bobby Isaac's run of 201.104 in the K&K #71 Daytona on another windy Alabama day at the same track later that year. The Baker effort will, however, forever stand as the first official NASCAR-legal lap in excess of 200 mph. Using Wallace's own calculations, Bobby Allison was rumored to have topped 200 mph during testing before Baker did it, but Buddy's time has always been the recognized record.

The team stayed overnight and were back at the track the next day, actually working with NASCAR on ways to help slow the cars. The side window glass was removed so the air no longer flowed smoothly over the side surfaces. That cost about 3 mph and a rule against removing side glass went into effect when the Grand National circuit returned for its second appearance at the Alabama track in April.

Hot Wings and Other Things

Petty's selection of Hamilton as his team's secondary driver was fully realized when the tour returned to the banks of Talladega for the Alabama 500 on April 12. The PDA walkout had faded soon after the hard days of that inaugural event, and things were cheerful in the pits. The track had been resurfaced, and Goodyear arrived with a new tire. It looked more like a drag slick than a circle-track tire; 102 round indentations were placed in the tire's track-facing surface. According to Goodyear, these were good for 35 laps. Because the fuel window was only about 32 laps, both qualifying and race day proceeded much smoother.

Hamilton's #40 car started the race from the sixth spot and was one of 11 wings on hand. He took the lead toward the end of the event, and, with favorable pits stops, the white flag found only his car and pole-sitter Bobby Isaac's #71 Daytona on the lead lap. The difference was too much for Isaac to overcome, and Hamilton took a second race title for 1970.

The third event at the track, the Talladega 500, was held on August 23, 1970, the week after the restrictor plates were added. Bobby Isaac and #71 again qualified first at 186.834, almost 13 mph slower than the 199.658 time he had used to take the pole in the spring. The final result was the same: Hamilton won a 1970 superspeedway event for the third time and Isaac was second.

After its day in the sun running 200 mph in 1970, the #88 chassis went to Don White. He ran it for several seasons, eventually with a 1974 Charger body. Collector Greg Kwiatkowski researched the lineage, found it on White's property, and is presently restoring it as the #88 car. (Copyright CR Racing Memories 0707017, Ray Mann Photograph)

However, Isaac won 11 other races, as well as the 1970 Grand National title. His efforts, coupled with others, also gave Dodge's McCurry and his White Hat team the NASCAR Manufacturers' Championship that year.

Due to issues with the fragile nose and overheating in traffic, the wings only flew at various times in 1970, not at every event. In addition to the wins by Hamilton and Isaac, Richard Petty took home the title at Rockingham with his 'Bird in early March. Bobby Allison in the #22 Mario Rossi Daytona won the Atlanta 500 late that same month. In June, the tour returned for a summer event on the road course in Riverside, California, and Petty and Allison finished 1-2 in wings.

This win followed a bad wreck at Darlington in early May when Petty hit the pit wall at speed and was injured, costing him four events and any shot at the 1970 season title. The cars ran some short-track races in the summer stretch, with Petty's #43 'Bird winning the Sheaffer 300 in Trenton, New Jersey. He used his conventional car to win on flat tracks at Maryville, Tennessee, and Ona, West Virginia, but a wing car was present at each of those events as well.

The first race with the plates, the Yankee 400 in Michigan, went to Charlie Glotzbach and the #99 Nichols-Goldsmith Dow-Corning Daytona, ending under caution due to weather. Ironically, this was the only Grand National series race in history that had winged cars finish in all top-five positions. Allison, Brooks, Isaac (all in Dodges), and Hamilton followed Glotzbach to the finish.

Hamilton then won the following event, held at Talladega, and Buddy Baker won the traditional Labor Day weekend race in Darlington in Cotton Owens' #6 Daytona. The final race won by a wing in NASCAR went to Petty at Dover, Delaware, on September 20. Meanwhile, during the off weeks when the teams were in traditional cars, the Chryslers dominated the 1970 Grand National season.

Records show that Bobby Watson drove the #8 Dodge Daytona at just one race, the 1970 ARCA 300 at Daytona. He either sold or rebodied it afterward. (Copyright CR Racing Memories 1402005, Ray Mann Photograph)

"Fearless Freddy" Lorenzen, once a Ford stalwart, came out of retirement to run seven events in 1970. Ray Fox built this Charger Daytona, reportedly under the aegis of track operator Richard Howard. (Copyright CR Racing Memories 0702001, Ray Mann Photograph)

One of the longest-running Mopar equipment competitors in circle-track racing was Buddy Arrington, seen here with #5. He drove Chrysler products until 1984. Today, this name is synonymous with late-model Hemi gear. (Copyright CR Racing Memories 1402001, Ray Mann Photograph)

Wings in Retrospect

After having won a huge 25 events in 1969, the Torino Talladega won only 4 in 1970. The aero Mercury Cyclone Spoiler again won 4 races, and non-aero Torinos won just twice in 1970 for a total of 10 Ford victories that year. As noted above, wings won 12 events in 1970, but non-aero Chryslers also took home a whopping 26 additional titles that year. All 11 of Bobby Isaac's victories had come at tracks of less than a mile, and he had no fewer than 32 top-five finishes.

So, although Dodge did not win the Daytona 500 until 1973, when Richard Petty captured victory in a Charger, it took home the 1970 manufacturers' title with 17 race wins and numerous top-five finishes. As Ford had won this accolade every single year since 1963, it was sweet indeed. The Plymouth effort had yielded 21 race crowns with less overall consistency for a close second.

Aero cars were only campaigned for two years on the Grand National circuit. During that period, Ford won 40

Dr. Don Tarr, seen here in a Superbird, was one of a number of weekend warriors who came out to race in Grand National competition during the pre-Winston era. In his 17 starts in 1970, this Plymouth wing only ran at the Firecracker 400 in Daytona; the rest of Tarr's aero cars were Dodges. (Copyright CR Racing Memories 0702007, Ray Mann Photograph)

events to Chrysler's 62 (of course, not all of these were in aero models). If the rules had remained unchanged, Ford and Chrysler aero cars would have likely continued to be winners on the faster tracks, but Bill France was not interested in seeing older vehicles showcased on the series.

Moreover, the development of specialized equipment, even if those cars were homologated for the series by creating street models, was not beneficial to spectator identification. When Ford greatly reduced its financial presence in racing overall, France recognized that the easiest way to keep competitors involved was to handicap the specialized body designs. Mandating a 305-ci limit to all aero models in 1971 took care of this.

Wings in the USAC and ARCA

These two organizations received the short shrift in the wake of the Grand National series, but information compiled by Frank Moriarty in his work *Supercars*, and resultant material gathered by the Aero Warriors club, give a great deal of data. Ironically, the Charger Daytona never proved to be as dominant as an aero purist may think. Some of this was simply due to the fact that Plymouth had an A-grade group of drivers with the two Petty

cars, Ramo Stott in ARCA, and the duo of Norm Nelson and Roger McCluskey on the USAC late-model circuit. All except Nelson won multiple events. Bobby Isaac was the only consistent winner on the Dodge side during this era, and he did not win with his wing car after the end of 1969 at Texas.

Although many other drivers piloted Charger Daytonas, they often faltered from mechanical failures, accidents, or plain poor luck when it mattered. In 1970, Allison and Baker each took a single win for the Dodge wing, with Glotzbach winning the Michigan race and one of the Daytona qualifiers.

Including the single 1969 victories by Brickhouse and Isaac, the Dodge Charger Daytona won six NASCAR races and only two other titles, both in USAC's late-model series: Don White's victory on the Milwaukee Mile in August of 1970 and Butch Hartman's win at Pocono in late September 1971. The only event in ARCA that included a Daytona Charger was the 1970 running of the 300-miler at Daytona. Long-time short-track pilot Bobby Watson finished second behind Ramo Stott's Superbird.

Superbirds, on the other hand, took home 17 wins overall: 8 in NASCAR, 7 in USAC, and 2 in ARCA. Ramo

Dick Brooks was in his second year on the NASCAR circuit and ran in 34 races, achieving 15 top-five finishes that season. He spun out during the Daytona 500 in this car. (Copyright CR Racing Memories 1402002, Ray Mann Photograph)

Norm Nelson and Roger McCluskey dominated the USAC series, and records show Norm ran #41 at nine events that season. This may have been at Sears Point, which was USAC sanctioned that year. (Copyright CR Racing Memories 141 0002, Ray Mann Photograph)

Stott's #7 'Bird ran in two NASCAR superspeedway events in 1970. Those were the spring races at Daytona and Talladega. Stott won the associated ARCA crowns in the same car at both of those events. He actually led two laps at the 1970 Daytona 500 as well.

Combined with his more standard Plymouth's effort, Ramo brought home ARCA season titles in both years. His #77 Superbird, driven by Lem Blankenship, ran six events in 1971 on the USAC circuit and finished all in the top 10. Ramo also ran a 'Bird as #47 at six USAC events himself in 1972, winning the 200-miler on the banking of Michigan International Speedway on July 16, beating Roger McCluskey's Superbird on the last lap.

McCluskey dominated on the USAC tour in the wing car era in perhaps the most colorful of the Superbirds; it featured a large roadrunner cartoon on the sides. In the 19 events that he drove Norm Nelson's second wing between 1970 and 1972, he finished first six times and was in the top three of 15 of those races. McCluskey was notably the last sanctioned winner in a wing when he topped all other entries at USAC's fast 200-miler at Pocono, Pennsylvania, on July 30, 1972. Nelson ran 6 events himself, with three top-five finishes. The team finished 1-2 on the circuit in 1970.

Sal Tovolla made 15 starts in a Superbird on the USAC series during this era without victory, while Bobby Unser made 4 USAC starts in a Ray Nichols–fielded Plymouth Superbird in 1972, finishing second twice.

Signs of the Times

Although the Mopar faithful did not feel it as quickly, the American muscle car era died a fairly swift death during 1970. General Motors made major changes to its performance marketing in the middle of 1970, while huge increases in insurance policies (which came to light during congressional hearings on auto safety in 1969) ended much of the potential youth market for those cars. Ford dropping out of racing conveniently gave Chrysler executives room to apply some of that funding to other (often now mandated) projects.

The election of Republican President Richard M. Nixon in 1968 and the increasingly aggressive Democratic Party–led 91st through 93rd Congresses between 1969 and 1974 were both bitter and successful depending on one's political allegiances. Each blamed attendant societal woes on the other side, yet foreign policy demands and the emotionally charged conflict in Vietnam made Nixon extremely malleable on domestic policy issues. As a result, he largely continued the policies of his two Democratic predecessors. The result included the new Environmental Protection Agency, the ban on tobacco advertising on broadcast media, and revenue-sharing with states to justify changes to tax and monetary policy.

For 1970, the Hemi's legacy, in both race and street designs, was unquestionably a dominating presence in Chrysler's vehicle marketing. Chrysler had taken an immense 38 percent of the performance car market, no doubt influenced by the engine's preeminence in competition. The year will be forever recalled as the best of times for supercar fans. The storm clouds of change were already gathered when Johnny Carson's *The Tonight Show* sold the last pack of Marlboros on television at 11:50 p.m., January 1, 1971.

This is the Funny Car final of the 1970 Super Stock Nationals at York, Pennsylvania, with Leonard Hughes beating Larry Reyes in Hawaiian for the title. The 1970s made drag racing a major sport. (Photo Courtesy Pit Slides Archive, quarter-milestones.com)

CHAPTER ELEVEN

1971
Winds of Change

The Factory Finale for the Street and a Racing Requiem

In the Wellborn Musclecar Museum's extensive file of Harry Hyde's personal papers is a short note penned to Hyde by Bill France in December 1970, thanking him for two cases of fine Kentucky bourbon for Christmas.

Hyde, the owner of the new World Champion #71 Dodge team, and many other Chrysler-focused racers, faced an uncertain future in the new year, for a variety of reasons.

By then, December 1970, Chrysler had already contracted with Hyde for the new season, as had sponsors WIX and Goodyear. After all, winning the NASCAR championship was a big deal. However, things were not perfect in Dodge City. Foremost had been dramatic cutbacks in race funding from the factory, leaving Hyde with a big credit for parts but no cash to go racing. In addition, that parts credit was now good with Petty Enterprises, which had been given the distribution business formerly belonging to Ray Nichels and Paul Goldsmith.

Nichels-Goldsmith and their Go-Fast Factory had been a unique enterprise. According to Ramo Stott, who won the ARCA Championship both seasons (1970 and 1971) and had raced circle track for most of the Hemi era, winter was often spent working in the huge Griffith, Indiana, warehouse with other racers, mainly USAC and ARCA competitors but also NASCAR teams.

Each man had a specialty (welding, sheet-metal fab, tube bending) and came to build Nichels' racers' chassis and suspensions for the coming season. You saw the basics of what everyone else saw, and you knew that the guy whose chassis you might be working on was doing something similar for you. It was a unique camaraderie, a far cry from what NASCAR became, or the way Petty Engineering operated. The Go-Fast guys did everything they could to win and all personally shared in the glory of being a part of every Chrysler's winning effort.

Due to the declining economic climate in the retail auto business and pressing nonracing needs, the 1970 NASCAR season ended with Chrysler pulling a large amount of funding from racers in the series, similar to what Ford had already done. Indeed, there were just two fully factory-backed drivers at the 1971 Daytona 500, Richard Petty and Buddy Baker, and Baker's #11 Dodge was being run from the Petty operation.

Nichels was partially funded to field a single car, but he too would be getting any fresh pieces from Level Cross. Pete Hamilton went to the Cotton Owens' operation,

Bobby Isaac did not run a full schedule following his 1970 championship, competing in 25 NASCAR races and winning 4 of them. This was the redesigned Charger body following the wing car era. (Copyright CR Racing Memories 0502018, Ray Mann Photograph)

The Petty team now had control of Chrysler's circle-track business. Richard Petty and Buddy Baker were the only major drivers on the payroll now, seen here at Daytona in 1972 after the STP sponsorship arrived. (Copyright CR Racing Memories 1102094, Ray Mann Photograph)

which switched to Plymouth that season. In the end, very few drivers raced in more than 40 of the 48 events that year. When the 1971 season ended, not including Petty, only two Chrysler racers were in the top 10: Jab Thomas out of Roanoke, Virginia, and Frank Warren of Augusta, Georgia.

There can be no mistake that Chrysler, from a business perspective, was wise to get Petty back from Ford. Although the cost of that change was perhaps borne by other competitors in some ways, Richard Petty gave the company winning accolades long after the Race Hemi was gone. Still, it was a bitter pill for Hyde and the others: Their toughest on-track rival had the exclusive factory parts that had once been under the disciplined responsibility of Ronney Householder.

Indeed, it has been privately stated that Householder was completely bypassed in the decision-making process. The edict for giving Petty Enterprises the parts business had been issued directly by Chrysler Board Chairman Lynn Townsend in the face of Plymouth's falling overall new-car market share.

From Bill France's perspective, 1971 and its rules could bring other dramatic changes, even though he noted in a personal follow-up letter to Harry Hyde that spring that NASCAR was asking Chrysler to reconsider making one race team the distributor of all circle-track parts. It should be noted that the Nichels-Goldsmith operation had never fielded an aggressive full-season effort as the company's distributor, choosing to mainly run plum events with name pilots. It should also be noted that Ford had already done what Chrysler was now doing, eventually leaving the legendary Holman-Moody operation out in the cold. Times were changing.

Rules and Repercussions

The ACCUS-FIA rules for 1971 were the tightest ever and, although created earlier, became the truest picture of what the future of auto racing looked like because of waning factory support despite popular interest in motorsports. For late-model Grand National racing, the 1969–1970 aero cars were not outlawed at the start of the year. They were, however, rendered uncompetitive. *Popular Mechanics* magazine laid out an excellent summary of the new rules in the January 1971 issue as part of its annual auto racing guide.

Foremost, the era of specialty body and engine creation was over. It was now 2,500 units or 1/250 of the prior year's production, whichever was larger; no half-year/midyear releases were allowed. Engines for racing approval needed to be installed in a minimum of 500 cars. It's not often stated that such engines for any new specially styled models had to meet a 5-liter threshold, no larger than 305 ci.

Any existing aero-styled car (Ford, Mercury, Dodge, or Plymouth) was required to meet that displacement for 1971 as well, but could do so without a restrictor plate. Although Chrysler had done some initial work on an aero wing package for the new 1971 B-Body redesigns, this ruling regarding body legality immediately rendered any such effort futile, and work was suspended.

Next for 1971, any newly offered production engine to be designated legal was limited to 366 ci (6 liters). Previously approved engines up to 430 ci remained legal, but the restrictor plate was mandated for them. The openings on this plate were subject to various changes at NASCAR's discretion. As you might imagine, the Chrysler Hemi and Boss Ford engines were given the largest amount of restriction, and therein lies the true reason the Hemi engine waned in NASCAR racing.

Port flow velocity and fuel availability were primary factors that had allowed these engines to have such incredible performance in the midrange through the upper end of the RPM band. If the engine could not get enough fuel to maximize port velocity it became uncompetitive, even when ram tuned for maximum availability. Add in a weight differential due to the physical dimensions of the engine, and it became even more difficult.

Just Petty Jealousy or More?

An unsigned letter in the Hyde files at the Wellborn Museum also brings to light another critical problem: rules enforcement. This was likely penned by Hyde, who is referenced throughout in the third person. It noted the non-aero car Richard Petty had been driving throughout 1970 was not legal by the current rules due to chassis changes. After getting no justice from NASCAR on the problem that season, when the same chassis returned in 1971 with a new body on it, Hyde complained more loudly.

That spring at Rockingham, #71 was given a smaller 1-inch-hole restrictor plate for a gas tank infraction. Based on Hyde's complaint, the Petty car had to run the same plate based on his violations, but Richard went on to win the event anyway.

In fact, Nord Krauskopft angrily pulled the #71 K&K Insurance Dodge of Harry Hyde and World Champion Bobby Isaac out of contention that same week despite it being the defending champion. He sent letters to promoters Larry Carrier of Bristol, Ned Jarrett at Hickory Speedway, and Richard Howard of Charlotte that the World Champion was not attending their spring races, and he included copies of the anonymous five-page letter to each.

The situation eventually thawed enough so that Isaac was actually back by Atlanta's Dixie 500 in April, but the team focused on other things that year. Isaac recorded four wins in an abbreviated year-long tour that consisted of just 25 dates, and the team prepared to run Bonneville (see sidebar "Flying Miles: A Look at Land Speed Efforts" on page 74).

Despite such setbacks, the 1971 season was good, even great, for Chryslers in NASCAR racing, winning more than half the events. Of 48 possible races, Isaac won 4, while independent Ray Elder won Riverside with a Dodge. Bobby Allison, now on his own, played musical cars between Chrysler and Ford equipment, but won 2 for Dodge that summer. Hamilton won 1 of the Daytona qualifiers in the Cotton Owens Plymouth, and Buddy Baker earned the Petty team its first win in a Dodge at Darlington. Like Isaac, Baker ran an abbreviated 19-race schedule.

Of course, topping all of this was Petty's new Plymouth, which won 21 events and had 41 top-10 finishes in 46 starts that year, a stellar season and proof that the new B-Body design was indeed better than expected even without extra aero refinement. It was not lost on anyone that Richard Petty had become the true superstar of NASCAR, a folk hero of racing fans, and a professional in the boardroom or behind the wheel. Regardless of how other contenders dealt with his success, King Richard was the true face of NASCAR's future and capably maximized his personality and talent to keep Plymouth and later Dodge in the limelight. He won the 1971 NASCAR championship. He did it again in 1972, 1974, and 1975. And he did it all in Chrysler products, whether Hemi-powered or not.

The (Final) Hour of Power

Late in 1971, *Stock Car Racing* magazine ran a cover story with this headline: "Is the Hemi Dead?" Several teams, including the Petty cars, had actually gone back to the circa-1964 Max Wedge heads mounted to the stronger Hemi engine blocks, a change that offered more breathing room in a literal sense due to larger-opening restrictor plates for wedge engine designs. A reworked bathtub intake and other Hemi-era technology helped make this package a strong one.

Although the Hemi did not fully disappear from NASCAR during a couple of years, it simply no longer was a dominant force. Indeed, on April 28, 1972, newspapers reported that Petty would again be running a Hemi engine in the race at Talladega for the first time that season, and the number 43 was on a Dodge for the first time.

Moreover, with Winston's sponsorship money arriving as a result of changes in tobacco advertising laws, the years between 1971 and 1975 resulted in some true challenges to points gathering and the attendant season-long prize money. Richard Petty proved to be very adept at making this system work despite changes each season and took Plymouth and Dodge body designs to Winston Cup World titles in four of those five years.

Driving his blue #43 Plymouth GTX in 1971, Petty won the championship, the Daytona 500 for the third time, and had a seven-race streak in July and early August. In USAC and ARCA, the 429.999-ci rule remained in effect, and the Hemi could still run there without restriction in 1971, and it did. Roger McCluskey and Ramo Stott took home season titles to give Plymouth all three major circle-track sanctioning body championships.

This is a Petty Enterprises big-block wedge on display at the Wellborn Musclecar Museum. A Hemi-style restrictor plate is why the wedge gained favor in 1971.

Ramo Stott and Doug Schellinger at the 2014 Mopar Collectors Guide Hall of Fame ceremony. Stott is holding the Daytona victory flag from 1970. He won event titles in this car in 1970, 1971, and 1972.

Among the changes for 1971 was that cars moved closer to the emerging idea of rolling billboards. Another was the advent of outside financing not seen during the factory wars. Businessman Chris Vallo (C. V. Enterprises) backed Ray Nichels' cars to the tune of a $1 million down payment to field a world-class team.

Heralded widely in the periodicals of the day, Nichels returned to Pontiacs that season with big-name drivers. In addition, a Plymouth was assisted by a modest STP sponsorship and campaigned part of the year by Freddy Lorenzen. However, Vallo proved to be less than honest, eventually going to prison, and after an additional promised $6 million never showed up, the huge initial outlay Nichels had made cost him his racing business. The following year, Petty Enterprises received a much larger STP sponsorship; that program continues today, almost a half century later.

One Final Flight on the High Banks

Chrysler's wing cars had a last hurrah of sorts in 1971, but without the Race Hemi. Mario Rossi and the #22 Coca-Cola Charger Daytona had been fairly successful in 1970 with Bobby Allison driving. Allison had gone out on his own (and taken the Coke money) for the new season, but Rossi and former factory driver Dick Brooks, who also was without a ride in 1971, agreed to make an attempt at the Daytona 500 under the new rules.

During 1969, Plymouth had used its former Petty budget to help field an Indy car program with STP that Art Pollard drove; a Harry Weslake–designed LA-series destroked 318-ci small-block engine powered it. Coupled with the development work from 1970 on the 305-ci engine for the Trans-Am series, Chrysler's small-block engine was beginning to show promise in endurance racing. For Rossi's car, Chrysler assisted in the financing of a stock car engine that Keith Black's people in California

built for this effort. The team made quite a spectacular showing at the 1971 Daytona 500.

The car qualified well by finishing third in its 125-mile qualifier race, and Brooks was actually the only competitor in the field racing without a restrictor plate. The announcers on the television broadcast echoed France's sentiments about how competition for 1971 had improved due to the rules changes. The fans went wild as Brooks pushed the screaming high-RPM gold-and-red 1969 Charger Daytona toward the front.

Brooks led the event on and off for a total of five laps before Pete Hamilton drifted into him on the exit of turn two. The damage was severe enough that Hamilton was done for the day. However, Brooks limped home two laps down and eventually finished seventh despite the body damage.

France is rumored to have issued a final decree that actually banned the aero specials after this event because of Brooks' strong showing. This has not been verified, but no aero cars ever ran after this race. With so much invested in Hemi and other big-inch technology at that time, it is possible that no other Chrysler team was willing to risk its success on the extended high-RPM running of the LA-series engine, and that may have been the case with other brands as well.

Development on small-block engines continued as NASCAR eventually settled on a 358-ci limit that basically rendered big-block structures uncompetitive due to weight and undersquare problems (when the stroke is longer than the cylinder bore diameter). In perhaps a fitting end, Dick Brooks later scored Plymouth's final NASCAR victory at Talladega on August 12, 1973.

Regarding 1971 NASCAR racing, I need to mention one final thing. In an effort to achieve some form of parity for small-block engines and perhaps in deference to a deal that Roger Penske had recently made with AMC

Although not a Hemi, Dick Brooks was the pilot of the final wing car to run in NASCAR, here alongside Pete Hamilton just before their accident at the Daytona 500. (Copyright CR Racing Memories 0412045, Ray Mann Photograph)

to develop racing equipment, for the first time since the Talladega debacle of 1969, drivers in unrestricted 5-liter Grand American pony cars began to run with the big dogs during the second half of the year. Allison won a couple of his Grand National races with a Mustang. Tiny Lund did likewise in a new Camaro with Pepsi backing.

This was simply more confusion wrought by new dynamics in motorsports marketing, changes in sponsorships, and the withdrawal of factory support. One thing was certain: The era of the American supercar had ended.

Rarest of the Rare

As the decades have passed, the 1971 Chrysler model year has gained notoriety for many muscle car fans. With emissions testing taking center stage, this year marked the end of the Street Hemi program. Although some basic work was done on a more compliant version of the engine with the A279 engine model, in the end it was decided to let the powerplant retire unaltered at the end of 1971 production that July.

After all, defanging the Hemi would not have served the company nor the engine's history well, and this decision certainly helped seal its legacy among aficionados of packaged American horsepower. The Charger received the same trap-door air-grabber design that had showed up on Plymouth B-Body designs in 1970. Both were restyled, and the performance model of the Coronet was dropped entirely. Today, however, no Street Hemi package is more coveted than the 1971 Hemi 'Cuda convertible, of which a mere dozen or so examples eventually came off the assembly line.

The 'Cuda featured a fairly radical reworking of the grille, immense side graphics with engine callouts, optional high-impact colors, and more in its second season. It was frankly over the top, even among a breed that set that standard. It and other designs for 1971 sometimes spark a love-hate relationship among Chrysler fans. The styling potential learned during earlier wind tunnel tests resulted in serious changes to the B-Body body lines, but those cars also grew an exponential option list of colors, spoilers, hood treatments, and options. With insurance rates up, all final-year Hemi vehicles can be considered rare. Because both the B-Body and Challenger R/T convertibles had also been discontinued, the Hemi 'Cuda was the sole survivor of this style; it warrants additional discussion, as it too was a winner.

Droptop Door Slammer

It has been said that the 1971 weight numbers filed with NHRA were massaged by the company to bring the Hemi 'Cuda convertible out of D/DA and into SS/EA as a result of the Ray Allen project. The bottom line was that a couple of these cars were custom-built specifically for racing. Racer Dave Wren ran one for a brief time in the middle of the 1971 season, and Terry Earwood won the U.S. Nationals with Steve Bagwell's example in 1973. The most famous 1971 Hemi 'Cuda in competition, however, went to Zanesville, Ohio, Super Stock racer Carroll Fink, who ran a car resale franchise with his brother Gale.

Fink had won the 1970 Super Stock Nationals and a number of NHRA event titles in an uncompetitive 1967 RO Plymouth in SS/DA. In early 1971, a 340 'Cuda convertible that had been wrecked was totaled-out under warranty and then turned over to Detroit area car builder Tom Tignanelli. Under factory direction it was rebuilt into a 1971 Hemi 'Cuda droptop specifically for racing and debuted for the 1972 season. Fink went on to record a fair number of final round appearances that year, including a victory at Sanair, Quebec City, Canada, at a new race called the Le Grandnational, which had been added to the NHRA schedule in 1971.

The 1971 styling for the Barracuda was quite dramatic, and all convertibles are in high demand today. Carroll Fink drove his homebuilt version in the early 1970s to several late-round showings and a win.

The Hemi 'Cuda convertible proved itself with several multimillion-dollar sales in 2014. This one, on display at the Muscle Car & Corvette Nationals near Chicago, sold at Mecum for more than $3 million.

At least one real 1971 Hemi 'Cuda ended up on the dragstrip for more than a time trial. It was a car owned second-hand by Nick Masciarelli, who, like Fink, was from Ohio. After buying the car, he also went with Tignanelli for power, and the car was raced for a handful of seasons before being retired. It also ran in SS/EA and once even raced Fink's version heads-up (unsuccessfully) at the 1972 Super Stock Nationals at York.

Fast-forward to 2014, in restored pristine condition, the Masciarelli B5 blue 'Cuda finally became a winner. It took home $2.4 million at an RM Auctions event in Arizona to record one of the highest-ever public selling prices for any post-1960 American production car. The sale of another 1971 Hemi 'Cuda convertible topping $3.5 million at a Dana Mecum auction firmly established the model as the true pinnacle of the era.

The Pros

In 1971, Larry Carrier formed the International Hot Rod Association (IHRA), so drag racing had a third sanctioning body. Based out of his race facilities in Bristol, Tennessee, he scheduled 7 races that season. Along with 10 Grand Americans on the AHRA tour and 8 NHRA nationals, traveling drivers had 25 big race dates, plus various points races and independent events. The result was more opportunity for exposure, plus a bewildering number of rules adaptations and interpretations.

In addition to continuing support of the clinic program of Dick Landy and Bill Tanner, Dodge marketing partially funded a very well-heeled effort for Gil Kirk's Rod Shop team that put new Chargers, Challengers, Demons, and even a Mitsubishi Colt into action across several classes with seasoned drivers.

Ronnie Sox (right) is in action during Indy qualifying in 1971. He won six of eight possible titles that season and lost only two rounds of NHRA racing that entire season. (Photo Courtesy Tommy Erwin Archive; University of South Carolina 012__1971)

Mike Fons was a noted Chevrolet racer before joining the Rod Shop effort and building this Challenger, which won the NHRA World Finals. It is seen here at its first event in Martin, Michigan, in August 1971. (Photo Courtesy Pit Slides Archive, quartermilestones.com)

Plymouth continued its support of the Wildlife Racing Funny Cars and the Pro Stock program for Sox & Martin and Don Grotheer. Both divisions also still had contract racers including Vanke, Griffith, and others as needed. NHRA records for 1971 show that Chrysler achieved a pretty amazing feat from this multipronged approach. It was the grand finale of Hemi power.

In NHRA Pro Stock, Ronnie Sox continued where he had left off in 1970, winning six of eight races. His loss at the Summernationals, now moved to Englishtown, New Jersey, was due to a deflated slick. He was outrun in NHRA competition that year just one time, at the World Finals in Amarillo, Texas (the former Dallas location had switched to the upstart IHRA organization). Mike Fons, in a Challenger running the Rod Shop colors, shut down Sox in the semifinal round with a fair-and-square 10.06 to 10.14. Fons won the 1971 NHRA season title when he beat Herb McCandless in the Sox & Martin team's other car in the final, 10.05 to an off-pace 10.40.

While Fons sewed up the NHRA crown, the new IHRA race series ended with Don Carlton and the *Motown Missile* crew winning the season-ending finals in Lakeland, Florida. Arlen Vanke won the AHRA Winter Nationals in Arizona at the start of the season to end his perennial "always a bridesmaid" title. Don Carlton, Carmen Rotunda, and Bob Lambeck drove Mopars to wins on the AHRA circuit. Lambeck, now on his own in an ex-Landy 1969 Dart, came into the AHRA final event of the season at Fremont, California, as a points-leading favorite after a win in Denver and several late-round finishes.

In the end, Jim Hayter wound up the AHRA World Champion for Chevy dealer Fred Gibb in the first ZL1 Camaro ever built. It was small consolation after the car's owner Dick Harrell had been killed in a Funny Car accident a month earlier.

Danger Zone

Ironically, Harrell had just attended a benefit race for Larry Reyes the weekend before his fatal accident in Toronto, Canada. Reyes, who had moved on from *Hawaiian*, had been badly hurt in a wreck in the new *Super 'Cuda* late that summer, a tragedy that left him without the use of his legs. The year saw a number of serious accidents as the Funny Car contingent stepped up performances. The *Ramchargers* and *Hawaiian* teams both suffered traction-related problems that resulted in losing the entire differential housing right on the track. Prudhomme had a finish-line engine explosion that, with the lack of aerodynamics, caused his *Hot Wheels 'Cuda* to literally fly over the timers at Seattle International Raceway.

Add to this mix a rash of fires, guardrail jousts, towing accidents, and thefts, and Funny Car costs increased in 1971. The same accidents gave pause to the sanctioning bodies as well. Better-equipped fire-fighting equipment at the track, new front tire rules, and well-designed fire suppression systems on the cars helped make such harrowing situations more survivable. Nonetheless, experiments with wings, underbody airflow, injector positioning, and body styling all continued to make Funny Car racing a place of innovation.

In terms of repeat championships for the "fiberglass flops," the Chargers did it. Gene Snow again captured the AHRA series crown for Funny Cars in his new Dodge, *Rambunctious*. At NHRA's winner-take-all World Finals now at Amarillo, Texas, the NHRA crown went to a New York–based Charger, *Custom Body Dodge*, under the control of Phil Castronovo.

Funny Cars with shaped-fiberglass Chrysler bodies remained in abundance nationwide, encompassing A-, B-, and E-Body layouts from both Dodge and Plymouth. The names *Chi-Town Hustler, Mr. Norms, Hawaiian, Color Me Gone, Super Duster, Rambunctious, Custom Body Dodge,* and others only added to their popularity. But the Funny Cars found the Top Fuel class a resurgent competitor for attention that season, and once again Big Daddy Don Garlits was leading the charge.

Going Forward by Moving Back

Once healed, and well enough to drive by June, Garlits ran the rest of 1970 in the same car that injured him so badly at Lions in April. Garlits began thinking about how to resolve the issue of sitting behind or over the engine and clutch/transmission (the tranny had been the culprit in his accident). He and his guys in Florida, Tommy "T.C." Lemons and Connie Swingle, began building a new car with the engine mounted behind the driver's seat.

This combination had been tried in dragsters before, often with ill-handling, car-destroying results. AHRA racer Duane Ong's *Torque Pawnbroker* had been the only current-era example that proved to be safe and competitive.

Funny Car racing continued unabated in 1971, with many Chrysler entries on hand. This is the new Mr. Norm's Super Challenger *in the pits at the* Popular Hot Rodding *race in Michigan. (Photo Courtesy Pit Slides Archive, quartermilestones.com)*

Multi-time event victor Larry Reyes is seen at the controls of Super Duster *at Dallas at the end of 1970. In a dangerous era for racing, he was injured in an accident at Norwalk, Ohio, that left him paralyzed. (Photo Courtesy Ray Mann Archive, quartermilestones.com)*

Garlits' revolutionary rear-engine dragster (bottom) is seen here running against Tom "the Mongoose" McEwen (top) in the uniquely-styled Hot Wheels *front-engine dragster. (Photo Courtesy Pit Slides Archive, quartermilestones.com)*

TOM HOOVER ON THE HEMIS THAT NEVER WERE

The success of the 426 Hemi was a major accomplishment for Chrysler, but a number of other experimentals were attempted from what had been learned. Here, engineer Tom Hoover recalls some specifics of these packages that never reached the production level.

A925: 1964

The so-called doomsday machine DOHC NASCAR engine was built as a valvetrain test fixture in the middle of 1964 but never ran under its own power. Progress on it was canceled after Bill France deemed the non-production engines of both Ford and Chrysler illegal at the end of the 1964 season.

Tom Hoover remembers, "The A925 was not only designed as a DOHC package, but there was a pushrod version as well, and that was what I favored. However, once NASCAR took a look at it, they didn't want to hear about it or our A864 Hemi either, and that was the end of that! I do not believe any parts were ever brought in for the pushrod version.

"You have to remember, Americans were always well versed when it came to pushrod valvegear activation. It had a solid background and I think it would have been a winner. The parts that were brought in were for the DOHC version, in which case the valves were activated by a tappet in a bore over the valve by the camshaft itself.

"The A925 ran only as a valvegear fixture; that is to say, it was never fired up with a carburetor on it. The guys then found some issues with the overhead cam version that would have to be resolved before the project could go forward, and that never happened because NASCAR had lowered the boom. As I remember, this was with the cam followers; the followers scuffed and broke and so forth.

"Personally, I think what we needed to do at that time was get some advice from the British racing people, either BRM or Weslake & Company. The Europeans had used actuation of the valves with overhead cams for years and years. Anyhow, that would have been the next step had we continued."

A148: 1966–1967

The A148 was actually an attempt to create an even larger bore block that could be destroked below 400 inches due to changes in the NASCAR rules. Begun in 1966, it would have used almost a completely

John Mahoney purchased the only surviving A925 in the 1970s, and he has displayed it periodically. This image of the engine in testing in 1964 is from the Tim Hoover collection. (Photo Courtesy Chrysler Group LLC)

different structure from the 426, and very little was interchangeable. Unfortunately, this project was politically motivated and came to no avail.

"We want to sort of step carefully about this, but fundamentally what happened was that a delicate political situation evolved after a management change at very high levels," Hoover says. "The powers that be reassigned Bob Rarey, who had run the Powerplant Engineering department, to run the Mound Road engine plant.

"The new chief engineer, one of the 'old heads,' took over at Powerplant and he took it upon himself to muster up the engine design department, Bill Weertman's department, to make improvements on the basic A864 Race Hemi engine. He wanted really big valves; well, didn't we all? I had wanted a .060 bigger valve for the A990 replacement aluminum head in 1966 and had not been successful. Anyhow, I'm thinking the A148 had a 2⅜-inch intake and 2-inch exhaust.

"He didn't invite any of the experienced race program people, including me, to help on the A148; he wanted to show the young whippersnappers the truth and the light. He didn't consult with Harry Weslake about what shape the port should be, and the intake port was poorly shaped. It was way too big; like 4 square inches.

"In my view, it just didn't work. The engine lab brought the parts in beautifully, and they ran the engine for several months, but it never put out the power the A864 did. I think the fundamental flaw was that, instead of talking to anyone like Weslake, they used the old conventional

TOM HOOVER ON THE HEMIS THAT NEVER WERE CONTINUED

Chrysler wisdom of going with the simple cross-sectional area of the port regardless of what the shape was. Shape matters; the old timers did not realize that.

"Still, they did a good job of keeping the port area constant, going through the runner from the opening to the valveseat. That was done at the expense of optimum shape, though, which Weslake could have provided to make a winner out of it. From the valveguide to the valveseat, you have to follow an accomplished airflow expert of Weslake's stature to get that right.

"The final thing was, they wanted a bigger exhaust valve, so they tipped the exhaust location outboard and added a pocket around it. They changed that 58.5 angle separation and they lost the hemispherical combustion chamber.

"Maybe the only good news was that ultimately, engineering established a position for a guy named Bob Miller to become our port flow expert. They gave him a flow bench and so forth, and later, things such as the D4 head with the high round exhaust port and the W2 version of the LA-engine head came from his benchwork. By the time he was functioning, we relied on him for the airflow work. Miller was a young guy not contaminated by all of the decades-old doctrine of the engineering establishment. He was our own in-house Harry Weslake.

"Anyhow, the A148; what a bummer. The money and engineering capacity was expended on it to no avail, not to mention the cost of tooling and experimental parts and so forth. And the reason was political. Well, it didn't work."

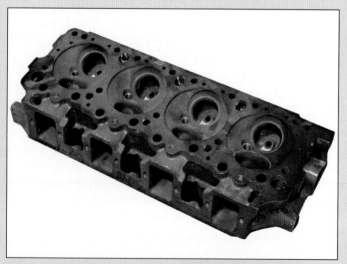

Few parts from the A148 program survived; this is a cylinder head from the program in Jim Kramer's parts collection. Note the port size and shrouding around the exhaust valve.

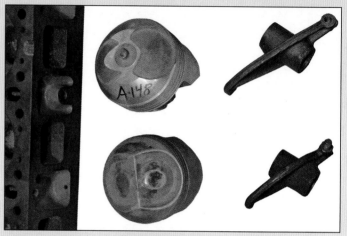

A comparison between the larger A148 piston and exhaust rocker (top) and the one used on the conventional A864/A102 Hemi engine. These examples were provided by Kramer Automotive.

A279: 1969

Worked on in 1969, the A279 project was positioned to bring both the Hemi and wedge engines into the 1970s, and it featured a number of improvements. It fell victim to mandatory emissions adjustments ordered by Congress that hastened the end of the American muscle car.

"The A279 engine, which we called the ball-stud Hemi, was the program to generate an engine to replace the basic B engine performance wedge A134 440 GTX/R/T, as well as the A139 Road Runner engine. Those already had the better intakes, a fresh cam, and streamlined exhaust, and this would have been the next generation of those packages," Hoover says.

"The A279 would have been a terrific engine in my opinion. First, it was a true Hemi, and second, it had the chamber rotated. If you were looking across the bore centerline from the fender and thinking of a clock, the intake was moved from its 12:00 position over to about a 2:00 position. The exhaust was spun around too, and what made that possible was the use of ball stud rockers, which had been on Chevrolets forever, and had just been adopted by Chrysler for the new 244-inch straight-6 being introduced in Australia. We took what had been learned in that program and applied it to the A279 V-8 program.

"One major benefit was it guaranteed increased swirl of the incoming charge from the runner into the combustion chamber. It would have been better than the A102 and A864 Hemis, and in turn would have made it

Tom Hoover's former Barracuda was on display at the Forge Muscle Car Show in 2007, after being bought by noted Hemi engine builder John Arruzza.

The A279 engine in the car was originally among Dick Landy's parts. John Arruzza rebuilt it and installed it in Tom Hoover's old street car. It's on display at the Forge Muscle Car Show.

a much better engine to beat the emissions compliance requirements that were coming along. Plus, it still had damn good output; it was not like it was a compromised package for the B-engine wedge. It was a real up-to-date Hemi using what we had found. Plus, there were no studs on the head for that fifth bolt location; you screwed the heads on just like the A134.

"We actually built 12 of those engines for the program in two displacements (440 and 396), and all but two were either used up in testing or scrapped. When the dust had settled, Maxwell gave one to Landy to work with, hoping he could play around and get something out of it. But we did enough piston work during development to see the real promise of that thing. It would have been a real wing-dinger.

"Then everybody puckered when they found out what the emissions compliance for 1971 would be, plus the insurance situation. There were actually two programs that were canceled in 1969: the A279 and the gas turbine engine that was to have gone into the Charger for 1970. It was simply economics. The boost the insurance industry had put onto cars like the Road Runner and GTX, plus the emissions compliance that was coming down, spelled the end to those kinds of engines. The compression ratios came down; they all ran at the lean limit on spark retard. The catalytic converter was on the horizon. It was over.

"Well, years later, I put my blue Barracuda, which I had owned for 32 years, on eBay. Jim Kramer and John Arruzza were the two guys bidding on it and Arruzza won. He had gotten the A279 engine from Gean Landy after Dick died. He stroked it a little, had some custom pistons made, and then built it up for the car. I never had it in there myself. After he was done, they put it on display at one of the Carlisle events. I was there and they interviewed me. About six months later, John sold the whole thing to a guy in Texas and, last I heard, it was on display in the museum in Auburn, Indiana."

Late in 1970, as he began testing his new car, Garlits ran into problems with the car darting around at 220 mph. Fellow driver and fabricator Swingle thought maybe they needed to reduce the steering ratio. After it was changed, the result was a quick trip down the straight and narrow.

Still, when Garlits showed up for the 1971 West Coast winter meets, the naysayers said it was just a nice novelty. A slew of new-car orders went out to the nation's chassis builders after Garlits found a home in the winner's circle at Pomona, Bakersfield, Dallas, and other places. Most drivers were happy to have the view and safety of the engine behind them as Garlits freely shared how he had solved the problem. Pete Robinson lost his life in his Ford-powered slingshot the same weekend Garlits won the Winternationals with the new car. The rear-engine revolution was on.

Drag Racing 1971

In hindsight, 1971 was perhaps the most successful year ever for Chrysler in sanctioned racing. The three championships in stock car racing, NHRA and IHRA Pro Stock championships, NHRA and AHRA Funny Car crowns, and the final Top Gas crown (to Austin Myers in a twin-powered blown Chrysler entry), were a big deal, but the Sportsman class domination was even more so. These cars were not always Hemi powered, but many were. Frankly, for 1971 win results by event, it is actually easier to list who weren't in Chryslers.

For example, Don Nicholson's Pro Stock victory at the Summernationals was the only non-Chrysler win for the day. At the Gatornationals it was George Owens in a Chevrolet in Modified. The company did the unthinkable at the 1971 U.S. Nationals, winning every single eliminator except Bike: Steve Carbone in Top Fuel, Ray Motes in Top Gas, Ed McCulloch's 'Cuda in Funny Car, Ronnie Sox in Pro Stock, Tom Trisch A/AA Hemi-powered altered in Competition, Bob Riffle's *Rod Shop* Demon in Modified, Greg Charney's SS/B stick 1965 Coronet in Super Stock, and Al Corda's 1964 wagon, the only non-Hemi of the group, winning in Stock.

The Super Stock World Championship went to a Mustang at Amarillo, but the Hemi cars thundered in that division all season, winning six of eight titles. After Jim Clark's 1965 *Hemi Express* Dodge posted a runner-up at Pomona, it was Carroll Fink's 1967 Plymouth over Dave Wren's SS/DA 'Cuda at the Gators. Again it was Fink over Judy Lilly's SS/AA 'Cuda at Dallas, Ken Montgomery's well-traveled *555* 1965 Plymouth over Wren at Englishtown, a heads-up SS/DA final when Tom Myl beat Dean Nicopolis at Sanair, and Charney's 4-speed over Terry Earwood in a Hemi 'Cuda at Indy. After Ken McLellen won Amarillo over Dick Panter's 'Cuda, Ron Mancini earned a win in his Dart at the Supernationals in Ontario, California, beating Doc Conroy's 1965 Dodge.

Arlen Vanke (inset photo) never earned an NHRA Pro Stock crown in his long career, but he did take his JEGS-backed Duster to a big win at the 1971 AHRA Winter Nationals. This is a re-creation of the car by Le Hodge that used many of Arlen's original parts.

In the end, Hemi cars were in 14 of the 16 NHRA final-round spots! At Sanair, 15 cars in the final 32-car field were in SS/DA, either 1970 Hemi 'Cudas or 1967 package cars.

Pro Stock was little different. Sox won six of eight possible titles, Fons won Amarillo, and Nicholson earned the dubious honor of the only non-Chrysler winner in Pro Stock. Wally Booth was in the other lane at the Winternationals for Chevrolet's only final-round showing of 1971. Sox took out Don Carlton at Gainesville, Nicholson at Dallas, had problems at Englishtown, came back to win Sanair over Carlton again, then beat Stu McDade in Billy Stepp's Challenger for the Indy crown. At Amarillo, Fons beat Herb McCandless, but Sox finished the season-ending Supernationals with a close win over McCandless (9.61 to 9.64, both in excess

Greg Charney's Dodge was the overall victor in Super Stock at the 1971 Nationals, a year when the Hemi cars ruled the division. (Photo Courtesy Tommy Erwin Archive, University of South Carolina 125__1971)

The Rod Shop had all current-model Dodges in 1971, covering a variety of classes. Bob Riffle had a just-released Demon with a Hemi installed in it to run in B/Modified Production. The biggest engine available for the street models was the 340. (Photo Courtesy Pit Slides Archive, quartermilestones.com)

Technological advances in Pro Stock include new independent runner (IR) intakes with added plenum area beneath the carbs. This was in part due to the rapidly increasing RPM levels that the cars were capable of, but required taller hood-scoop designs. This example was provided by Kramer Automotive.

Chrysler's unique crank-trigger ignition sensor allowed for near-exact timing. It gauged ignition events directly off the movement of the crankshaft rather than through a gear on the camshaft. This example was provided by Kramer Automotive.

of 140 mph) in a new 'Cuda the shop had just built for Milwee Construction.

Now track-proven, the Milwee 'Cuda was to be driven by Super Stock racer Geno Redd, but in a testing accident at Orange County the following day, Redd wrecked the car and was killed. The increased speeds in Pro Stock soon resulted in more safety rules, but other rules from the NHRA's high sheriffs affected Chrysler much more than other manufacturers.

For instance, Francis Crider had been a dominant force in Comp in an injected Hemi C/Dragster, the Dodge Super Bee, winning three events. For 1972, the combination was no longer legal. In Super Stock, the NHRA first proposed to blend the whole group into Modified, leaving Stock Eliminator as the door-car–only division. Instead, the organization opened up several more half-second classes at the bottom of the field, now to encompass 40 possible classes for 1972. Hemi cars were still at the top but greatly outnumbered. This change alone made a Hemi-only Super Stock final a thing of the past.

The real change came in Pro Stock, as all three sanctioning bodies adopted a more dramatic sliding scale for 1972. This was still based on a ratio of pounds to cubic inches, but adding physical weight to certain engine designs. As in NASCAR, the Hemi was not dead yet, but 1971 was indeed the high-water mark for the engine in the Pro Stock and lower classes. Perhaps just like the Street Hemi, the Race Hemi went out with pure FirePower in 1971.

The Street Racers

To this point, I have mainly covered how the Race Hemi wrought woe upon organized racing, but before leaving the halcyon days of 1971, I'd like to take a look at where the engine made waves on the boulevards. Truth is everyone from Tom Hoover and Mike Buckel, with their late-night exploits on Woodward Avenue, to Street Hemi buyers nationwide, who chose to "breathe on them" with race-originated parts, helped the reputation of the engine. Indeed, production of the Hemi was never great compared to, say, the 396 Chevrolets or Cobra Jet Fords. But for those who ran with the night conquistadors, it was always some supposed Hemi car rumored to be just one town away, one weekend past.

For more documented examples, turn to the metro areas of big-city America: New York, Chicago, Detroit, Los Angeles. Here, it became a money proposition. Perhaps the apocryphal pink slips were not in play, but cash was. Sometimes lots of it, sometimes with guns, and cops, and liars, and losers. In Detroit, the most notorious Hemi car was a 1967 WO-type Coronet for which Ted Spehar claimed responsibility, ran out of his old Sunoco station, and owned and driven by Jimmy Addison. Powered by extra displacement and Spehar's careful assembly, the car was known as *Silver Bullet*. Tom Hoover admits that he no longer needed his street Coronet to defend the corporate reputation after Addison got his Dodge running.

Two others, both African-American, really stood out in Hemi heritage. They were located on opposite sides of the nation.

Big Willie

In Los Angeles, a 6-foot-4 former Green Beret named William Andrew Robinson III became known as "Big Willie" after his picture showed up with that tagline in a 1966 expose on street racing in the *Los Angeles Times*. That year, following the exploding racial tensions of 1965, the police were surprised to find black, white, Hispanic, and other ethnic groups racing one another for money. They sent a cruiser to find Big Willie, who hoped he was not in trouble.

Indeed, he was not. The city council did not want a repeat of the Watts riots and convinced Robinson to go undercover as a street race organizer, complete with a paycheck. Having come out of a Southeast Asian firefight with serious injuries, living thanks to the courage of a Hispanic soldier, Big Willie wanted peace in the streets and could look the part with his physical stature (he was a power body builder who had competed in a Mr. Universe contest). They gave him all-night access to a boulevard, the assistance of some other officers as officials, and let him run the show.

The colors of the Street Racers of Los Angeles jackets were similar to those worn by the Hells Angels (most were off-duty cops and city employees). Kids showed up by the thousands to participate: surfers, greasers, gangsters, and lone wolves. Dragsters, altereds, street rods, low riders; you name it, they all ran. Two guys lined up, one winner collected any money posted fair and square, and the drunks learned early on there was no hell-raising on Willie's watch.

The morning after Martin Luther King, Jr.'s assassination in 1968, Willie and a mixed-race group cruised the blocks of South Central together, telling people to be cool. Amazingly, Los Angeles didn't burn when other places did. This cannot be laid solely on Robinson, but his reputation and respect no doubt had a calming effect.

So, when a local dealership still had an unsold Hemi Daytona in 1970, the owner came up with the perfect

Still larger than life, Big Willie (right) is seen in 2009 with Jim Kramer, an honorary member of the Brotherhood of Street Racers.

Big Willie Robinson and his wife Tomiko toured the United States representing the International Brotherhood of Street Racers from Los Angeles. This low-quality photo shows how Queen Daytona *appeared in 1971 at Union Grove, Wisconsin. (Photo Courtesy Dale Mathews)*

promotion: Give it to Robinson as a public gesture. Robinson's wife Tomiko, of Afro-Japanese descent, was given a second Hemi Daytona by another area Dodge dealership. Various California engine builders and parts companies helped build them up for performance. However, Willie wanted his King Daytona to go faster still, so he took it apart and the body went to AeroChem for an acid bath. Unfortunately, it stayed in the tank a little too long and came up full of holes. "I killed my car," he lamented. Tomiko, in her still-unmolested *Queen Daytona*, told him point-blank, "Willie, you are not *touching* my car!"

With their popularity growing and the Street Racers evolving into an all-night scene at Orange County International Raceway, the couple went on tour nationwide, and the remaining car began to get modified. It went faster and faster, with Tomiko as the pilot and Willie as the crew chief. Then, during an evening track event in Knoxville, Tennessee, she hit a full water barrel in the wrong place of the shutdown area, which totaled the rare Dodge.

With help from friends in the mayor's office, Willie founded a racetrack on Terminal Island in the Los Angeles Harbor after Lions Drag Strip closed in 1972. Unfortunately, helping black racers on the streets of Los Angeles was never good political theatre for those climbing into the mayor's seat. The track was a political football, opening and closing on and off for decades. Unimpressed by midnight basketball, Big Willie Robinson truly believed in the brotherhood of street racing until his death in 2012 from complications related to diabetes.

The Mutt Brothers

The other team came out of Brooklyn and was made up of several young men who parlayed money into buying a car to race on Conduit Avenue. Eugene Coard was one of them. This was serious stuff; equipment for street racing came to the Big Apple from drivers such as Sox, Jenkins, Harrell, and Nicholson. Coard's team consisted of John "Mutt" Lyles, his brother Ronald, Bennie Durham, and Jessie Johnson. Their car was based out of J&B Automotive at the corner of Willoughby and Bedford. In late 1968, the so-called Mutt Brothers team had an L88 Chevelle, a fast Hemi GTX, and the chance to buy a 1968 Hemi Dart from S-K Speed Shop.

"We bought that S-K Dart for $6,000," says Coard. "The car had just gotten bounced in tech at Indy. We asked how much, and he told us. We figured it to $1,000 each and we could sell the Chevelle. A friend repainted it for us; it was a beautiful car, but it was just black when we got it. We also hid the GTX in a garage, so the myth on the street was that we had just swapped that Hemi into this Dart body."

The car became infamous when the team had a chance to make some money in a big race against John Edward, who had a worked 427 Camaro that Dick Harrell had built.

"The night of the big race, the one people said was for a quarter-million dollars, there were people lined up along the street, thick, for the whole quarter-mile. That was the third time we tried to run the car. The first time, the Dart dumped the driveshaft, so we called it off. The second week, the Camaro broke something when it was started and began to lose power, so we agreed to try again a week after that." The racers also paid the local police $200 per event, whether the race happened or not, to allow them five minutes to unload, race, reload, and leave.

"When you street raced, the owners of the cars got a pot together, and somebody held it. Plus there were a lot of side bets that we didn't have anything to do with. There'd be $20s and $50s going back and forth. That happened at the track, too."

As with many stories, the pot on the big night grew to exponential levels over the years. "The pot wasn't $250,000; one writer said he thought it was $1,250, but I'll never forget how much it was," Coard reminisces with a grin. "The pot was actually $8,000 for that race. It built up during the period of three weeks. Like I said, you sort of had teams, and your team put the money together for your car and you kept a list. If you bet $50 of the $2,000, the payoff was $100; we ran for $3,000. That was parlay money; you just kept using it to race."

In the final and third big-money race, John "Mutt" Lyles shut down the Edward Camaro fair and square, took his winnings, and bought a BSA motorcycle. He was unfortunately killed on it soon afterward.

The team decided it could get a car to run on the dragstrip next. Team members talked to Buddy Martin and bought Ronnie's 1969 match race car, selling the S-K Dart for $6,500 and buying the old Sox car for $8,500. Besides, although the Dart never lost a street race, the cat was out of the bag on its origins.

"That lasted about 10 months, until after the big race; then a bus driver from Manhattan came into the shop with a magazine that had a story on the S-K car," Coard says with a laugh again. "We used to always keep the car up on the lift, so people could see it had no traction bars, as that was a no-no. He came in, looked at it, looked at the magazine, and said, 'This is that car.' There was an army canteen as the radiator overflow, and it was in the pictures; you could see it from under that car."

Next, they turned the 1969 Barracuda back into Sox & Martin and ordered all-new pipe. Once finished, Joe Fisher drove this Barracuda with J&B lettering during 1971. Then Ronald Lyles took over for 1972. As the only competitive black racers in Pro Stock, the team members proved to be very popular, netting a magazine cover and numerous bookings, plus touring with the new United States Racing Team Pro Stock circuit.

Later, they went so far as to build a little Colt for match racing, but Eugene and Ronald had to hang it up as costs and frustration mounted in the middle of the decade. By then, for them and many other Hemi racers, the end had come.

The Coard family stands with a match race Duster tribute to the Mutt Brothers and (the late) Ronnie Lyles, reflecting a history of racing involvement that has come into the twenty-first century. Eugene Coard and Ronnie Lyles were both licensed to drive Pro Stock back in the day.

CHAPTER TWELVE

1972-1979
Upheaval
Hemi Racing in the 1970s

This history of the Chrysler Race Hemi ends at the same time the street engine disappeared. The simple reason is that 1971 was the high-water mark for Chrysler in racing competition.

Indeed, it could be argued that Chrysler, more specifically Dodge, did not return to this level of competition excellence until 2012, when Brad Keselowski locked up the NASCAR Sprint Cup title in the Roger Penske #2 Miller Lite entry and Allen Johnson prevailed in NHRA Pro Stock in his Hemi-powered Mopar Dodge Neon.

Nevertheless, the Hemi legacy has been maintained through today by accolades and on its own merits. The second-generation version of the engine released by the factory in 1964 continued to excite enthusiasts during the decades that followed. Detailing this era could entail an entirely separate book, but I will take a look at some of the Hemi highlights that began in 1972. Like the new-car lists at the dealerships, things indeed had changed when the NHRA season opened at the Pomona Fairgrounds for the Winternationals that year.

The late Bill Jenkins was one of the true geniuses of drag racing. Following his efforts in 1966 against Jere Stahl, Jenkins admitted later that Chevy promotions boss Vince Piggins began writing "research" checks to Jenkins Competition the next year. The Hemi had stood

in the Grump's way at almost every turn in the American supercar era. At the same time the engine disappeared from Chrysler's production options, however, Jenkins was busy in his Malvern, Pennsylvania, shop putting the finishing touches on the next generation of Pro Stocks.

With the muscle car era now basically over, the NHRA was looking for solutions to keep all brands involved, much as NASCAR had done. In 1971, the AHRA had tried a sliding scale of weight breaks, adding a pounds-per-inch ratio based on cylinder head configuration. As in NASCAR, hemi-type engines from Chrysler and Ford carried the most weight, and Chrysler racers actually boycotted a handful of the early 1971 AHRA events as a result. The NHRA had also wearied of the "Sox Nationals" in what was considered a premier division, and the automotive print media often concurred.

So although the high sheriffs of drag racing had mildly tweaked Pro Stock rules in 1971, the NHRA went to a sliding scale in 1972: a 7.25 lbs/ci for hemis (Chrysler/Ford), 7.00 for canted valves (big-block Chevy rat/Cleveland–type Ford), and 6.75 for inline wedges (small-block Chevy/Ford Windsor/small-block Mopar), which made Grumpy Jenkins excited. Although he was best known in Pro Stock for big-inch Can-Am and iron 427-ci cars, nobody had forgotten that Jenkins still worked with small-block

The most advanced E-Body Pro Stock on planet earth was the new Motown Missile 'Cuda. However, the rules had changed and the car won just one title that season. (Photo Courtesy Jon Steele Archive, quartermilestones.com)

Chevrolets for racing and development. Dave Strickler had won the Super Stock world crown in a Jenkins-built 302-ci Z28 in 1968.

Jenkins had another advantage that year. Chevrolet had released a subcompact car, the Vega, in response to the immensely popular Ford Maverick. Jenkins did some math, built the lightest example he could (about 2,200 pounds under NHRA rules for that year), and then put together a 331-ci small-block Chevy Pro Stock engine to maximize the weight break in the rules. After some sorting out, the package proved to be exactly what the NHRA ordered and then some. Like *The Boss* 'Cuda of Sox during the previous season, *Grumpy's Toy* won six of eight NHRA events, including the World Finals and a special PRA race in Tulsa, Oklahoma, that Don Garlits organized with AHRA's Jim Tice. The latter was held the same weekend as the Indy Nationals as a boycott of purse payouts by the NHRA; it paid $35,000 to win.

As a result, even *Time* magazine reported that Jenkins' fat $250,000 gross haul made his earnings equivalent to the NBA's Wilt Chamberlain, considered the highest-paid athlete of the era. Jenkins' victory was more important for another reason. Racing sanctioning bodies were now using the rules, which could be changed virtually on a whim, to create favorites. The following seasons saw other combinations rise and fall based on how weight breaks, body wheelbase design, and cylinder head style were quantified in the rules.

One result is certain: None of the Pro Stock World Champions after 1971 in NHRA won with a Hemi car. The only Chrysler Pro Stock championship of the 1970s, after Sox' run of 1971, came in 1979, when Bob Glidden dominated one season in a Plymouth Arrow body using a new W2-series small-block engine derived from the 340 LA-series design.

Direct Connection

The factory did not give up on the Race Hemi after 1971. They continued through outside research, as much of the NASCAR work was now in the hands of Petty Enterprises (plus the efforts by Harry Hyde, who had no problem getting answers when calling friends still working at Chrysler). Spehar and company were the hands-on guys in the drag racing efforts.

One change was that Mopar's performance parts division was now known as Direct Connection, and it was through this arm that Larry Shepard, Tom Hoover, and others interfaced with racers, both Sportsman and Pro, and ongoing parts evolutions continued. For 1972, the dealer clinic program ended, but Sox & Martin, Dick Landy Industries, and the *Motown Missile* effort remained

Bob Riffle in a Colt and Don Carlton in a Duster square off at the NHRA Nationals in 1975 in Competition Eliminator. The Colts were never legalized in NHRA Pro Stock and gained a nasty reputation for crashing. (Photo Courtesy Ray Mann Archive, quartermilestones.com)

the primary torchbearers for the company, although not the sole leaders. According to Larry Griffith's paperwork, at least 13 other teams, plus the Rod Shop, received support of one sort or another under contract from Dodge at the beginning of 1972.

Many other racers stayed loyal to the cause during the next several years, but any Hemi effort would be bittersweet for one and all, and all but the most diehard switched by mid-decade. Fewer and fewer Hemis were running in NASCAR. If the drag racing weeklies and magazines reported one Chrysler team or another was running competitive times, soon after, the rules were adjusted to make the other competitors faster or weigh down the Hemi cars again.

The issues of vehicle size and frontal area came to the forefront. Unlike Chevy's Vega and Ford's follow-up Pinto, Chrysler had no body that met the new 93-inch minimum wheelbase rule. The imported Mitsubishi Colt was 92 inches, and therefore was only legal in Competition Eliminator in NHRA.

Later, a handful of Hemi Colts ran in AHRA and IHRA Pro Stock competition. Their most noted efforts were under the tutelage of Roger Denney, who recorded an 8.21 on nitrous oxide with his example at a California match race. Nose-heavy, stubby, and short, the Colts also built a nasty reputation for ill-handling at speed, putting Bill Flynn into the hospital and ending the legendary Don Carlton's life in a testing accident in 1976.

As Jenkins rose to the top, factory attention was focused on developing exotic pieces for the E- and A-Body models to reduce vehicle weight, and experimental head designs that culminated in the D5 (an aluminum version of the D4 replacement head, which had been cast with the new D-shaped exhaust port). This focus was evident on the 1972 *Motown Missile* piloted by Carlton, warranting the cover story of *Hot Rod* magazine.

The 500-inch Hemi in John Hagan's Plymouth shows that the era for the engine ended in NHRA Pro Stock. The return of the brand in the late 1980s used a Dave Koffel-designed wedge-style head.

Ron Butler completed a number of competitive entries for Chrysler racers, which is why engineer Tom Coddington came to watch him fabricate a car under factory purview. He was known from his Ramchargers days as "The Ghost" for his quiet demeanor that shielded both brilliance and strategic thinking. Coddington documented the process to allow the Chrysler engineering department to ascertain what could be done to advance the cause.

In the budget-tight environment of the early 1970s, even this was an expensive proposition, all to no avail due to the ongoing rules adjustments as well as advances being made with other competing engine combinations. Ironically, Jenkins' formerly competitive package quickly fell to the factory-favored Cleveland Ford in 1973 and 1974. Then he returned with a big-block Camaro to win again, with Larry Lombardo as driver.

As things became more frustrating, Chrysler actually sent the remaining supported drivers into Super Stock at one point for 1974. Butch Leal took a very trick Butler-built 1965 A990 Plymouth to several late-round showings and a win at the 1974 Summernationals. He followed that up with a win in Modified in his "uncompetitive" Pro Stock Duster at Gainesville the next season.

Although there was some leeway in saving weight by dropping displacement, there was not a lot of benefit in using the Hemi block in undersquare configurations in drag racing. Several combinations between the 366-ci NASCAR designation and 400 ci were tried. The RPM capability using the 7-liter crankcase at the smaller sizes could not do what equivalent competing designs were capable of. Moreover, the swirl effect that Harry Weslake

had been concerned about in the earliest days was now being practiced in non-Hemi combustion environments, and the quench area of the Hemi combustion chamber was actually too large for flame control as compression ratios rose.

With the writing on the wall, by 1975 any development work still being done on the Hemi was solely in the hands of independent racers and engine builders.

Winners, Also-Rans and Diehards

The factory-associated *Motown Missile* 'Cuda won Chrysler's only 1972 NHRA Pro Stock crown at the Gatornationals and then posted a 1973 win as the newly-designated *Mopar Missile* Duster at the Springnationals, which by that time had been relocated to National Trail Raceway near Columbus, Ohio. The *Missile* had been a trendsetter with spectacular qualifying efforts and good showings at many events during 1970 and 1971, but was badly handicapped as were the other Mopar entries.

Butch Leal posted the biggest professional Mopar win of his long NHRA career in his Duster at Sanair that same summer. That trio of victories, however, were Chrysler's only major showings other than a couple of runner-up finishes until the era of Glidden's small-block.

After the NHRA went to a flat 500-inch Pro Stock program for 1982, several competitors made attempts to run Hemi-powered cars in the category. By that time, however, higher RPM levels and ongoing valvetrain development on the big-block Chevrolet and, to a lesser extent, the Boss-type Ford had allowed those combinations to take over. By 1983, both combinations were aided in part with factory development, as the factories were involving themselves in motorsports again.

By 1980, Chrysler was fighting for its very survival; the W2 Pro Stock effort of Bob Glidden ended abruptly as a result. He went back to Fords with no small success following the big-inch rule. Tuned by noted driver Greg Anderson, John Hagan's runner-up in a Hemi-powered

John Hagan was the last Hemi competitor to go to a final round in NHRA competition, doing so at the 1981 World Finals. Clark and Colleen Rand now own this restored car.

HEMI DRAG RACERS THEN AND NOW

Many drag racing drivers associated with Hemi notoriety continued in racing. Following is a brief look at a few of them, including their careers and accomplishments.

Ronnie Sox

After 1971 Ronnie Sox never won another national event in NHRA competition. He and Buddy Martin dissolved their partnership in 1974 as their race car business had all but disappeared. Sox went on to win an IHRA season title in the early 1980s in a Mustang owned by Dean Thompson. He posted a single runner-up to Glidden at Gainesville in 1979 in a 1979 Dodge Challenger (by then another import design from Mitsubishi) reportedly rebodied from a Colt by Clyde Hodges.

He told me that, years later, NHRA founder Wally Parks saw him at an event and apologized for the rules mismanagement of the 1970s. Sox, usually upbeat, grimly replied with a short litany of what he had lost thanks to the prejudiced revisions and ended by simply telling Parks, "A lot of good that [apology] does me now."

Ronnie Sox lost his battle with cancer in 2006.

Dick Landy

Dick Landy fared better. He won the 1973 AHRA World Championship and remained, as Sox did, a prolific personality in racing circles. Also, his longtime relationships with members of the media on the West Coast kept his Dick Landy Industries (DLI) engine-building business in Northridge very viable. The DLI tag was on most of the remaining Hemi-powered competitors after 1977, and the shop led ongoing efforts to return the Hemi to glory in the class. Landy himself eventually turned the driving chores of the team's little Dodge Charger over to Mark Yuill before parking the car for good when the 500-inch era arrived.

Dick Landy passed away in early 2007 after an illness.

Herb McCandless

Driver Herb McCandless actually found 1972 to his liking. After the Sox & Martin shop built a Dodge Demon for him to drive, he did very well with it that season. Going to the final round against Jenkins at both the big-money AHRA Tulsa race and NHRA Summernationals, the man known as "Mr. 4-Speed" wowed the crowd at the latter

Ronnie Sox posted a runner-up in NHRA Pro Stock in this Challenger, but he ran it in A/FX on other occasions. He and Buddy Martin closed their shop in 1974, although they teamed up on occasion for these later projects. (Photo Courtesy Bryan Flach Archive, quartermilestones.com)

when he went into a powerstand that he carried to half-track due to a broken wheelie bar.

McCandless also won most of the races on the new United States Racing Team circuit, a match race program consisting of all big-name Pro Stock racers. In the late 1970s, his McCandless Performance Parts bought tractor-trailer loads of parts being made obsolete by Mopar, and he became a major hardware supplier to the Mopar hobby. The Demon is now restored and in the possession of collector Todd Werner.

A Dart Sport that Dick Landy built himself and raced during the mid-1970s was found and restored. Collector Marco DeCesaris now owns this historic machine.

Herb and Marie McCandless and their sons pose with his 1972 Demon, a car he considered to be his favorite due to its accomplishments. Todd Werner owns it today.

HEMI DRAG RACERS THEN AND NOW CONTINUED

Butch Leal

One of the most visible racers who continued on was Butch Leal, who became the final Hemi Pro Stock winner when he beat all comers in his Duster at Quebec's Le Grandnational in 1973. This car was built by Ron Butler in 1971 and put "the California Flash" into the media spotlight with wheelstands and fire burnouts. In 1972 and 1973, it also put Leal into the winner's circle at AHRA national events, the famed *Popular Hot Rodding* magazine race twice, the March Meet at Bakersfield, Orange County International's biggest match races, and others.

To top it off, Leal became the NHRA's first national event competitor to run in the 8-second zone with 8.98 at Englishtown in 1973. He posted two NHRA final-round appearances in 1973 in addition to the Sanair title.

Due to even more rules changes, in part because of this showing, Chrysler boycotted the NHRA Pro Stock in 1974, and the car's A-Body successor, also by Butler, ran mostly in Modified, giving Leal additional national event titles. Coupled with his Super Stock prowess in the trick 1965 A990, Butch took home *Car Craft* magazine Driver of the Year accolades for four consecutive years in the mid-1970s. Before he stepped away for other pursuits as a semi-professional golfer in 1977, the Arrow he was running reportedly became the first Pro Stock car in the 7-second zone, clocking a 7.96 at a California match race.

Roy Hill

One diehard who kept going during the 1970s was Roy Hill, whose Dusters were noteworthy in that they were helped by Petty Engineering. Maurice Petty built horsepower for Hill, who lived only a few miles away in the Randleman area, and also built one of his race cars in its entirety. After a stint with Sox & Martin as a crewman in 1969, Hill bought a 1968 'Cuda from the team and went racing himself. Following that, he ran his own string of Dusters, a Colt, and an Arrow before finally moving to Jon Kaase-powered Boss-type Fords in the early 1980s. Hill's personality and business sense have made him a noteworthy part of the drag racing community to this day.

"It's amazing how, in the 1970s, the NHRA could take a pencil and put you out of business. All it did was try to make us find a way to take advantage of a situation," he grins.

Hill posted one NHRA runner-up finish at Columbus in 1975, but also did very well on the IHRA circuit, the sole Hemi racer still placing high in any sanctioning body's yearly points. He told the following story about match racing back then.

"One year, when Larry Lombardo was driving for Bill Jenkins, Jenkins had built a NASCAR engine for the DieGard Chevy. Donnie Allison was driving it. The car sat on the pole at Daytona, so Bill went over to Maurice and Richard Petty and says, 'Hrmmph! All you guys do is build tractor engines. Hrmmph!' So they came home from Daytona and called me to ask me when I was going to run Jenkins.

"As it was, I had a big match race set up at Cecil County with him in March. So Maurice said, 'We've got you a crankshaft, a block, heads, a set of rods and pistons, and we'll build you an engine; you get some of that nitrous.' I called Dave Braswell and told him what we were doing, so they took one of the Weiand Hemi manifolds and built the system inside, underneath the plenum. We used to always mill out the ends and runners so you could see, but we didn't on that one, and the nitrous was hidden in that.

"So I get up to Maryland, and you know Jenkins, he waited until the last thing to make an appearance. He unloads that thing, raps the throttle two or three times, and takes the lane he wants. You know, I'm just Roy Hill. He came over to talk to me and I asked him, 'How fast are you going to run?' He's got his nose up and says, 'I'm planning on running an 8.70. Hrmmph.' At that time, most guys were still in the 8.90 to 9.10 range, so I said, 'Man, how in the world will you do that!?' But the air was really good that night.

"So, Larry leaves and he's got about a fender on me; I shifted into second and flipped the switch. I go by him. Larry went 8.70 at 156; I went 8.62 at 163. Unheard of! So we get back, we were letting the car cool off, and Jenkins comes over to me. He looks the engine over and then asks me, 'What have you got in that thing, Hill!?' I said, 'Oh, that's just one of those old tractor engines Maurice and Richard put together for me!' [laughs]. His next response was 'Hrmmph!' He knew exactly what I said and what it meant.

"Later, when Grumpy came down to race at Piedmont Dragway, he'd stop in and see Maurice and he and Maurice became pretty good buddies. Yeah, that was the last time he talked about their tractor engines."

Hill also remembers the Colts and Arrows: "I bought the Colt that Francis Crider had, and it was a tough piece. I raced it and the Duster, and decided it was time for a smaller car. That's when I got the Arrow. That was a car Ron Butler built. Going from a Hardy car to the Butler car

Roy Hill was always a major Mopar contender in Pro Stock in the 1970s, even as other drivers ended up in competitors' equipment. He is seen here with his Duster at the 1975 U.S. Nationals. (Photo Courtesy Ray Mann Archive, quartermilestones.com)

Roy Hill's 2.2-style Dodge Charger was notable in that he ended his Mopar driving career in it. Like Sox, he moved to Ford products but maintained fond memories of the Hemi era. (Photo Courtesy Bryan Flach Archive, quartermilestones.com)

was no comparison. That Butler car was outstanding, and when Butch Leal got his and got it loosened up, the Arrow model was better still. I stayed with Butch when I was on the West Coast.

"A lot of it was the way the engine was mounted; the height of the engine. Learning to keep the car low on the ground meant everything in the world. The Arrow was faster than the Duster, but it only had a 94-inch wheelbase, which was stretched from the stock 92-inch wheelbase. It hooked really hard.

"With the Duster, we had always put all the weight to the back to get it to hook. It took us a while to realize that we needed to add the weight underneath the Arrow. We set that up under the seats. There were two sets on each side, 4 inches wide, and the weight fit into trays beneath

the car, and a bolt dropped through it. It made the floor lower, and all of a sudden, we were picking up more speed and keeping the nose down. It actually helped keep the car itself lower to the ground, so it even had some aero advantages."

Aero Arrow or not, the frustrating rules program continued on, and Hill found the evolved Boss Ford Pro Stock engine was close enough in basic design to the Chrysler Hemi that making the transition was relatively easy when he finally abandoned the Hemi.

Arrow at the 1981 Winston Finals is the last NHRA Hemi final-round appearance on record. Hagan was tragically killed in this car's Hemi-powered successor at an NHRA event in Brainerd, Minnesota, the following season.

Circling on USAC and ARCA

The Hemi era ended in NASCAR when the 358-ci rule was formally enacted overall for 1974; there was no way to destroke the Hemi effectively. Still, the big inches ran in USAC and ARCA even after that; 1972 was the end of the aero cars in that sanction.

"The final win for a wing car was at USAC's Pocono 500 in 1972, but as an FIA race, select NASCAR competitors were brought in by the Pocono promoter as well," Doug Schellinger notes. "As a result, this was the first and only heads-up fight between the unrestricted Hemi-powered Superbirds driven by the likes of USAC

Roger McCluskey had the dubious honor of driving the final wing car to win in circle-track competition, seen here at Pocono Raceway in 1972. (Photo Courtesy Doug Schellinger DSAC Collection)

The wing era closes in 1972 as Ramo Stott leads Richard Petty over the tunnel turn at Pocono during the FIA-sanctioned USAC race. This was the only event in which the USAC and Winston Cup-legal cars raced each other. (Photo Courtesy Doug Schellinger DSAC Collection)

stars Roger McCluskey and Ramo Stott, running against the conventional 1972 Road Runner of Richard Petty. McCluskey put his Superbird on the pole and then completely dominated the race, turning qualifying lap speeds near the end.

"Petty's car also ran strong early on, but DNF'd with engine failure. When he was asked about racing heads-up against the Superbirds, Petty said, 'I would have run a wing car, but I couldn't find one!' Both of the 1970 Petty team Superbirds had been sold in 1971."

USAC and ARCA continued to allow engines up to 429.999 until 1984. The victorious era faded, but one diehard competitor was Gordie Blankenship of Keokuk, Iowa, long a hotbed of circle-track racers. He raced until the end in Hemi equipment, often assembling engines from parts he scrapped together for his #17 *Mirada*.

"I won some qualifying races, a big one at Dequoin State Fairgrounds in 1981, but we broke a lot of stuff by the time the racing got going," Blankenship says, recalling that overheating was a big concern. "We never had a lot of money, so I ran a lot of castoff parts. Junk. Still,

when it ran well, it would go and we could run up toward the front. USAC finally set a rule that you could still run 440 inches as long as it was a small-block; then ARCA went to a 355-inch rule for 1985."

A handful of other drivers ran Dodges in 1983 and 1984, but the Hemi era was formally over on September 2, 1984, when the final big-blocks competed in the USAC sanction.

Super Stock Rock n' Roll and Modified Muscle

Hemi-powered cars continued to win in the Sportsman ranks. After the twin-engine Top Gas class was canceled, the NHRA created the Pro Comp class, which featured dragsters, Funny Cars, and altereds on alcohol; many were Hemi powered. In Modified, the Rod Shop stayed with Chrysler for several years after 1971, with Francis Crider, Bob Riffle, and Don Carlton winning event crowns. In Stock, Ray Cook used a 1970 Hemi Challenger convertible with the T/A-type fiberglass hood to win the 1978 NHRA World Championship, but it was years later, in 1997, before Al Corda did likewise (and in a similar hardtop Challenger) with Mopar sponsorship.

Hemi winners continued in the Super Stock ranks, but as in Pro Stock, none of the famed package cars again recorded a season-long title victory. Judy Lilly won several more events, as did Carroll Fink, Terry Earwood, and Ken Montgomery.

Montgomery found his greatest success in the tried-and-true 1965 *Triple Nickel* Plymouth, even though he did convert his 1968 Barracuda first to a match race Pro Stock and later campaigned it as an A/Modified Production car. That car remains today in as-raced condition circa 1972, a time capsule of the glory and challenges of

An old autographed handout photo shows Gordie Blankenship's Mirada. He ran Hemi engines until USAC outlawed big-blocks. (Photo Courtesy Doug Schellinger DSAC Collection)

In the early 1980s, Richard Griffen launches hard at Baton Rouge in the car Ron Butler built for Butch Leal. This was the car Leal raced during the 1974 Pro Stock boycott. (Photo Courtesy Bryan Flach Archive, quartermilestones.com)

Old Hemi cars never died; they just kept going faster. George Vignogna hoisted the nose high against Ken Montgomery during the era when Mopar sponsored the NHRA Summernationals in Englishtown, New Jersey.

John Friel was one of several racers who helped put SS/AA racing back on the map. He ran one of the first competitive Darts in years during the early 1990s.

However, as this image of a Friel qualifying engine from Indy shows, speed costs money. How fast do you want to go?

the era. The 1965 car, on the other hand, is the epitome of the modern vintage Super Stock car.

After leaving Bill Tanner, Earwood went on to drive for Steve Bagwell, a Georgia businessman who had no problem spending money to go Super Stock racing. By the mid-1970s, rules changes had begun a true transition of Super Stock into its modern format, with aftermarket replacement differentials, big tires, radical suspension changes, and newly legalized engine combinations. Bagwell spent his money and moved the bar forward accordingly. Earwood and driver Richard Griffen continued the legacy of Hemi dominance for several years, and by the mid-1980s, everyone was realizing just how special the Hemi package cars were.

That resulted in two opposing directions: Cars that had not been overly molested (cut up) were retired and entered the collector's market; ones that were still capable of remaining competitive became even more so. A handful of 1964, 1965, and 1967 cars were still in competition, no longer the ire of the sanctioning body or class. Drivers including Frank Lupo, Lou Vignogna, Phil Roar, Rick Johnson, and Bob Marshall were among those now welcomed. Today, Marshall remains one of the final competitors in the big 1965 models, racing against a slew of late-model SS/BA Mustangs in 2014.

Meanwhile, the remaining national magazines began devoting pages and stories directly to the SS/AA class at Indy, where the 1968 Race Hemi faithful still gathered

year after year. This returned that particular class title to a level of notoriety availed by no other in NHRA Sportsman racing. Mopar Performance, the eventual successor to Direct Connection following a number of changes in Chrysler's ownership, posted significant prize money for the class win beginning in 2001. Since then, Hemi cars in SS/AA now run under the moniker SS/AH, a revival of Hemi interest and excellence, with technological advances to boot.

New "Old" Hemis

The Hemi revival was due in part to a commitment that Chrysler made to the racing community in the early 1990s. By that time, NHRA-legal iron blocks were becoming worn out, very expensive, and difficult to find, especially in light of the growing collector car market for good examples. Joe Hilger, an avid gearhead who had moved into a senior-level executive position at Mopar,

Larry Griffith (left) and Joe Hilger (right) stand with Griffith's restored Dart. Hilger was responsible for getting the 426 Hemi back into production in the 1990s.

knew there was pent-up demand for a new cast-iron replacement block. This was not only from muscle car enthusiasts, but also from long-loyal racers competing in the NHRA and IHRA Stock and Super Stock ranks.

As quickly as possible, Hilger approved the funding for new tools for the block; he also had new OEM-design Hemi head tooling created. Indeed, Hilger's vision, along with the diehard employees who served in the Mopar Performance Parts group, was to actually revive the 426 Hemi engine. He wanted to do it both in parts form and as crate engines, a turnkey package done mainly to meet the demand of a cadre of new street enthusiasts.

Ray Barton, a relocated Canadian engine builder who had become one of the primary purveyors of Hemis racing in Sportsman class, worked with Mopar Performance engineer Larry Shepard and he recommended revisions and improvements in the design. Their work made this new-generation 426 block much stronger. Even more interest grew in the legendary SS/AA class (now SS/AH) where the 1968 Hemi Barracudas and Darts still raced head to head. Although Al Corda's 1997 NHRA Stock Eliminator World Championship was with one of the earliest examples of this reborn 426 Hemi in competition, the real barometer for Hilger's foresight happened in 2001.

That year, Mopar Performance Marketing Manager David Hakim saw the opportunity to really promote the Hemi's Super Stock heritage on the dragstrips across the country. Hakim, who had raced in Stock and owned a real 1971 Hemi Charger, spearheaded an effort that resulted in the popular Mopar Hemi Challenge just for those cars. Eventually, the company created a special Super Stock Hemi block with unmachined lifter bores just for racing. The Hemi Challenge race, managed as part of promoting the Mopar Hemi parts line, is still running at the NHRA's U.S. Nationals over Labor Day every year.

Wings over Europe:
One Final Hurrah for the Twentieth Century

Had it not been for Joe Hilger's passion and love of the brand that gave the world a reborn Hemi, we may have not seen its most notorious wing entry run again, the original #71 Dodge Daytona of Bobby Isaac and Harry Hyde. Tim Wellborn and his wife Pam are noted for their outstanding car collection in Alexander City, Alabama. Most people do not know that Tim was at the first Talladega race in 1969, that his father bought a 1971 Hemi Charger brand new and had been involved in one way or another with the track since its inception, and that Tim still owns a real Dodge Daytona he converted to Hemi power as a teenager, using a wrecked 1968 Road Runner as the donor.

Fast forward to the late 1990s. Tim had overseen a very successful revival of his family's Wellborn Forest Products cabinet business and had the money to begin a car collection. He also had a NASCAR driving license and an invitation to take the K&K Insurance Dodge to Europe. The car, donated by Harry Hyde with a dummy engine in 1976, was in the collection of Talladega's International Motorsports Hall of Fame Museum, where Tim is an executive director.

"In 1995, I put in a call to Chrysler and talked to executive Bob Lutz about getting an engine for the K&K car," Wellborn recalled later. "And he agreed the car needed to get back together. He was very excited about it."

This was no sitting-in-a-corner mill either. It was the first production crate-engine Hemi to be run on one of the factory dynamometers since 1971. It displaced 528 inches as the factory was planning to make stroker crate engines available. Getting the car exhibition ready in

Tim and Pam Wellborn at the Hall of Fame inductions at Talladega. Tim drove #71 in Europe as the largest-displacement Hemi stock car to ever run at speed with help from Chrysler's Bob Lutz.

1998 with help from Roger Gibson, Wellborn put more than 100 miles on the new engine on the banks of Talladega, being very careful because of the car's historical significance. It was then shipped to Goodwood for the yearly Festival of Speed.

Through Chrysler's fresh connections in Europe and the Viper's ongoing international racing efforts, a schedule of historic racing events kept the Wellborns in Europe in 1999 for several weeks. After Goodwood, the largest engine (Hemi or otherwise) to run in an American stock car took fast laps at England's Silverstone and Germany's Nürburgring road course. On exhibition laps with the Viper team, Wellborn took the car to 140 mph. No restrictor plate needed, and it was the only car on the property running without mufflers.

And Then Came the Fuel Racers

Of course, there was no way to denigrate the Hemi in the nitromethane ranks, no matter what the sanctioning bodies thought. By 1972, the number of racers still in non-Chrysler cars was minuscule, led by Jim Bucher's Chevrolet dragster and a handful of survivors in the Funny Car ranks. Big changes had taken place as the Street Hemi exited, and none was more critical than the advent of aluminum blocks.

There are obviously explosive results when parts inside an engine fail under the pressure of burning supercharged nitromethane. An aluminum crankcase offered not only simple weight reduction, but also the ability to replace, or resleeve, a damaged cylinder with minimal effort. Moreover, if the event was not too catastrophic, damage to the aluminum case itself could be patched much easier than the high-heat furnace brazing required by an iron example. By this time, the rigors of competition had become so serious that it was possible to blow the entire crank and reciprocating assembly out of the bottom of an iron

"Kansas John" Wiebe smokes the tires in his slingshot during the development phase of the Donovan engine. (Photo Courtesy Jon Steele Archive, quartermilestones.com)

engine onto the race course. However, the first aluminum example was not for the 426, but for the old 392.

By the late 1960s Ed Donovan was among the many parts suppliers who could see the writing on the wall for the eventual unavailability of early 392 Hemi block cores. Donovan decided to take the plunge and develop a 417-ci (from a 4.00 to a 4.10 bore) version of the engine, primarily for fuel-racing dragster customers who had remained with the familiar combination. The block, created with major revisions for strength and maintenance, made its debut in early 1972, with "Kansas John" Wiebe and the Mike Kuhl/Carl Olsen Good Guys teams among its cheerleaders. Donovan sold the block on its improvements and ease of maintenance over any iron engine, and found a lot of customers very quickly.

However, a version of the 426 engine was not far behind, just months in fact. It came as a result of Don Alderson and Milo Franklin's Milodon company, which, like Donovan, had begun primarily as a parts manufacturer. The Milodon-derived block was called the VII Liter, and, like Donovan's innovations, showed design improvement from the OEM passenger car configuration. Engine builder Ed Pink was among its first proponents,

James Warren receives the shut-off sign as he blows out the side of a cast-iron Hemi block during the PRA National Challenge in 1972. (Photo Courtesy Jon Steele Archive, quartermilestones.com)

and the basic engine won world titles for Garlits, Shirley Muldowney, and others. Like Donovan, Milodon also found a ready market for its replacement cylinder heads as well as kit-type complete engine assemblies.

Pink had a longtime non-acrimonious business rivalry with horsepower guru and Chrysler associate Keith Black. Already considered one of the best engine builders in the business by 1972, when Black began moving forward on an aluminum block, he was methodical and cautious. Moreover, he had some serious assistance from former Chrysler engineer Bob Tarozzi, who came to South Gate, California, at the invitation of Holly Hedrich, who was Black's shop manager (fellow Chrysler alumni Bob Mullen was helping Donovan).

By this time, the tooling for the Hemi engine was no longer needed by Chrysler and had actually been scrapped. Using Frank Bialk's original set of blueprints from Chrysler's files, Tarozzi made serious adjustments for a fresh aluminum casting that could be sleeved up to 550-ci (bore size of 4.340). A prototype was cast. The Candies & Hughes team, which had recently decided to move into Top Fuel, performed the first track development work on the engine at Irwindale Raceway and convinced Black to make the investment in tooling.

Wildly successful because of its greater adaptability to multiple environments than its counterparts, Black's engine dominated the fuel ranks for more than a decade. Following Black's development, Chrysler helped promote the product line, assigning them Mopar parts numbers and listing them in their catalog. Black's products continue to be used by many racers today. A handful of other suppliers also create similar equipment specifically for NHRA's long-standing 500-ci displacement limit in fuel racing.

Winners . . . All of Them

So, although many Chrysler fans were frustrated with what was happening in the door-car ranks, the fuel cars continue to use the engine. It has been refined over and over; today, even on the 70-percent nitromethane maximum NHRA imposes and a shortening of the dragstrip's measured distance for these cars to 1,000 feet, the supercharged engine based on Bialk's original design is capable of producing in excess of 10,000 hp. Of course, that effort lasts mere seconds under full load, managed by the fuel system, supercharger size and positioning, and clutch lock-up components, which modulate how much of that horsepower makes it to the rear tires.

As of this writing, dragsters can cover that 1,000 feet in 3.7 seconds, with speeds topping 330 mph on rare occasions. Funny car models, computer-styled and capsule-shaped with body identification coming primarily from graphics, are only a short distance behind them, running times in the high 3.9s and 320-plus mph. The Hemi legacy Chrysler began 50 years ago is indeed alive and well. Nobody did it better. Ever.

This modern testimony to the potential of nitromethane is on display in the Garlits Engine Room. Unfortunately, this particular example cannot be fixed by simply resleeving it.

Raw power: The Hemi legacy continues in professional drag racing. Today's Top Fuel cars reportedly make a calculated, albeit momentary, maximum 10,000 hp during a 3-second 1,000-foot sprint.

Hemi: Everything Changed but the Legend

I t was 1998. Chrysler had begun looking for a global merger partner under CEO Robert Eaton. Germany's Daimler-Benz AG acquired the company under a stock-swap deal to gain a 92-percent share of the firm.

Although the inside joke of the newly formed DaimlerChrysler company was that the entire word Chrysler was still pronounced silently in the corporate halls of Stuttgart, the truth was that this infusion of cash and technology brought the company full circle to position it for the twenty-first century marketplace.

By this time, the LA-series small-block had become the Magnum engine line, featuring upgrades in manifolding, valvetrain, and cylinder head design. The changing demands of emissions had forced some of the changes, but the basic structure had met a majority of the company's global gasoline V-6 and V-8 needs. It had even been the starting point for the V-10 engine in the sporty Viper.

Perhaps fortuitously, Joe Hilger had the Hemi nameplate trademarked when doing work on reviving the 426-ci Gen II–style engine. Shortly thereafter, that name was used as the descriptive foundation of a whole string of what are now referred to as late-model or Gen III Hemi engines.

Return to NASCAR and New Hemi Engines

These new engines were again found on both the street and racetrack through the Dodge and Mopar brands. The company made a huge return to NASCAR in 2001 using engines first derived from the Magnum block architecture and created a string of competition-focused powerplants that took Dodge to no fewer than 55 event wins through 2012. The Charger nameplate returned to a performance-oriented rear-wheel-drive platform (albeit four-door) in 2006. Added to this new street model was a new Hemi engine, which made use of both old and new ideas.

First introduced for the Ram truck line in 2003, the new engine displaced 345 ci and was called out as the 5.7L engine. It became part of the passenger vehicle line in 2005. Unlike the earlier true spherical/hemispherical combustion chambers, the head/piston shape took advantage of swirl technology. Indeed, Tom Hoover worked as a consultant and recommended the squished chamber, as well as moving the single block-centered cam higher and dual spark plugs for greater emissions control.

By working with modern materials and advances in engine design, the bottom end (both block and reciprocating assembly) was

Wheels up, Charlie Fitzsimmons, Jr. brings the heritage of Hemi power full circle as he races toward the winner's circle at the 2012 Gatornationals; blueprinted power came from Arrington Performance.

strengthened considerably, horsepower rose, and the weight of the engine was less than that of the 5.9 (360-ci) Magnum design it replaced. Rated at 345 hp, one horsepower per cubic inch, the engine took the Hemi legacy into the modern marketplace. Power jumped up considerably, to 370 horses, when new technology was added in 2009, including Chrysler's VCT (variable camshaft timing) and MDS (multidisplacement system) advances. The 5.7L uses a 3.92-inch bore and a 3.58-inch stroke.

The next Hemi iteration was a superior performance version displacing 369.7 ci, or 6.1 liters, created by increasing the bore size from 3.92 to 4.06 inches. Compression rose from 9.6 to 10.3:1. This version was created to power the new line of SRT8 (Street and Racing Technology) vehicles in the Dodge, Jeep, and Chrysler model lines.

Released in 2005, the 6.1L Hemi engine reached the legacy 425-hp rating that the original 426 Hemi had been noted for 40 years prior. This was done via changes to head and manifold designs, plus new technology in reciprocating part cooling and lubrication. However, this displacement did not benefit from the technical advantages the 5.7L did in 2009. Those changes went on another legacy displacement the company had just released at 6.4 liters, or 392 ci.

The new 392 Hemi gained its displacement by a bore increase to 4.09 and a stroke increase to 3.72; this was basically an all-new design building upon what had been learned. Lightweight racing-type pistons, scientifically proven high-flow heads with larger valve sizes, and an intake manifold that physically modifies runner volume at higher RPM ranges helped push the power numbers even higher. At 6,000 rpm, this engine is rated at 470 hp, higher than any previous passenger car V-8 in Chrysler's history, and 470 ft-lbs of torque. Mopar Performance Parts also offered a crate engine version of the 392 rated at 540 hp and 490 ft-lbs.

Don Garlits built a supercharged Gen III 392-ci Hemi engine that runs on nitromethane in exhibition cackle and racing. This was a special program supported by Mopar Parts, with which he still maintains a relationship.

Garlits' efforts to run the new engine in fuel applications gave him the opportunity to stress the new technology. He says the engine performs well.

The 392 Hemi arrived in 2011, just as Roger Penske and his Dodge NASCAR team reached their pinnacle. By then, major changes had occurred to the company. Daimler had returned to Germany, selling a majority share of Chrysler in 2007 to a group of investors led by Cerberus Capital Management. However, the banking crisis of 2008 ended with the government and President Barack Obama managing a bailout of the company, shuttering many loyal dealerships and resulting in a majority purchase by Fiat.

Although Penske driver Brad Keselowski won the 2012 NASCAR Sprint Cup championship for Dodge, the circle-track effort was terminated when the company did not offer Penske a longer-term contract starting in 2013 and he quickly accepted an opportunity from Ford.

Quarter-Mile Muscle for a New Generation

Following the popular introduction of the retro-styled 2005 Ford Mustang, Dodge began laying the groundwork for a two-door model based on the same LX vehicle platform of the Charger. Naming the result Challenger was a given. Its retro styling was incredibly successful, and the car reentered history in 2008. Right on its heels came a midyear announcement that Dodge planned to offer a new Drag Pak model of the Challenger, its first drag-specific race package since 1968. A pair of prototypes created for Stock Eliminator debuted at the NHRA's Mopar Mile-High Nationals that June and were piloted by Don Garlits and Judy Lilly.

The new cars were sold as a body-in-white package to be finished by the end user and could be equipped with the 5.9L Magnum, 5.7L, or 6.1L Hemi crate engines offered through Mopar, with either automatic or manual transmissions. Due to the level of work associated with getting these cars ready to race, it took some time before

The Teuton crew from Louisiana and three Drag Paks: one with a wedge engine, one with a new Hemi engine, and one with a V-10 Viper engine.

The return to 426 cubes also helped put racers David Barton and Kevin Helms into winner's circles of the Factory Stock normally aspirated class. This was done by an NHRA allowance to install the engine in the previous V-8 Drag Pak models. It meant affixing a tag to them as special production changes because a 426-inch option had not been part of the original Drag Pak offering.

Pro Stock and Funny Car Champions

Another modern Hemi engine had a specially created block structure for NHRA Pro Stock racing. Like the Gen III design, the engine takes advantage of many changes in engine technology; the parts are sold unmachined so that end users have full control over valve and combustion chamber use.

As it was from the beginning, much of what is located beneath the carburetors and valve covers in Pro Stock racing is proprietary. Racers in this class are often separated in qualifying by the smallest margins in professional motorsports. Suffice it to say that it works. Today, the Johnson & Johnson team out of Greenville, Tennessee, has been the flashpoint for this latest Chrysler factory hot rod effort, taking back-to-back World Championships in 2012 (driver Allen Johnson) and 2013 (driver Jeg Coughlin, Jr.). Other Dodge Pro Stock drivers have included V. Gaines and Matt Hartford.

In Funny Car, Don Schumacher Racing emerged as one of the sport's biggest players following the noted driver's long retirement until the 1990s. Today, the team fields multiple Hemi-powered nitromethane teams, with son Tony Schumacher taking home no less than seven NHRA Top Fuel season crowns. The Funny Cars of Gary Scelzi (2005), Jack Beckman (2013), and Matt Hagan (2012 and 2014), won World titles as well.

Full Circle: Bringing a Bazooka to a Gun Fight

Ford and Chevrolet's increasing involvement in drag racing was due in part to supercharged editions of the new Mustang and revived Camaros. In the middle of 2014, the renamed Fiat Chrysler Automobiles N. V. (FCA) announced the release of the most powerful production

The Hemi engine in the Teuton entry run by Kevin Helms won the 2014 U.S. Nationals Factory Stock crown in the B category and the 2015 Gatornationals.

the 2008–2009 examples arrived on the track, but they began making history by winning major NHRA events with Jeff Teuton and Charlie Fitzsimmons, Jr. driving, plus assorted class titles.

The next big step was a Drag Pak that used the V-10 Viper engine, which displaced 512 ci (8.4L). It proved difficult to compete with due to NHRA's horsepower factoring and increasing involvement by Ford and Chevy in the heads-up Factory Stock class, which had started in 2012, the year after the car arrived. Fortunately, something new was in the offing: a return to the true 426-inch displacement from Mopar for the Gen III Hemi engine.

This displacement was achieved by using a 4.125 bore and 4.0 stroke. Although it is possible to attain the same 7.0L using a conventional iron block, Mopar offers this as an all-aluminum engine package, allowing for steel cylinder sleeves to ensure greater bore stability. The engine was coupled with CNC-cut cylinder heads, improved cam timing, lighter weight, and even the ability to run on 93-octane pump gasoline due to its tuned engine management program.

Jeg Coughlin, Jr. (left), Allen Johnson (right), and a real elephant showcasing 50 years of Hemi power in 2014. Both drivers won world titles for Mopar and Dodge in recent seasons.

This is Matt Hagan and the special 50th Anniversary Hemi Dodge Charger he ran at select 2014 races for car owner Don Schumacher. He won his second championship that year.

vehicle in American manufacturing history, the Hellcat Challenger and Hellcat Charger. The new 707-hp engine used a slightly destroked version of the 6.4L 392 at 6.2L (378 ci) via the 4.09 bore and a 3.58 stroke. Displacement was changed to increase overall strength for the engine in the forced-induction environment. The block was cast iron, topped by a low-profile twin-screw supercharger. It required completely revised hardware for engine durability. In fact, more than 90 percent of the internals were reengineered for the release.

So it came as no surprise that, at the 2014 NHRA U.S. Nationals, Mopar announced the Drag Pak program would continue. Once approved for racing, it is possible the next Drag Pak could be released using both the all-aluminum 426 and the new 6.2L Hellcat engine technology. The car would be similar to the previous releases in terms of design, and enthusiasm for its potential in competition is high.

As this book went to press, this latest and perhaps greatest addition to the Hemi legacy had not been released yet. It stands to reason, however, that the Race Hemi Hellcat and its street counterpart could indeed be a modern finale worthy of a standing ovation.

The 2015 Drag Pak test vehicle during its first track test in August 2014 carried on the legacy of the 426 Hemi and its ultra-stock heritage for Fiat Chrysler Automobiles. (Courtesy FCA/Mopar Performance, Troy Wood Photo)

REFERENCE SOURCES

Burgess, Phil, *Larry Reyes: "The Flyin' Hawaiian and Other Stories,"* National Dragster "Insider," March 20, 2009

Garlits, Don, *Don Garlits and His Cars Garlits,* Museum of Drag Racing, 2009, ISBN 978-0-615-30266-9

Hunter, Jim, "Ford's OHC Dilemma," *Stock Car Racing* magazine, September 1966 pp. 8-11

Huntington, Roger, "Why the Street Hemi?" *Super Stock & Drag Illustrated,* Sept. 1966, pp. 36-37

Ladow, William, *Conversations with a Winner: The Ray Nichels Story,* LaDow Publishing, ISBN 978-0-9723623-0-6

Matune, Mike, "Plymouth Belvedere Goes Continental," *Vintage Motorsport,* Nov/Dec 2013, pp. 58-64

Modern Rod magazine editorial, "The Chrysler/NASCAR Hassle," February 1965

Moriarty, Frank, *Supercars: The Story of the Dodge Charger Daytona and Plymouth Superbird.* 1995 Howell Press, ISBN 978-1574270433

Rockwell, David, *We Were the Ramchargers: Inside Drag Racing's Legendary Team,* SAE Books, 2009, ISBN 978-0768019322

Schild, James, *Maximum Performance: Mopar Super Stock Drag Racing 1962-1969,* Motorbooks 2006; ISBN 978-0760321928

Schild, James, *Original Dodge and Plymouth B-Body Muscle 1966-1970,* Motorbooks International, 2004, ISBN 978-0760318607

Schorr, Martyn, *Mopar: The Performance Years,* Stance & Speed, 2009, ISBN 978-0982173312

Vestal, Anthony, NHRA Media Guides, IHRA Media Guide 1997

Voegelin, Rick, "The Rivalry: Bill Jenkins, Jere Stahl and Top Stock Supremacy in 1966," *Elapsed Times* magazine Annual, 2012

Weertman, Willem, *Chrysler Engines: 1922-1998,* SAE International 2007, ISBN 978-0768016420

Weertman, W., *Chrysler Corporation's New Hemi Head High Performance Engine,* with R. L. Lechner, SAE 660342, April 11, 1966, Courtesy Steve Lasday.

www.allpar.com, Chrysler reference summaries

www.racing-reference.info, NASCAR, USAC, ARCA results

www.ultimateracinghistory.com, NASCAR, USAC, ARCA results

Young, Anthony, *Hemi: History of the Chrysler Hemi V-8 Engine,* 2002 Motorbooks International, ISBN 978-0879385378

INDEX

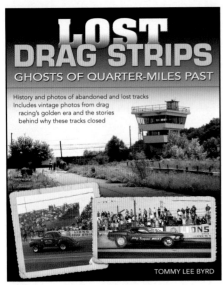
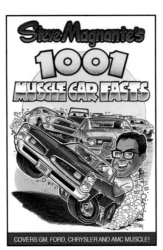
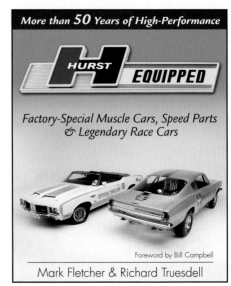
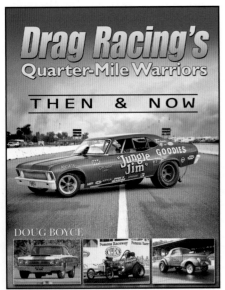